For my wife, Elaine, whose support, encouragement, and discerning eye helped me build my collection

Preceding pages
Left: A. M. Cassandre's famous group of posters (see pages 197–200) form the backdrop for André Kertész's photograph *Dubo, Dubon, Dubonnet, Paris* (1934).
Right: A passerby looks at posters on the Boulevard de la Madeleine in Paris in this 1927 photograph by André Kertész. A. M. Cassandre's poster for Au Bûcheron is in the background (see pages 138–139).

Below: King George V and Queen Mary get into their coach in front of a wall of posters at the foot of Blackfriars Bridge, circa 1920.

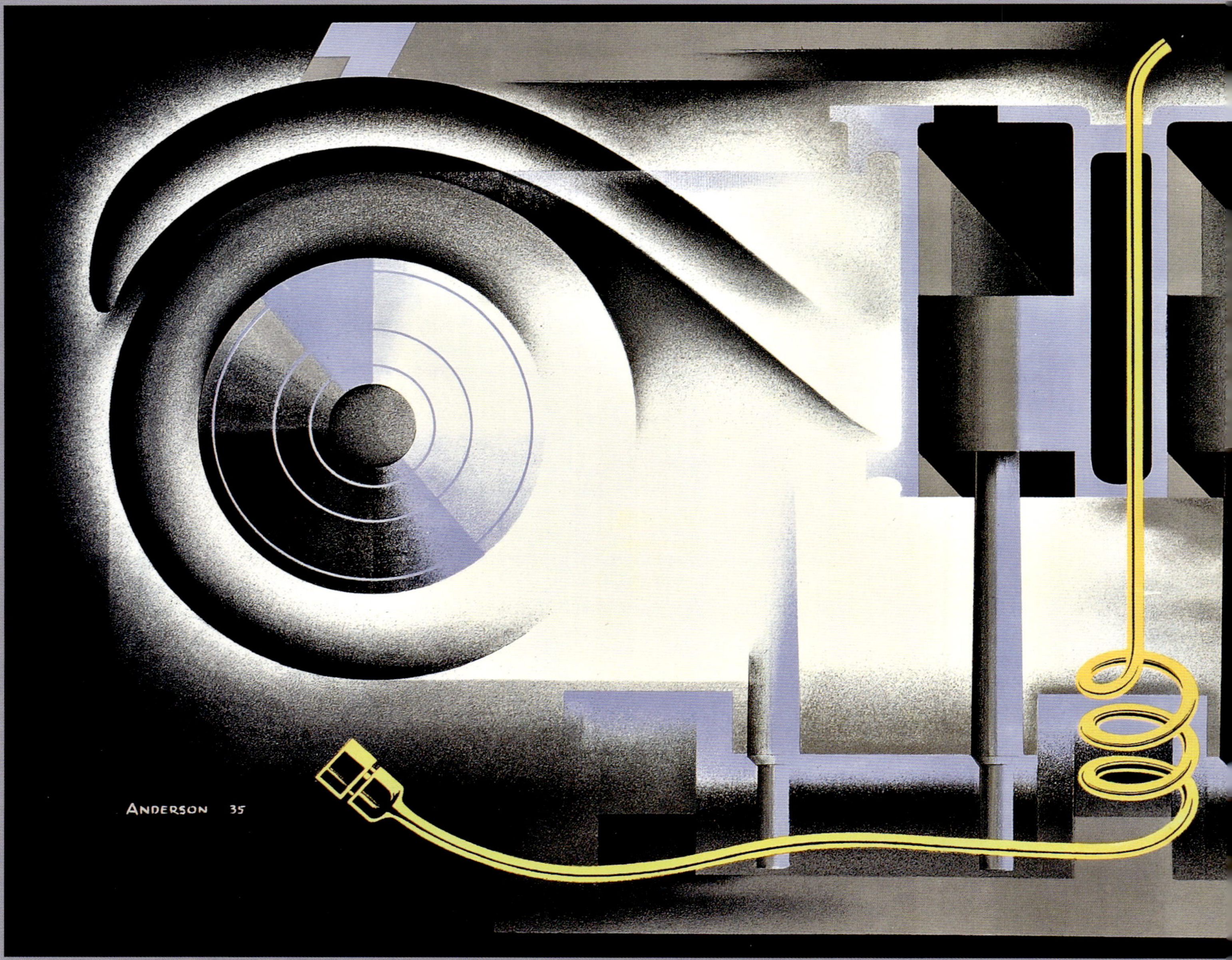

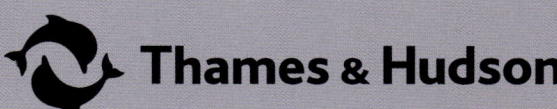

Thames & Hudson

THE
ART
DECO
POSTER

WILLIAM W. CROUSE

Introduction by **ALASTAIR DUNCAN**

with 367 illustrations

8	INTRODUCTION
13	A NOTE ON POSTER COLLECTING
15	AVIATION
43	AUTOMOBILES AND MOTORCYCLES
71	CONSUMER AND INDUSTRIAL PRODUCTS
101	LEISURE
133	FASHION AND ENTERTAINMENT
163	MOTOR RACING
189	FOOD, BEVERAGE, AND TOBACCO
223	OCEAN LINERS
247	RAILWAYS
273	TRAVEL AND TOURISM
308	ACKNOWLEDGMENTS
309	BIBLIOGRAPHY
310	INDEX
312	CREDITS

INTRODUCTION

THE FOLLOWING pages present an embarrassment of art deco riches from the William W. Crouse collection—an expertly selected group of early twentieth-century posters that span a variety of subjects, from ocean liners to musical revues to aperitifs. Crouse, an authority on and longtime avid collector of works in the medium, focuses on the dynamic, mostly linear compositions of the interwar years rather than on the flowery, often whimsical, carryover works from the Belle Époque era. Many of these forceful geometric images fully capture the buoyant mood of the 1920s, as Europe rebounded from war and celebrated the machine's innate power and rhythm. Others capture the restrained mood of the 1930s, as the world slipped into an economic depression.

The Roots of Art Deco

The art deco graphic style originated in, and was anticipated by, book and fashion magazine illustrations that evolved in Paris during the years 1910–1914. Inspired by Sergei Diaghilev's Ballets Russes, which arrived in Paris in 1909, and by Léon Bakst's vivid stage and costume designs, French artists introduced the same orgy of colors and mélange of Russian, Persian, and Oriental influences into their book illustrations, fashion plates, and theater sets. Couturiers such as Paul Poiret provided further opportunities for artists by commissioning them to illustrate brochures promoting the designers' latest fashions. By the outbreak of the First World War, Bakst-inspired pochoirs and aquatints dominated the pages of Paris's foremost fashion magazines and showcased the talents of myriad artists, including George Barbier, Edouard García Benito, Georges Lepape, Robert Bonfils, Umberto Brunelleschi, and Bernard Boutet de Monvel. These developments introduced commercial art as a bona fide profession—and the graphic designer as its foremost practitioner. Advertising became an industry, and the industry gave birth to poster art.

The 1920s poster artists drew on the rich and enduring turn-of-the-century tradition of Henri de Toulouse-Lautrec, Théophile-Alexandre Steinlen, and Alphonse Mucha. Works ranged

from the transitional high-style interpretations made by Leonetto Cappiello prior to World War I to the rigorous geometric compositions created by A. M. Cassandre a decade later. Most designers, however, favored as their point of departure the soft-edged, fanciful stylizations found in Cappiello's work. Jean Carlu, Charles Loupot, and Paul Colin, for example, embraced a light and engaging graphic style that traced a clear progression from their fin de siècle forebears.

The Poster as Art Form

Posters, in the form of notices and proclamations, first appeared on public walls after the invention of the printing press in the fifteenth century. But poster art, which marries image and text, came into existence in the second half of the nineteenth century after the Industrial Revolution had created a consumer economy and a newly prosperous middle class, fueling demand for goods and services. Artists designed posters to persuade, and sell products to, this newly affluent clientele. Inspired by circus posters from the 1840s, the French lithographer Jules Chéret (1836–1932) created posters to attract audiences to the theater. He perfected the lithographic printing process and introduced the high-volume printing press to France. Chéret's then-unique approach of combining text and illustration as elements of equal importance made the poster a powerful promotional tool.

By 1900, passersby could read posters on France's ubiquitous *colonnes d'affiche*—bollards or kiosks—on which public notices were posted. At first, these posters announced mostly performances: the music hall, burlesque, and cabaret. After 1918, they evolved into an art form with a decorative vernacular all its own, one that competed directly with radio. Posters promoted travel, vacation resorts, sports competitions, Grand Prix races, and art exhibitions, including the annual salons staged in Paris at the Musée Galliera and the Grand Palais. In Germany and Italy, Hitler and Mussolini used posters as a significant instrument of fascist propaganda.

Opposite page, left and center: Léon Bakst designed these and other costumes for the 1910 Ballets Russes production of Nikolay Rimsky-Korsakov's *Scheherazade*, choreographed by Michel Fokine. Bakst also served as the production's set designer.

Opposite page, right: Choreographer Michel Fokine dances with his wife, prima ballerina Vera Fokina, in Rimsky-Korsakov's *Scheherazade*.

Couturier Paul Poiret and his models present French fashion in the streets of London, circa 1925.

A B C D E F
G H I J K L M
N O P Q R S T
U V W X Y Z

Above left: The Broadway font was designed by Morris Fuller Benton in 1929.

Above right: Designer Paul Poiret shifted fashion's emphasis from the art of dressmaking to the art of draping, freeing women from the rigid couture traditions of the nineteenth century.

The Evolution of a Style

In the 1920s, dynamic design became the most effective means of persuading customers to buy a particular product. Advertisers and artists sought powerful symbols and visual techniques. Poster designs were simplified, their images reduced to the essentials of product and brand name. Reduction was key: saying more with less became the goal. Sharp linear compositions floating on flat areas of background color quickly drew the eye of passersby in busy twentieth-century cityscapes. Other gimmicks, such as aerial points of view, diagonal compositions, and vanishing perspectives, helped capture viewers' attention. The overall intent was to startle the unsuspecting audience, a must in a message-laden environment. A. M. Cassandre, the preeminent posterist of the interwar era, downplayed his profession's creative contribution to the consumer economy by defining his role as merely that of a catalyst: "The poster is only a means," he noted, "a means of communicating between tradesmen and public, something like a telegraph. The poster artist plays the role of the telegraphist; he does not emit messages, he transmits them."

With pared-down graphics came the need for new sans-serif typefaces that both streamlined the message and delivered a powerful visual impact. Poster artists derived inspiration from the reductionist alphabets of the constructivist and Bauhaus movements. Clean, crisp lines and bold, mechanical-looking typography, such as M. F. Benton's high-contrast Broadway font (1929), fit precisely with Machine Age aesthetics and the ideal of standardization. Such typography, which today is routine, was revolutionary at the time.

Women were prominently featured in 1920s poster designs, often in the guise of a chic demoiselle: willful, coquettish, sporty, and puffing on a cigarette to symbolize her newfound independence. The couturier Paul Poiret had sparked this transformation by freeing women from the Victorian whalebone corset, a fashion milestone that created a stir not unlike the miniskirt furor of the 1960s. Clad in tubular dresses, wearing the latest garçonne coiffure, women were portrayed in print in a crisp illustrative style, sometimes swinging a golf club or twirling a parasol at water's edge.

Perceptive readers will also observe that the angular machine imagery in 1920s posters underwent a stylish transformation in the wake of the global Great Depression. At the behest of industrial designers (a profession newly introduced during the Machine Age), artists rendered their images in a more fluid, streamlined form to show that energy-efficient motion was the best means to jump-start failing industrial economies.

Art Historical Influences

Art deco graphic artists drew on many techniques introduced by avant-garde painting movements in the early years of the century to create a new grammar of decorative ornament. Cubism and Italian futurism, in particular, provided a powerful range of stylistic tools with which commercial artists solved

problems of design and composition. Cubism added geometric fragmentation, abstraction, distortion, and juxtaposed or overlapping images and color. Futurism, established in 1910 with the "Technical Manifesto of the Futurist Painters," signed by Gino Severini, Giacomo Balla, and others and inspired in part by the new century's obsession with speed and power, translated brilliantly into potent images of the era's giant ocean liners and express locomotives. From the Dutch De Stijl and Russian constructivist movements came a mix of pure line, structure, asymmetrical balance, and color. By borrowing concepts from these rather esoteric and cerebral art movements, poster artists helped to bring them into the cultural mainstream and in so doing helped make them more comprehensible to the public at large.

The teachings of the period's vanguard design schools, including the Deutscher Werkbund, Wiener Werkstätte, and Bauhaus, all of which, to varying degrees, sought to reconcile art and industry—that is, to exalt in the precision of the machine and its ability to inject beauty into everything—further influenced interwar poster designs.

Notable Practitioners

After 1919, several poster artists in Paris embraced the seminal art deco style with vigor and innovation. Jean Carlu, for example, showed great diversity in designs. His posters for the Compagnie Aérienne Française (CAF), an airline, and Monsavon, a brand of soap (for which he served at one point as artistic director), remain among his most appealing. Swiss-born Charles Loupot settled in Paris, where he worked as an illustrator for *Femina* magazine. His light, charming poster designs portrayed young women with a rather Louis Icart–like sentimentality. In 1930, Loupot was invited by A. M. Cassandre to join his Alliance Graphique, where Loupot's engaging style provided a spirited counterpoint to Cassandre's sharp linear imagery.

Born in the provinces, Paul Colin settled in 1913 in the French capital, where he created posters, paintings, and set and costume designs for the Paris Opéra. His fame rests primarily on his long association with Josephine Baker, which began in 1925. Colin's entertainment posters, including the one for *The Blackbird Revue*, were invariably designed in a lively, angular style that, especially after 1926, traced the emerging influence of the machine.

René Vincent, another notable poster artist, forsook his architectural studies at the École des Beaux-Arts for a career in the graphic arts and, to a lesser extent, in ceramics. An illustrator for *La Vie Parisienne*, *The Saturday Evening Post*, and *L'Illustration*, Vincent also designed posters for the automaker Bugatti, creating compositions in a crisp illustrative style heightened with contrasting blocks of color. He often distorted perspective and scale to create illusions of speed, power, and dynamism. Several other French painters and graphic artists provided the world of poster art with memorable works—including the prolific artist known as Orsi, whose identity remains an enigma but

Above left: The Spanish artist Juan Gris painted this cubist still life, *Breakfast*, in 1915.

Above right: *Speed Lines (Speed + Landscape)*, by the Italian futurist Giacomo Balla (1913), is one of a series of images in which the artist explored the automobile as a symbol of speed and power.

In addition to posters, the artist A. M. Cassandre designed typefaces, painted portraits and landscapes, and designed stage sets, especially during the latter part of his career.

whose name appears on more than a thousand art deco posters (including one for Gold Starry fountain pens).

It was A. M. Cassandre, though, who emerged as the art deco era's ultimate communicator. Born Alphonse Mouron in the Ukraine, Cassandre introduced new visual tools with which he transformed the advertising business. Following his studies at the Académie Julian in Paris, he launched his career across a broad spectrum of the graphic arts—painting, theater design, and typography. It was in poster design, however, that he made his most dramatic and lasting impact. Cassandre comprehended fully the function of a poster; he knew that the elimination of superfluous detail would sharpen the message. He transformed poster art into a dominant twentieth-century advertising medium through simplification, translated into a vigorous interplay between geometric elements and references to the machine. His designs for the national railways—*Nord Express*, *Étoile du Nord*, and *Chemin de Fer du Nord*—and for the ocean liners *Statendam* and, the most celebrated, *Normandie* quickly achieved the status of poster classics.

Beyond Paris, poster artists adopted the art deco style in various ways and to varying degrees. In Switzerland, Herbert Matter—known principally for pioneering the photomontage technique—and Otto Morach designed posters for the fashionable men's clothing store PKZ. In Belgium, the Swiss-born Léo Marfurt formed his own studio, Les Créations Publicitaires, where he produced the masterful *Ostende-Douvres*, advertising ferry service between Ostend and Dover. Two other artists from the Low Countries, Willem Frederick Ten Broek and Kees van der Laan, produced posters for Dutch clients in an arresting, Cassandre-like modernist style.

In Great Britain, Edward McKnight Kauffer, Alexandre Alexeieff, and Austin Cooper captured the interwar mood with verve and imagination. Elsewhere, Marcello Nizzoli in Italy and the team of Stefan Osiecki and Jerzy Skolimowski in Poland applied modernist graphic designs to their poster commissions.

Today's reader should bear in mind that the essence of these posters is intangible: the success with which they captured the mood of modernity in the interwar years. Whether consciously or unconsciously, graphic designers captured the spirit of the age, and as a result, these posters are largely uplifting and optimistic, reflecting the zeitgeist in western Europe following the Great War as economies rebounded. A walk down memory lane also awaits those who can recall the cruise ships, automobiles, monoplanes, and passenger trains of travel's golden era.

—Alastair Duncan

A NOTE ON POSTER COLLECTING

VINTAGE POSTERS produced from the late 1800s through the mid-1900s are rare and often valuable. Posters of this period were created through an exacting, labor-intensive, and expensive process known as direct-transfer lithography, which has fallen out of favor for commercial use. In this process, a printer transferred a design to a block of limestone or a zinc plate using a grease pencil, etched the design in place with acid, inked the stone with a single color, and hand-pulled a sheet of paper through a printing press containing the stone or plate. For most posters, the printer repeated this entire process for each of four colors—blue, red, yellow, and black. The printer's main challenge was to keep the colors aligned with each other (in register) as he pulled the paper through the press on each of the four pulls. Because this process was so time-consuming, printers only made posters in small runs.

Several other factors make original posters rare. Printers used their stones and plates over and over, erasing the etched image and drawing a new design on the newly blank stone or plate. Thus it was almost impossible to create subsequent printings after the first. In addition, because posters were normally intended to last only a few weeks or months, printers used the most inexpensive paper available. Once pasted to kiosks, columns, or buildings, posters were impossible to remove without damaging them; and in any case they had usually been marred by weather, pollution, and graffiti. As a result, only a tiny fraction of the first runs of printed posters have survived, largely because collectors saved them—and, in a few cases, printers preserved them as unused extras before the stones were ground down for the next job. In the last decade, virtually no other class of antiques has increased in value more dramatically than posters.

Posters specific to events and locations were typically discarded once the event was over, so they are much less common than posters advertising consumer products such as spirits and cigarettes, which were printed in larger quantities and posted wherever these products were sold. Furthermore, posters from the south of Europe are harder to find than those from the north of Europe because northern Europeans had a robust history of collecting that was absent in the south. Posters from outside Europe are even scarcer, as advertisers less commonly employed the medium in other parts of the world.

Posters promoted virtually every type of product, event, and service imaginable. As such, it is possible to collect posters of a certain artistic style (art deco, art nouveau, Impressionist), time period, subject matter (cars, trains, radios, expositions, sporting events), product or service (London Underground, Shell Oil, PKZ, Modiano, Campari), country of origin, artist, or frequency (the annual Dartmouth Winter Carnival; the Grand Prix de Monaco)—the possibilities are nearly limitless. A strong collection requires striking images that are masterfully composed in terms of both layout and color. The historical significance of a product, event, or service (Davis Cup tennis, Works Progress Administration) also adds value.

This collection focuses exclusively on art deco posters printed between World War I and World War II (1919–1939). It excludes movie posters, political posters, and Russian works. Although they were made between seventy-five and ninety-five years ago, these art deco posters look as contemporary as any twenty-first-century advertisement. —W.W.C.

AVIATION

HUMANS HAVE always wanted to fly. Ancient myths and legends, like that of Icarus, are replete with heroic tales of flight. In more recent times, rapid advances in technology and science turned this millennia-old dream into an everyday event. A mere century and a quarter passed between the first manned hot-air balloon flight, in 1783, and Orville Wright's twelve-second flight in the powered spruce biplane *Wright Flyer I*, in 1903. Flight then became an attainable reality, and with the establishment of commercial airlines around 1920, the aviation industry began to flourish.

During World War I, fighter planes played an important role for the Allies and the Central Powers alike. In the war's aftermath those pilots, newly unemployed, used their decommissioned planes to form the world's first airlines, initially hauling mail throughout Europe. Founded by former military pilots in 1919, KLM remains the oldest commercial airline still in existence: the United States would not have its own airline until 1926, when Stout Airways was founded. Stout was eventually absorbed by what is today United Air Lines.

In 1927, Charles Lindbergh made his historic nonstop solo flight from New York to Paris, covering 3,600 miles in thirty-three and one-half hours in his plane, the *Spirit of St. Louis*. Five years later, Amelia Earhart would become the first woman to make the crossing. These historic moments contributed to the growing popularity of air shows and air races, which quickly became the world's most well-attended spectator sports. Still, flight was nowhere near as advanced as it is today. Runways frequently consisted of nothing more than a small strip of grass or gravel. Outside the West, even grass and gravel were a luxury, as most planes in Africa and Asia had to land on water.

Boeing Air Transport (which would later become United Airlines) hired the world's first female flight attendant in 1930. Twenty-five-year-old Ellen Church, a pilot and a registered nurse, had convinced the company's management that she could reassure passengers and calm their fear of flying. Her first voyage as a "sky girl" was a twenty-hour, thirteen-stop trip from Oakland, California, to Chicago. In addition to taking care of passengers, a flight attendant in those days hauled luggage, fueled planes, and assisted in pushing the aircraft back into its hangar. Job standards specified weight (between 100 and 118 pounds), height (between five feet and five feet four inches), age (between twenty and twenty-six), and marital status (single). Physical examinations were required quarterly to "assure the bloom that goes with perfect health."

Aviation was bringing the world closer together, and poster art captured the traveler's imagination, glamorizing destinations as well as the speed, comfort, and security of a new and exciting industry. The very best graphic artists—A. M. Cassandre, Jean Carlu, Edward McKnight Kauffer, Anders Beckman, Umberto di Lazzaro, Tato, Francis Bernard, Otto Baumberger, Munetsugu Satomi, and others—were hired to promote air travel throughout Europe and the United States.

Ala Littoria: Linee Aeree Italiane, 1934
Tato (Guglielmo Sansoni, 1896–1974)
37 x 29 inches (94 x 73.7 cm)
Barabino & Graeve, Genova

This extremely rare poster by the Italian futurist Tato elevates the tail section of an Ala Littoria aircraft to monumental status, aggressively thrusting the tail toward the viewer as the craft's orange vertical stabilizer rises majestically skyward into the space occupied by the airline's name. The result, while a bit imposing, is monolithic and unforgettable. Formed in 1934 through a merger of four existing airlines, Ala Littoria was supported by the Mussolini regime and was the Italian national airline from its founding until World War II. Mussolini named the airline Ala Littoria, or "winged lictor." A lictor was the ancient Roman soldier who carried the fasces—the bundle of reeds wrapped around an ax—which was the symbol of Roman authority and the object from which fascism drew its name. Ala Littoria serviced a total of twenty-nine destinations throughout Europe and Africa and also provided transport for the Italian military. An interesting side note: the last legitimate job held by the notorious Italian swindler Charles Ponzi (1882–1949)—considered to be one of the greatest con artists in history and the man for whom the term "Ponzi scheme" is named—was at the Ala Littoria office in Brazil.

Italian Aerial Lines, ca. 1935
Umberto di Lazzaro (n.d.)
38 x 23½ inches (96.5 x 59.7 cm)
Grafiche I.G.A.P. (Impresa Generale Affissioni e Pubblicità), Roma and Milano

In relation to Tato's epic Ala Littoria design (left), this rare di Lazzaro poster is lighthearted and breezy. By using green lettering below the red and white biplanes, the designer flies the colors of the Italian flag in an inventive manner, romanticizing speed and travel in a carefree cubist fashion. The artist's "coming-and-going" approach not only shows the airline's diversified fleet of planes but also implies that it provides both passenger and mail service. The high-wing trimotor craft on the bottom, which has wing "spats" to cut down the draft, appears to be a Caproni Ca.133, used by the airline on its routes to Ethiopia. This is the English version of the poster; it also was printed in French and Italian.

Aerotransport: Swedish Air Lines, 1935
Anders Beckman (1907–1967)
39½ x 24½ inches (100.3 x 62.2 cm)
Esselte, Stockholm

In this striking poster, Beckman places an Aerotransport Fokker F.XXII as close as possible to the viewer while maintaining its altitude over the airport. It is an outstanding design choice, one that creates an incredibly solid impression. The Fokker comes across as a more concrete entity than even the architecture below, which is shrouded in light fog. The F.XXII was the last Fokker airliner built prior to World War II. Only four were manufactured: each of them, powered by four Pratt & Whitney Wasp engines, could carry twenty-two passengers and a four-member crew. Officially established as Aktiebolaget Aerotransport in 1924, Swedish airline AB Aerotransport initially operated between Stockholm and Helsinki, but shortly thereafter expanded its passenger route to Berlin. It carried mail from Stockholm to Malmö, Sweden, and then on to Amsterdam and London. Moscow was added to the route in 1937, followed by Paris, Oslo, and Prestwick, Scotland, during World War II. In 1948, the government-owned ABA was merged with privately owned SILA (Svensk Interkontinental Lufttrafik) to create a new entity, ABA, which today is a part of the Scandinavian Airlines System, or SAS Group.

United Air Lines, 1938
Arthur C. Radebaugh (1906–1974)
42½ x 27 inches (107.9 x 68.6 cm)
Printer unknown

Similar to Anders Beckman's design for Swedish Air Lines (left)—in fact, the two are nearly mirror images of one another—this poster promotes United Air Lines' "coast-to-coast" service with an extremely substantial aircraft coming in for a landing at a fairly indistinct airport. However, unlike Beckman's Fokker, Radebaugh's sleek, streamlined DC-3 is depicted in painstaking detail. Arthur Radebaugh, who described his work as being "halfway between science fiction and designs for modern living," was celebrated for his virtuosic airbrush technique, and that mastery is magnificently displayed in this poster. The Douglas DC-3—an American-made, fixed-wing, propeller-driven aircraft generally considered to be the workhorse of aviation during the 1930s and '40s— revolutionized air transport with its speed and range. December 17, 2010, marked the seventy-fifth anniversary of the DC-3's first flight, and there are still a number of small operators around the world that use the aircraft for passenger and cargo service. United Airlines is the oldest commercial airline in the United States, initially founded as an airmail service in 1926 by Walter Varney (1888–1967), who also founded Continental Airlines. It is interesting to note that the United States Department of Justice approved the merger of these two aviation companies on August 27, 2010.

Sabena: Rapidité, 1938
L. Keizer (n.d.)
39½ x 24¼ inches (100.3 x 61.6 cm)
Studio E.L.K.A.

Sabena is an acronym for Société Anonyme Belge d'Exploitation de la Navigation Aérienne. It began operations on May 23, 1923, as the Belgian national carrier, and its first paying flight, on April 1, 1924, carried passengers from Rotterdam to Strasbourg via Brussels. The artist's art deco indicators of speed, apart from the obvious dial, are the trio of stylized eagles cutting across the trail of the soaring airplane, conveying rapid movement, or *rapidité*. The most telling elements of the design, however, are the silhouette of the aircraft—which appears to be a three-engine Savoia-Marchetti SM.83—and the dial, which is climbing swiftly toward the 250-kilometers-per-hour mark, the cruising speed of the aircraft. The typography at the bottom, which looks a little like a neon sign, puts the final touch on the best Belgian aviation poster of the era. Sabena operated until 2001, at which time it filed for bankruptcy.

Scandinavian Air Express, 1931
Anders Beckman (1907–1967)
40 x 24 inches (101.6 x 61 cm)
Ivar Haeggström, Stockholm

Formed in the late 1920s, Scandinavian Air Express was a joint venture between Royal Dutch Airlines (KLM) and Aerotransport AB of Sweden. It provided fast, reliable service from Scandinavia to France and England via Amsterdam. Here, Anders Beckman gives us a cool, stylized airplane that follows the enticing trajectory of the text toward its destination. What may not be obvious in this seemingly simple design is that Beckman was one of Sweden's major artistic talents. He contributed to the design of the glorious Swedish pavilion at the 1939 New York World's Fair and formed an eponymous design school within his native country. Although his work had a global impact, perhaps his best compositions are the hundreds of richly graphic advertising posters he created for Sweden's most famous companies (see page 18). Each of his many images for the aviation industry gives the viewer a taste of the twentieth century's romance with modernity, as if they are all leading toward the final famous scene in *Casablanca*. It's that palpable swell of excitement within his images that makes posters such as this one stand out from others in the genre.

K.L.M., 1933
Munetsugu Satomi (1900–1995)
39 x 24⅜ inches (99.1 x 61.9 cm)
Poster Novia, Paris

Upon viewing Munetsugu Satomi's poster for KLM (an abbreviation of Koninklijke Luchtvaart Maatschappij, or Royal Dutch Airlines), one doesn't have to think long or hard to come up with the name of the artist who, clearly, most inspired and influenced the lesser-known Satomi. That artist is, of course, Cassandre, the art deco genius whose stylistic impact spanned the globe. In fact, shortly after attending the École des Beaux-Arts in Paris, Satomi briefly studied with Cassandre. Unquestionably, it was under Cassandre's tutelage that Satomi learned to distill a subject down to its essence, blending pictorial representation and lettering into nearly pure graphic design. Using the sparest possible graphic elements and without tonal excess, the artist instantly makes us aware of the airline's global reach. The text along the border is included for specificity's sake. KLM was founded on October 7, 1919, five years before Imperial Airways (see pages 22–23), and although it is now a subsidiary of Air France, it has continued to operate under its original name to this day, making it the oldest scheduled airline in the world to do so.

AVIATION

Travel in Comfort by Imperial Airways, 1935
Edward McKnight Kauffer (1890–1954)
40 x 24½ inches (101.6 x 62.2 cm)
Stuarts, London

In this poster for Imperial Airways, as in *Use the Telephone* (page 106), Edward McKnight Kauffer employs a photomontage to create a superb example of simplicity and specificity. In both posters, the artist uses only two colors (blue and black) and angled text. But here, instead of focusing on the instrument—in this case, the aircraft—he uses Imperial Airways' minimalist "Speedbird" logo soaring through an indigo sky and a dotted route map overlaid on a globe to draw our attention to the far-flung destinations the airline serviced. Imperial Airways, an early British long-range commercial airline in operation from 1924 to 1939, serviced parts of Europe but was especially noted for its "empire routes" to South Africa, India, and the Far East. The airline partnered with Qantas (Queensland and Northern Territory Aerial Services) in Australia and TEAL (Tasman Empire Airways Limited) in New Zealand to further extend its reach. Imperial Airways was formed in the hopes of prolonging and modernizing the British Empire, using modern transport to foster increased settlement, expanded colonial government, and stronger trade, but its growth lagged behind other European carriers, such as Air France and Lufthansa. After World War I Great Britain had a surplus of pilots and aircraft, but the secretary of state for air, Winston Churchill, refused to subsidize the commercial airline industry. By November of 1939, Imperial and British Airways were merged into a single, state-owned national airline, British Overseas Airways Corporation, or BOAC.

Imperial Airways: By Air in Comfort, ca. 1937
Steph Cavallero (n.d.)
19¼ x 12¼ inches (48.9 x 31.1 cm)
Stuarts, London

While Edward McKnight Kauffer's design for Imperial Airways provided a practical, informative approach to promote air travel (left), this Steph Cavallero poster takes a more persuasive tack, with simplified art deco forms and text providing the public with all the information they need. One way to calm passengers' fears of air travel was to assure them that an airplane's cabin amenities were as comfortable as, or more comfortable than, those on a train. The snug-looking armchair emphasizes the new level of comfort available on Imperial's fleet of so-called Short Empire flying boats, or amphibious aircraft, which were obviously preferable to the wicker seats and utilitarian feel of previous aircraft. The inclusion of a smartly dressed flight attendant holding a tray of beverages is a nice finishing touch, because ultimately it's hard not to be tempted by individual attention.

CAF: Tous Voyages Aériens, 1919
Jean Carlu (1900–1997)
38 x 28 inches (96.5 x 71.1 cm)
Les Imprimeries Françaises Réunies, Paris

This early and recently discovered poster by Jean Carlu highlights Compagnie Aérienne Française (CAF) and its contributions to aviation history. CAF was a pioneer and leader in aerial photography; images captured by the company were used by cartographers, industrialists, and city planners. The nineteen-year-old Carlu designed the poster with such minimalism that its brilliance can almost be overlooked. He was known for his use of color, simple lines, and geometric shapes to create subtle abstractions of the products being advertised. Here, with the globe nestled into the curve of the initial *C*, the aerial camera is Carlu's inspiration. The tail of the plane forms the shutter opening, while the camera lens, the wingspan, is focused on a view of France's post–World War I sphere of influence. The text simply lists specific destinations and reinforces the information that the graphic elements have already conveyed: "All Voyages by Air."

Aeroput Jugoslavija, 1930
Hans Wagula (1894–1964)
37 x 24¼ inches (94 x 61.6 cm)
Tipografija D. D., Zagreb

The headline that accompanies this day-and-night image loses some of its Slavic snap in translation, but its sales pitch couldn't be any clearer: "Train travel leaves you tired; air travel leaves you rested." Yet with its windows glowing invitingly against the dark, the train possesses an undeniable romantic allure. It is an interesting composition, one that pits expediency against leisure in a palette of primary tones. Founded on June 17, 1927, Aeroput was the national airline of the Kingdom of Yugoslavia. Like many airlines, Aeroput ceased operations during World War II. Unlike many airlines, though, it did not do so because of bankruptcy—the war simply created too many obstacles and hazards for this fledgling company. But thanks in large part to the tremendous efforts of Aeroput's staff and technicians, the airline took flight again on April 1, 1947, under the new name JAT Airways—Jugoslovenski Aero Transport. Still in business today, JAT is now the national air carrier of Serbia.

Misr Egyptian Airlines, 1938
İhap Hulusi Görey (1898–1986)
39 x 28 inches (99.1 x 71.1 cm)
Misr Press, Cairo

Two iconic monumental structures immediately set any scene as taking place in Egypt—the Great Sphinx and the Giza pyramid complex. Görey chooses the latter in his promotion for Misr Airlines, adding a fourth, diminutive pyramid to the existing three—from largest to smallest, they are Khufu (or the Great Pyramid), Khafre, and Menkaure— and tidily aligning them in an arid expanse with a Misr four-engine de Havilland DH.86B Express gently banking above them. It is interesting to note that the aircraft is named *Al Fostat*, which was the first capital of Egypt under Muslim rule and which is today part of the neighborhood known as Old Cairo. Misr Airlines (*Misr* is the Arabic word for "Egypt") was established in 1932 as a commercial carrier operating between Cairo and Alexandria. The Egyptian government took control of the airline shortly before the outbreak of World War II. In 1956, it merged with Syrian Airways to form United Arab Airlines, or UAA. UAA split in 1971, and a new airline was formed—EgyptAir, which is the name under which the airline operates today.

Air Union: Orient, 1929
Jean Olivier (n.d.)
38⅝ x 28 inches (98.1 x 71.1 cm)
Les Imprimeries Françaises Réunies, Paris

Jean Olivier's design is simple, direct, and economical, putting a minimalist spin on the classical use of perspective and vanishing point to effortlessly convey the expanses that Air Union is willing to traverse in order to deliver mail to the East. As stylish as it is arresting, the sight of the silhouetted three-engine Short Calcutta seaplane, stripped to its barest essentials and miles from land, evokes a cinematic association that in turn bolsters the image of reliability. Air Union was established on January 1, 1923, the result of a merger between the Compagnie des Messageries Aériennes (the pioneering French airline that provided domestic commercial, mail, and freight service as well as international service between London and Paris) and Grands Express Aériens (another pioneering French airline that flew domestically and to Geneva as well). In 1933, Air Union, along with four other French airlines—Air Orient, Compagnie Internationale de Navigation Aérienne (or CIDNA), Compagnie Générale Aéropostale (see pages 28–29), and Société Générale de Transport Aérien—was folded into the new entity known as Air France.

In 2 Tagen über den Ozean, ca. 1936
Ottomar Anton (1895–1976)
33 x 23¼ inches (83.8 x 59.1 cm)
Mühlmeister & Johler, Hamburg

Although zeppelins were used for sightseeing and domestic transportation purposes in Germany as early as 1909, the director of the corporation that owned the airships resisted the Nazi Party's desire to use them as beacons of propaganda. So the German Ministry of Aviation simply seized the corporation in 1935. Adorned with swastikas, these zeppelins would make appearances at public functions, blasting music and speeches from their speaker systems to the large crowds below. The DZR also used the airships for transatlantic crossings. Here, we do not know if the poster is advertising the company's North American or South American route, or if the airship depicted is the LZ 127 *Graf Zeppelin* or the now infamous *Hindenburg*; however, the text informs readers that in only two days' time—obviously outpacing the antiquated method of traveling by boat—they can be on the other side of the Atlantic. The composition follows the same formula mastered by Leni Riefenstahl in the many films she created for the party—the central figure is made larger than life by being viewed from below, while all other options or rivals are depicted in miniature. Although the *Hindenburg* disaster in 1937 certainly put a damper on the popularity of airship travel, the entire fleet was not grounded until the outbreak of World War II.

Right: This photograph, taken in January of 1936, shows the zeppelin *Hindenburg*, tail emblazoned with Nazi Party swastikas, landing in a field as spectators rush toward it. An unidentified dirigible soars above.

Aéropostal, 1930
J. Besson (n.d.)
31½ x 23½ inches (80 x 59.7 cm)
Avenir Publicité, Paris

This incredible art deco image, which ties the tradition of high-seas couriers to the airborne new guard, is an exquisitely dramatic example of the way airmail service was being presented to the public in the 1930s. In this design, the silhouetted frigate and the seas upon which it sails are eclipsed by the streamlined fleet of Compagnie Générale Aéropostale aircraft, in essence creating a lithographic dividing line between the antiquated and the modern. Compagnie Générale Aéropostale began operations in Toulouse in 1918 with the goal of serving the French colonies in Africa and South America.

Flèche d'Argent: Aéropostale, 1929
A. M. Cassandre (Adolphe Mouron, 1901–1968)
39¼ x 24½ inches (99.7 x 62.2 cm)
Société Anonyme Courbet, Paris

Airmail service was started after World War I by former wartime pilots looking for new lines of work. At first, airplanes were not powerful enough to carry the number of passengers required to make a profit, so they relied on carrying mail to stay in business. Posters—such as this one, commissioned from Cassandre by the Compagnie Générale Aéropostale—helped to sell what seemed to be a somewhat outlandish concept to the public. Indeed, the wing of the sketchily drawn plane (itself a kind of *flèche d'argent*, or "silver arrow") seems to slice an opening into the sky through which it makes its entrance into our reality. Although CGA was one of the largest and most successful French airlines at the time of this poster's production, with 131 aircraft and routes throughout France, Africa, and South America, it could not withstand the pressures of the Great Depression, and what was left of it was amalgamated into Air France in 1933.

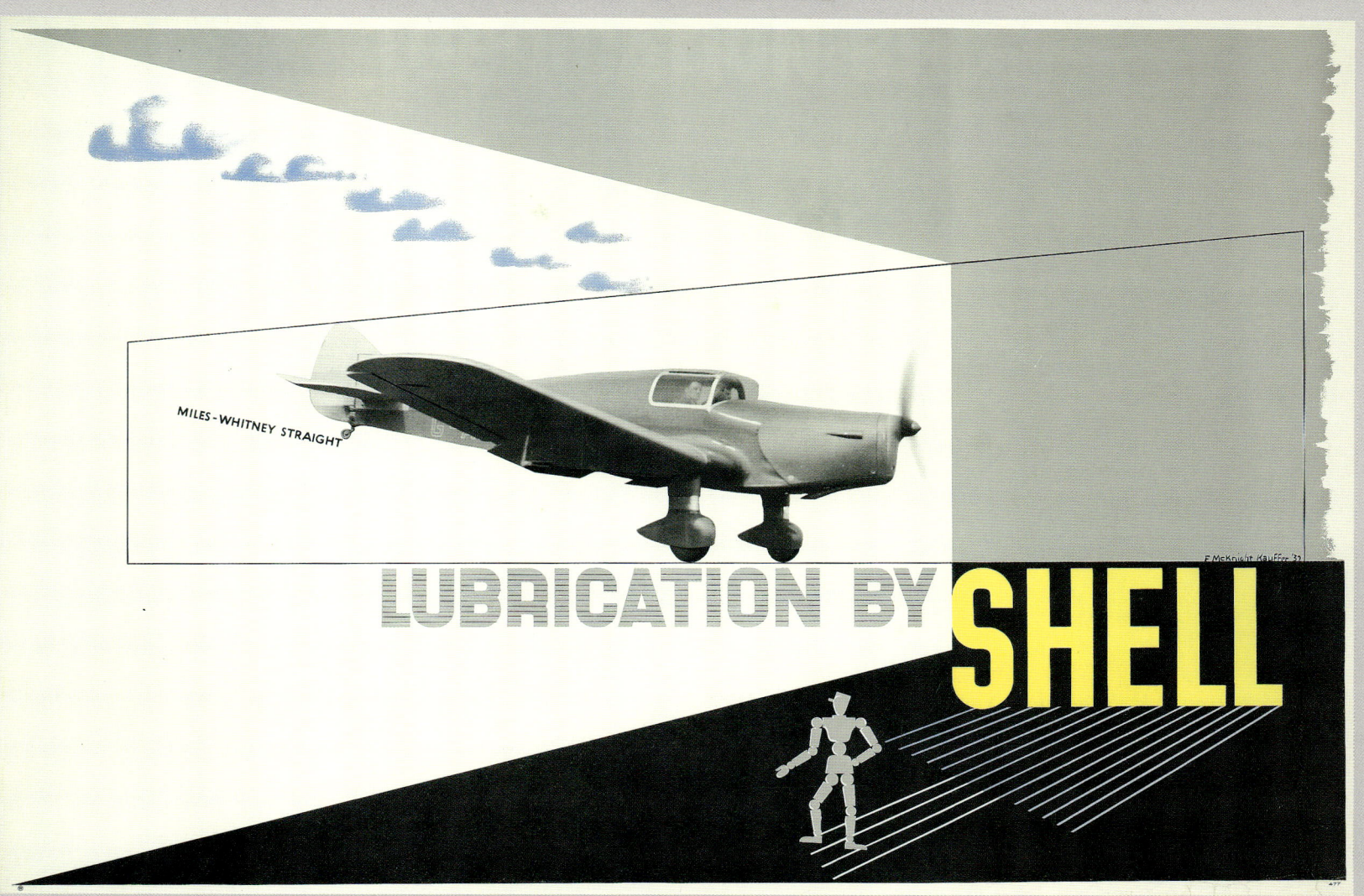

Nationale Luchtvaart School, 1932
Kees van der Laan (1903–1983)
35¼ x 23¼ inches (89.5 x 59.1 cm)
Kühn & Zoon, Rotterdam

One of Europe's oldest aviation academies, the Nationale Luchtvaartschool was formed in 1927 by the Rotterdam Aero Club as a means of encouraging the average daredevil to learn how to fly. Here, the school's three Dutch branches—in Rotterdam, Amsterdam, and Enschede—advertise a reduced introductory fee below the thrilling image of a high-wing monoplane flying toward the viewer's face, so close that it might buzz off the top of the text with its propeller. The soft gray-white spray of wispy clouds around the plane instantly creates an atmosphere of excitement and drama: there is no definition to either the horizon or the ground, no bearings or landmarks. The aircraft could be inches away from a crash or soaring high above the sea, and that mystery and freedom are part of what fuels future pilots' desire to take to the sky. The design itself plays on that romanticized passion, as it suggests an advanced level of technique to a presumably unskilled group of students. The mundane and difficult aspects of practice, preparation, and study are obviously not touched upon—just the glory of potentially being the next Roland Garros, the famous French aviator from World War I whose name appears on the tennis stadium in Paris where the French Open is held annually (see page 117).

Lubrication by Shell, 1937
Edward McKnight Kauffer (1890–1954)
29¾ x 44¾ inches (75.6 x 113.7 cm)
Waterlow & Sons, Limited, London and Dunstable

In this poster, Edward McKnight Kauffer employs an ingenious convergence of rectangular components, one solid white with blue airbrushed clouds, the other a frame that showcases the design's centerpiece—a photomontage of a Miles M.11 Whitney Straight aircraft, which creates the spatial illusion of a flat plane. The typography serves perfectly as a landing strip and adds yet another dimension to this graphic masterpiece. The artist was also savvy enough to use the newest, sleekest aircraft on the market as the sole focus of Shell's lubricating prowess. Introduced in 1936, the Miles M.11 Whitney Straight was a low-power, economical two-seater aircraft with a side-by-side cockpit configuration, the result of a collaborative effort between Great Britain's Miles Aircraft and Whitney Straight (1912–1979), the American-born entrepreneur and Grand Prix race car driver who would later serve as director of the British Overseas Airways Corporation. The fifty M.11s built during the model's two-year production span were intended for civilian flying enthusiasts, but during World War II they were primarily used by the Royal Air Force as communications aircraft.

Gordon Bennett: Basel, 1932
Fritz Bühler (1909–1963)
50 x 35 inches (127 x 88.9 cm)
Graphische Anstalt W. Wassermann, Basel

Challenge: Gordon Bennett, 1934
Tadeusz Gronowski (1894–1990)
49 x 35 inches (124.5 x 88.9 cm)
K. Kczianskich, Warszawa

James Gordon Bennett, Jr. (1841–1918), was a millionaire sportsman and the publisher of the *New York Herald,* a newspaper founded by his father. His flamboyant, sometimes scandalous behavior led him to relocate to Paris, where he launched the *Paris Herald,* the Paris edition of the New York paper. He would raise the international profile of both publications by backing two historic expeditions: Henry Morton Stanley's 1869 quest to find David Livingstone in Africa and George DeLong's ill-fated voyage to the North Pole via the Bering Strait. Bennett also established a total of three international Gordon Bennett Cup competitions: one for auto racing, one for yacht racing, and one for ballooning. The latter, inaugurated in 1906, remains the world's most respected and oldest hot-air balloon race. Fritz Bühler's design for the 1932 event (left) turns a soaring orange balloon into the sun itself, hovering in the flat black space above planet Earth. Thomas "Tex" Settle and Wilfred Bushnell, a pair of United States Navy officers flying a balloon sponsored by the United States Army, won the competition that year with a 963-mile flight from Basel, Switzerland, to Vilnius, the capital of Lithuania, which in 1932 was under Polish rule. Tadeusz Gronowski's poster for the twenty-second running of the event, in 1934 (right), clearly shows the influence of Cassandre (who actually introduced Gronowski to airbrushing techniques on one of his many sojourns in Paris between the world wars). The influence is especially evident in the interplay of cloud and tether upon the surface of the balloon, which creates the suggestion of a globe. Although Gronowski places an airplane front and center in his design, planes had not actually been active Bennett Cup participants since 1920. The winners of the 1934 competition were Poland's Captain Franciszek Hynek and Lieutenant Władysław Pomaski, who departed from Warsaw's Pole Mokotowskie airfield and landed at the Soviet city of Anna, in the Voronezh oblast, traveling a total of 828 miles.

Left: Balloons stand in an airfield near Zurich at the start of the 1909 race for the Gordon Bennett Cup.

Scintilla: Lindbergh Byrd Chamberlin, 1927
Ernst Ruprecht (1891–1954)
26¼ x 18⅛ inches (66.7 x 46 cm)
Société Polygraphique, Laupen

S*cintilla* means "spark" in Latin, so it's a completely appropriate name for the Swiss company that produces magnetos—an alternator with permanent magnets used to generate the current in an internal combustion engine. Ernst Ruprecht's poster uses three historic landmarks—the Statue of Liberty, the Eiffel Tower, and the Brandenburg Gate, all separated by an expanse of blue—to play up the fact that Scintilla magnetos were an essential component of Wright Whirlwind engines. These were the engines used in the historic flights of three pioneering American aviators competing for the Orteig Prize, the $25,000 award given for the first nonstop flight between New York City and Paris: Charles Augustus Lindbergh (1902–1974), the winner of the prize, who made the journey aboard the *Spirit of St. Louis* on May 20–21, 1927; Richard Evelyn Byrd (1888–1957), the American aviator and polar explorer whose plane was being repaired when Lindbergh made his successful flight and who, undaunted, made his own transoceanic crossing between June 29 and July 1, 1927; and Clarence Duncan Chamberlin (1893–1976), the all-but-forgotten aviator who was the second man to pilot a fixed-wing aircraft across the Atlantic, which he did between June 4 and June 6, 1927. Chamberlin chose to fly to Berlin so that he could set the record for distance. Scintilla, a Swiss company headquartered in New York City, would move its magneto manufacturing operations to Sidney, New York, in 1925. The Bendix Aviation Corporation purchased Scintilla in 1929.

4th International Aviation Meeting Zürich, 1937
Otto Baumberger (1889–1961)
50¼ x 35½ inches (127.6 x 90.2 cm)
J. C. Müller, Zürich

With the outbreak of World War II on the horizon, the fourth International Aviation Meeting became an opportunity for soon-to-be-fighting countries to compare their military aircraft side by side. Although previous air shows were replete with examples of the latest advances in commercial aircraft, the focus switched to planes as tools of war for the 1937 event. Most notably, Germany arrived with a prototype for its Messerschmitt Me 262 Schwalbe (or Swallow, in English), the world's first jet-powered airplane. It was powerful without being heavy, as so many of the planes coming out of America were at that time. Its construction completely surpassed that of the once impressive biplane, adding unprecedented speed, agility, and accuracy to the realm of flight. It would also go on to become one of Germany's key weapons in fighting the war. Here, Otto Baumberger presents a faceless fleet of planes ominously funneling in formation across the sky. The feeling in this design has less to do with the wonder and excitement of a new technological advance in aviation than it does with a disconcerting fear of what humanity will now be able to achieve with this type of power. It is a foreshadowing of the dangers to come.

Fête Aviation 21e: Nancy, 1929
M. Planchaërt (n.d.)
47¾ x 31⅝ inches (121.3 x 80.3 cm)
Imprimerie Arts Graphiques, Nancy

The wing-top roundel instantly identifies the biplane in this poster as a craft in the service of the French Air Force, but the superior perspective set down by the artist gives the viewer the opportunity to fly in lithographic formation with Nancy's Twenty-First Bomber Wing Squadron, the primary organizers and performers in the August air show promoted here. While no specifics are given regarding what one would see at the show, the artist does provide a definite hint as to what type of missions the Régiment d'Aviation de Bombardement Nancy (RABN) flew: the black silhouetted craft, a stylized Lioré et Olivier LeO 20, won a 1926 competition held by the French Ministry of War for a new night bomber.

Fête des 21ème et 33ème d'Aviation: Essey, 1935
Brée (n.d.)
47 x 31 inches (119.4 x 78.7 cm)
Imprimerie Arts Graphiques, Nancy

In a manner very similar to Planchaërt (above left), Brée utilizes the French Air Force roundel, silhouetted airplanes, and a lofty point of view to draw attention to this June aviation festival featuring the Twenty-First and Thirty-Third Bomber Wing Squadrons, stationed at Nancy. In fact, the central roundel acts almost literally as a bull's-eye to secure the viewer's attention; thus centered, the eye is then free to roam over the graphically converging aircraft and take in the essential information. Not to be confused with the commune in France's Côte d'Or *département,* the Essey referred to in this poster is the Nancy-Essey Airport, a former military airfield that was closed in 1926 due to a lack of space for runway extension. Although it continued to be used for exhibition purposes, the French Air Force converted it into a grass airfield and reopened it in 1936, primarily for training purposes.

Allentown Air Meet, 1930
Anonymous
20 x 12½ inches (50.8 x 31.7 cm)
Printer unknown

With minimal use of color, an uncredited artist sets a midnight scene, anchoring it with the silhouette of downtown Allentown, Pennsylvania. The skyline is dominated by the Pennsylvania Power and Light building and the H. Leh & Co. department store, from which a brilliant beacon emanates, illuminating and attracting a squadron of aircraft to the Allentown Air Meet. Intended in part to dedicate the Allentown Airport (now known as the Lehigh Valley International Airport, one of the few airports in the nation that continues to serve its community from its original location), the historic one-time 1930 event was organized by the American Legion's Herbert Paul Lentz Post and was sponsored by John Leh of the Allentown department store family and his wife, Dorothea, both of whom were avid pilots. Mrs. Leh was, in fact, a close friend of Amelia Earhart and a member of the Ninety-Nines, an association of the leading female fliers of the day. The meet, in which approximately 150 pilots participated, was a huge success, attracting a crowd of some ninety thousand spectators. The event included an air parade between Bethlehem and Allentown, air races, stunt flying, and parachute jumps. Flying demonstrations were also given by pilots from the army, navy, and marines. Additionally, for a supplemental fee, those in attendance could take to the skies themselves, either riding aboard airplanes or on a Goodyear blimp named *Miss Mayflower*.

Right: This "first day cover," or collectible stamped and canceled envelope, commemorates the Allentown Air Meet in Allentown, Pennsylvania, which took place for the first and only time in 1930.

Crociera Aerea del Decennale, 1933
Umberto di Lazzaro (n.d.)
55 x 39 inches (139.7 x 99.1 cm)
Grafiche I.G.A.P. (Impresa Generale Affissioni e Pubblicità), Roma and Milano

This poster is an extremely rare and masterful design that promotes the second transatlantic mass-formation flight jointly sponsored by the Società Italo-Americana pel Petrolio (Italo-American Petroleum Society) and the Italian government, in celebration of the eleventh anniversary of Benito Mussolini's rise to power. In a corridor formed by a huge Italian flag and an equally impressive, yet reversed, American flag, di Lazzaro's imperious and rather intimidating squadron of Savoia-Marchetti amphibious aircraft stretches into the distance as far as the eye can see. Not only did these flights provide a remarkable demonstration of the growing reliability and seemingly limitless potential of aviation, they made it obvious that human flight had the power to shrink the globe. The twenty-four Savoia-Marchettis that flew from Rome to the Century of Progress International Exposition in Chicago, then returned to Rome via New York, were under the command of the Italian marshal of the air force, General Italo Balbo (1896–1940). The heir apparent to Mussolini, Balbo was an outspoken foe of Italy's alliance with Hitler and an outspoken proponent of an alliance with Churchill. He also led the first transatlantic mass-formation flight in 1930 (from Orbetello, Italy, to Rio de Janeiro). He was killed in 1940 when his plane crashed at Tobruk, Libya, apparently shot down—suspiciously—by Italian antiaircraft artillery.

Plzeň: Mezinárodní Letecký Meeting, 1931
Monogrammed JH; artist unkown
49⅜ x 39⅝ inches (125.4 x 95.6 cm)
Unie Vilím, Praha

The western Bohemian city of Plzeň, including the city's central Cathedral of Saint Bartholomew, is portrayed in layered silhouettes, providing a tranquil promotional backdrop for an early May international aviation (*mezinárodní letecký*) meeting sponsored by the Associated Congress of Czech Republic Aero Clubs. Without the interference of urban bustle, the unknown artist—identified only as JH—draws the viewer's eye immediately to the flags of the participating nations and the swarm of white aircraft descending on the city. While the majority of the flags are immediately identifiable, the one on the bottom may not be quite as familiar. The reason is that the four color blocks don't represent a nation but rather the city of Plzeň. The fourth-largest metropolis in the Czech Republic may not be famous for the aviation events it hosted, but it does have one global claim to fame—a city-owned brewery produced the first batch of modern pilsner beer in 1842. Plzeň is the home of Pilsner Urquell (the Czechoslovakian *plzeňský prazdroj* and the German *pilsner urquell* both mean "original source of pilsner"), a brand that is marketed worldwide to this day.

XVᵉ Salon de l'Aviation, 1936
Dolbeau (n.d.)
45½ x 32½ inches (115.6 x 82.5 cm)
Imprimerie de Léonard Danel, Paris and Lille

First held in 1909, the Paris Air Show remains the most important aviation exhibition in the world. Although interrupted by the First World War, the air show started again on a semiannual basis after 1919 and continued on that schedule until it was shut down once again by the onset of World War II. This poster advertises the penultimate exhibition before the war and masterfully expresses the desire to push air-travel technology ever farther forward. Looking more like a modern-era jet than a 1930s airplane (prototypes for jet-powered planes would not appear until the following year), this steel-blue craft shoots like a razor across the sky. It is indeed so fast that its tail end cannot be visually defined. This may have marked the first time that safety and reliability were taken for granted—technology had finally evolved to the point where one could focus on speed and power rather than on simply keeping the plane aloft. Such confidence seems to have greatly inspired this design: it is as though we are no longer looking at the aircraft of the present but rather at the one we hope to fly in the future.

13ᵐᵉ Salon de l'Aviation, 1932
Theodoro (Theodore Pfeifer, 1896–1973)
39¾ x 29½ inches (101 x 74.9 cm)
Les Belles Affiches, Paris

Theodoro's rare lithographic recreation of forward thrust begins with a red propeller but draws us into its vortex with clearly defined wedges of progressively lighter shades of blue. Its minimalism is powerful and eloquent, a vivid expression of the force behind human aviation. Couple this superior artwork with linear and curved text, and the end result is targeted marketing that draws attention to the thirteenth Paris Air Show, which convened at the city's Grand Palais. The most significant aircraft introduced at the 1932 show was the Morane-Saulnier M.S.225, a fighter plane designed to serve as a stopgap while more advanced aircraft were still under development. Impressed with the parasol-wing monoplane's prototype, the French minister of air, Paul Painlevé (1863–1933), ordered seventy-two of the single-seat fighters to be distributed between the air force and the navy.

Right: This photograph provides an overview of the show floor at the fifteenth Salon de l'Aviation, held at Paris's Grand Palais in November of 1936. The show was relocated to Le Bourget Airport in 1953.

13ᵐᵉ SALON DE L'AVIATION

DU 18 NOV. AU 4 DEC. 1932

AU GRAND PALAIS PARIS

THEODORO 32

les belles affiches. 43. Rue de Dunkerque. PARIS

AUTOMOBILES AND MOTORCYCLES

OF THE DELUGE OF PRODUCTS that were increasingly available to the masses in the 1920s and 1930s—a result of the economy and productivity of assembly-line manufacturing—the automobile had perhaps the most dramatic impact on our mobility, lifestyles, and social customs. Cars—and, to a lesser extent, motorcycles—freed people from their dependence on railroads and virtually ended rural isolation. In the United States, car sales increased from 1.6 million in 1919 to 4.5 million a decade later. Similar growth also occurred in Europe, particularly in France and Germany. By the end of the 1920s, automobile manufacturing was the largest industry in the world.

In the 1930s, despite the Great Depression, car sales continued to increase as advances in manufacturing and design produced bigger, more comfortable, more powerful, and more affordable vehicles. Automobile dealerships sprang up to cater to the demand, and, to further accommodate this burgeoning industry, new roads and bridges were built. In turn, other industries (such as petroleum, steel, tourism, etc.) experienced increased demand, thus providing desperately needed employment. In 1919, there were 350,000 miles of state-owned and state-maintained paved roads in the United States alone; by the 1930s, that number had increased to more than 1.2 million. In 1937, San Francisco's 4,200-foot-long Golden Gate Bridge, the longest span in the world at the time, was opened to vehicular traffic. As the number of travelers grew, motor courts, hotels, restaurants, and campgrounds sprang up along highways and popular back roads. Similarly, the demand for gasoline and oil required the construction of service stations.

Carmakers and the sellers of car-related goods and services relied on radio, newspapers, magazines, and posters to advertise their products. Somewhat surprisingly, sellers preferred different media in different countries. For example, in the United States, magazine advertising was much more widely used than it was in Europe, which held on to its long-standing and rich relationship with poster advertising. Consequently, art deco posters that were designed, printed, and displayed in the United States are a rarity. Even posters advertising American automotive brands—such as Ford, Chrysler, Pontiac, Chevrolet, Plymouth, and Pierce-Arrow—were almost always designed and displayed in European markets, as this collection demonstrates. Likewise, motorcycle and transportation exhibition posters are also mostly from Europe. Automobile and motorcycle posters made by some of the most influential graphic artists of the art deco movement—A. M. Cassandre, Charles Loupot, René Vincent, Giuseppe Riccobaldi del Baza, Roger de Valerio, and Marcello Nizzoli—constitute outstanding examples of first-rate advertising in the period between the two world wars.

Chrysler, 1930
Roger de Valerio (1886–1951)
47 x 62 inches (119.4 x 157.5 cm)
Devambez, Paris

Chrysler, 1929
Otto Ernst (1884–1967)
49 x 35 inches (124.5 x 88.9 cm)
A. Trüb & Cie., Aarau

A DeSoto CK-6 roadster hugs the curvilinear contour of the road as it surges forward, its galvanized driver beginning to blur with the speed that appears to be the car's key selling point. This extraordinarily rare de Valerio poster also features a stylized Chrysler insignia at the bottom right, further promoting the company that manufactured and marketed the DeSoto from 1928 to 1961. The marque was founded by Walter Chrysler (1875–1940) and was intended to narrow the market gap between Chrysler and Dodge in the midprice class. Shortly after the DeSoto was introduced, however, Chrysler successfully purchased Dodge, and it is believed that the DeSoto might never have been produced had the transaction been completed sooner. Regardless, the DeSoto was an incredibly successful brand for Chrysler; slightly more than two million vehicles were manufactured during its thirty-two years in production. The car was named after Hernando de Soto, the sixteenth-century Spanish explorer and conquistador who was the first European citizen to have (verifiably) crossed the Mississippi River. A stylized likeness of the explorer appeared in the DeSoto logo and on a majority of the hood ornaments that adorned the vehicles.

This extraordinary art deco design by Otto Ernst served to introduce Chrysler automobiles to the Swiss market. Set against a stylized backdrop composed of spherical clouds and ice-blue, triangular Alps, a speeding red Chrysler roadster surges into the foreground. It is as if we are seeing the transition of a product from the conceptual to the actual, inviting an automotive fantasy that effectively turns the Chrysler into a machine of dreams.

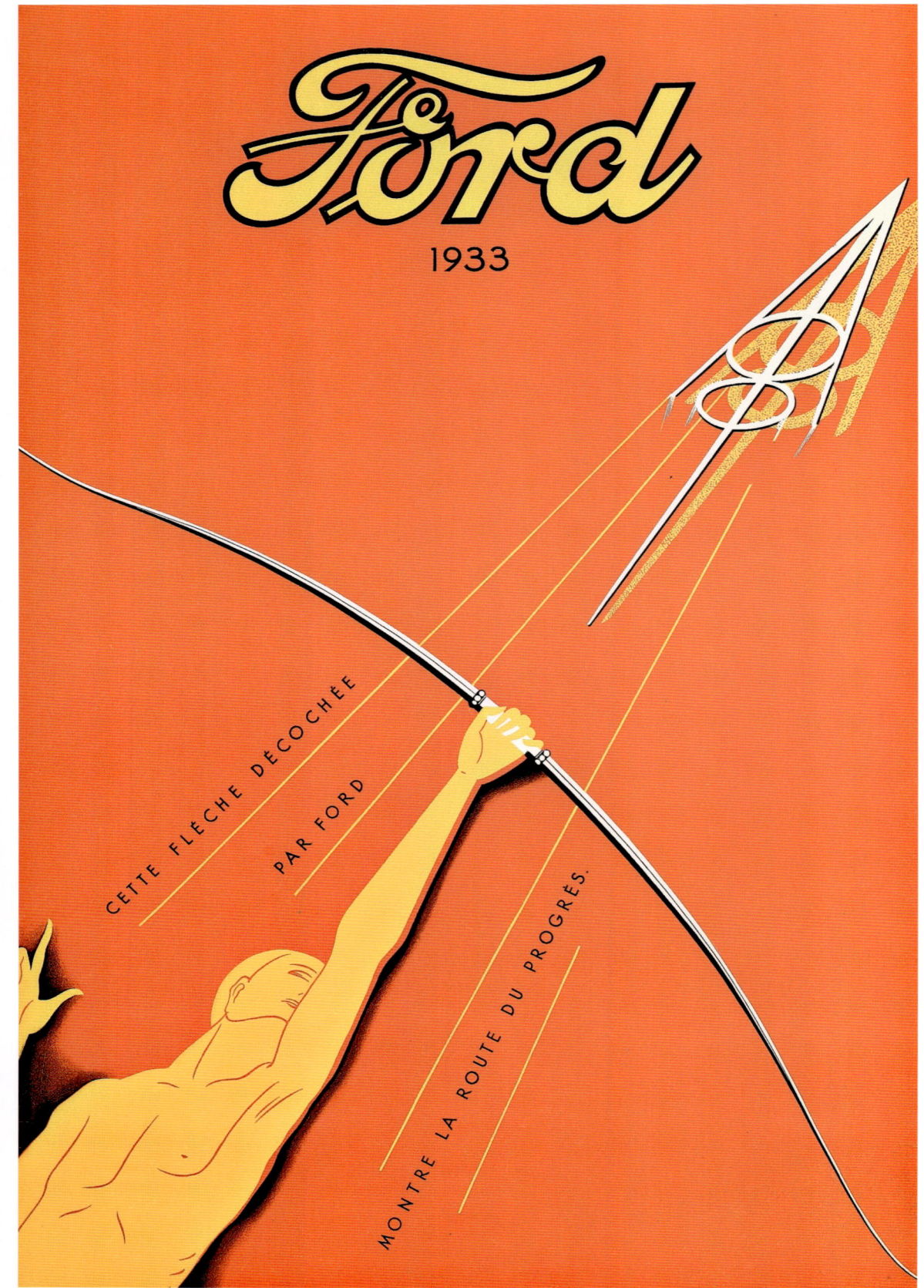

Ford: V-8, 1933
Anonymous
46 x 30⅝ inches (116.8 x 77.8 cm)
Printer unknown

Ford introduced the V-8 engine in 1932, and this poster for the following year's model showcases its promotional message ("Ford lets fly this arrow to show the road of progress") with a striking art deco take on classicism. Ford was the first company to cast a V-8 engine block in one piece. It was many years before the company's competitors learned how to mass-produce a reliable V-8; in the interim, the car and its powerful engine became the preferred choice of performance-minded motorists worldwide. After a couple of failed starts, Henry Ford (1863–1947) founded the company in 1903 with the explicit goal of making a car that the middle class could afford. He introduced the Model T in 1908, developed the "moving assembly line" in 1913, and when Model T production was stopped in 1927, more than fifteen million of the vehicles had been sold, a record that stood for forty-five years.

Chevrolet, 1932
Alfred Cardinaux (1905–?)
62½ x 46¾ inches (158.7 x 118.7 cm)
Office d'Éditions d'Art, Paris

Powered by a six-cylinder engine that produced sixty horsepower, a Chevrolet Confederate sedan glides through the urban evening like a powerful yet elegant phantom. Alfred Cardinaux's impressive and handsomely colored design for General Motors' French market (the company's cars had been available in France since the early 1920s) receives an additional promotional jolt, not to mention a touch of American pizzazz, from the golden illumination atop Detroit's Fisher Building, an ornate limestone, granite, and marble art deco skyscraper located across Grand Boulevard from the General Motors Building in Detroit. Named after Louis Chevrolet (1878–1941), the race car driver and cofounder of the Chevrolet Motor Company (which was acquired by General Motors in 1917), the cars had become the backbone of GM by the time of the Great Depression, largely because of their solid, reliable reputation.

Pierce-Arrow, 1929
Robert Louis (n.d.)
25¾ x 39½ inches (65.4 x 100.3 cm)
Imprimerie Weissenbruch, Bruxelles

The horizontal, arrow-shaped, metallic silver composition of this extraordinarily rare Robert Louis design emphatically implies motion: the overall feeling is that an automotive force is about to be unleashed. Based in Buffalo, New York, Pierce-Arrow was active between 1901 and 1938. Although they were best known for their pricey luxury cars, they also manufactured fire trucks, camping trailers, commercial trucks, motorcycles, and bicycles. Pierce-Arrows were noted for their solid build and powerful but quiet engines. Above all, however, they were a status symbol—a proudly displayed possession of Hollywood stars, corporate tycoons, and foreign royalty. Interestingly, Pierce-Arrow was the period's only luxury brand that did not also produce a lower-priced vehicle to generate cash flow, a deficiency that would prove to be its undoing. In 1928, to avoid bankruptcy, the company was sold to Studebaker for two million dollars. They tried to ride out the Great Depression with well-received vehicles like 1933's streamlined Silver Arrow and slogans such as "Suddenly it's 1940!" But because of the Silver Arrow's high price tag (it cost ten thousand dollars at the height of the Depression), Pierce-Arrow simply couldn't generate sufficient sales to stay in business. In 1938, the company closed its doors and declared insolvency.

Donnet, 1928
Alexey Brodovitch (1898–1971)
30½ x 23 inches (77.5 x 58.4 cm)
Grau, Nerfi et Cie., Paris and Lille

Alexey Brodovitch's superb Donnet poster tells its promotional tale with very few narrative strands: a well-heeled couple, out for the evening, are stopped in their tracks by the sight of a Donnet sedan in a showroom window. Lit by softly varied fields of pink light, the car becomes a thing of beauty desired by even the most sophisticated passersby. Founded in 1914 as Donnet-Denhaut by Jérôme Donnet and pilot François Denhaut, the French manufacturing company, located in Neuilly-sur-Seine, a Paris suburb, achieved a great deal of success with the flying patrol boats they produced for the French navy. After Denhaut left the company in 1919, Donnet stopped building aircraft and purchased the Swiss automobile manufacturer Zedel. He relocated operations to Pontarlier, France, and began manufacturing cars under the name of Donnet-Zedel. In 1928, he sold the Pontarlier factory and changed the name back to Donnet. The company would continue to expand its automotive output throughout the late 1920s and early 1930s, but the economic hardships of the Great Depression would cause the firm to halt production in 1934.

Pontiac 6, 1928
Greif (n.d.)
63 x 47 inches (160 x 119.4 cm)
Office d'Éditions d'Art, Paris

In order to promote the Pontiac Six to the French consumer, General Motors' French graphic arts agency, Éditions d'Art, called upon Greif to make an attention-getting advertisement. His solution was to present a driverless sedan (presumably so that passersby could mentally picture themselves inside the vehicle) streaking uphill below the lofty presence of the Pontiac Indian (which also served as the vehicle's hood ornament). The 1928 Pontiac Six introduced several new features that had not been available in previous models, including a new body, four-wheel brakes, a cross-flow radiator that minimized the loss of coolant, a dashboard gas gauge, and mohair upholstery. These new features, coupled with a step up from a four-cylinder to a six-cylinder engine, resulted in a car that became wildly popular within a very short time. The first Pontiac debuted in 1926, but the marque's history actually dates back to 1893, when Edward M. Murphy established the Pontiac Buggy Company in Pontiac, Michigan. Pontiac initially produced horse-drawn carriages, but in order to remain commercially viable, Murphy shrewdly founded the Oakland Motor Car Company in 1907. General Motors acquired half of Oakland two years later and bought the rest when Murphy died unexpectedly that same year. But it was not until 1926 that Oakland made an impact with the introduction of the Pontiac. Within months, Pontiac was outselling the Oakland brand, which resulted in the discontinuation of Oakland altogether in 1932. Pontiac is the only companion brand in automotive history to outlast the parent company that introduced it.

Plymouth, 1928
Ashley Havinden (1903–1973) and **Terence Prentis** (n.d.)
25⅞ x 36½ inches (65.7 x 92.7 cm)
W. S. Crawford, Ltd., London and Berlin

In July of 1928, wanting to compete with Chevrolet's and Ford's moderately priced vehicles, Chrysler introduced the Plymouth. Although it was only slightly more expensive than the competition, the Plymouth came with a host of nonstandard features that made it the better and more luxurious choice. To announce this new model in Germany, Chrysler hired the duo of Terence Prentis and Ashley Havinden to bring visual excitement to the brand. As Piet Mondrian's tricolored paintings were on the forefront of contemporary European art at the time, it seems almost impossible that the two artists are not referencing his work in this poster. There is the same variance in the thickness of the lines; the same offbeat, gridlike structure; even the same use of red, yellow, and blue. However, the addition of figurative elements takes the design from the simple, straightforward world of De Stijl into that of art deco. Where Mondrian's lines give order and purity, those in this image give thrilling movement. It is this sense of speed that makes us want to "look at the new Plymouth" and salute along with the bell-bottomed sailors. Chrysler was so pleased with this poster that Prentis and Havinden were hired again the following year to create a very similar image for the release of the Chrysler 65.

Fiat 520, 1927
Plinio Codognato (1878–1940)
76 x 54¼ inches (193 x 137.8 cm)
G. Ricordi & Co., Milano

This striking poster by Plinio Codognato was made for the 1928 introduction of the Fiat 520T—also called the 520—which replaced the 520 "Superfiat" V-12. The more modestly sized and powered 520T was one of the first cars manufactured with the steering wheel on the left side, presumably due to an Italian edict requiring that all vehicles drive on the right side of the road in order to deal with an increase in traffic. Only six hundred examples of this model were produced during the three years it was on the market (1928–1930). The poster features a bold red "520" mounted on a massive platform, under which the buyer is reminded that the Fiat 520 is "optima!" The car itself is drawn in outline form, facing the viewer, in a dominant, head-on position, with the Fiat name (in the early days, an acronym for Fabbrica Italiano Automobili Torino) prominently displayed on the grille. The poster's four-sheet size adds to the grandeur of the car.

Fiat 1500, 1935
Giuseppe Riccobaldi del Baza (1887–1976)
77⅞ x 55½ inches (197.8 x 141 cm)
Barabino & Graeve, Genova

It is nighttime on the Appian Way: a midnight blue sky and silhouetted black structures serve as the backdrop for the newly introduced Fiat 1500, which blazes across the Italian countryside with tree-blurring speed—although the whoosh of the tree is subtly rendered. A study in deliberate contrasts, this rare and important Riccobaldi poster "perfectly fuses the excitement of the Machine Age with the glory of the Roman Empire," according to Jim Lapides of the International Poster Gallery in Boston. Riccobaldi instantly fixes our sights on the vehicle, making it obvious that this new technological advancement in automotive production is the only thing worthy of our undivided attention. One of the first cars to be tested in a wind tunnel, the Fiat 1500 was produced from 1935 until 1950; only 42,500 of them were made. Its unparalleled aerodynamic efficiency and progressive styling far surpassed that of any touring car that preceded it and belied the then-prevalent notion that an aerodynamic vehicle could have little consumer appeal. Says Jim Lapides, "Even the lettering of the poster emphasized its streamlined styling. This art deco masterpiece is considered to be one of the great auto posters of all time."

Left: A 1938 Fiat 1500B is displayed with other classic cars in this 2007 photograph.

Voisin, 1923
Charles Loupot (1892–1962)
47⅛ x 31 inches (119.7 x 78.7 cm)
Devambez, Paris

Following World War I, Gabriel Voisin, who, along with his brother, Charles, was a pioneer in the French aviation industry, acquired a Citröen prototype in order to develop his own unique luxury vehicle. While Voisin ultimately focused his talents on automotive transportation, he never completely abandoned his love of aviation: his line was known as Avions Voisin ("Voisin airplanes"), and the vast majority of the vehicles' hood ornaments were avian by design—a detail that the artist, Charles Loupot, subtly reinforces with the shadowy wingspan upon which the car's moniker is set. This poster was one of two Loupot designed for the company in 1923. Here, with surprisingly few scenic elements and sparse use of color, he neatly places a Voisin automobile in its rightful place—on top of the world.

Bugatti, 1930
René Vincent (1879–1936)
54¼ x 37¾ inches (137.8 x 95.9 cm)
Imprimerie Joseph-Charles, Paris

René Vincent, the artist responsible for this gorgeous, iconic, and rare Bugatti poster, specialized in elegant automobile advertising. He set the standard for snob appeal in poster art during this era, which was known for sleek cars, elegant women, and an abundance of refined taste. Vincent was also one of the first French citizens to have a driver's license and was one of the first Parisians to have a garage built onto his house. With his love of the automobile, it is no surprise that he simply displays this Bugatti Type 46, with its bumblebee hubcaps and an elegant occupant, against an uncluttered background, allowing the vehicle to entice the public essentially unassisted. The T46—about 450 of which were built between 1929 and 1933—was a large enclosed touring car that was known for providing a rough ride, mostly because of the placement of the gearbox in proximity to the rear axle. Ettore Bugatti (1881–1947) produced some of the most fabulous automobiles in history. After creating cars for the De Dietrich, Deutz, and Hermès companies, he opened a factory of his own in 1909 in an unoccupied dye works in Molsheim (then in Germany, but today in France). What set his company apart from other automotive manufacturers was the meticulous attention to detail given to both the engineering and the artistic aspects of production. Ettore's father, Carlo Bugatti (1856–1940), was an important art nouveau furniture and jewelry designer, so it shouldn't come as a surprise that Ettore, too, was an amazing aesthete. His cars were as much works of art as they were machines. Only a few examples of each of Bugatti's creations were ever built—approximately 7,900 in total. Like so many other high-end automobiles, the original Bugattis failed with the onset of World War II. The company struggled financially and released one last model in the 1950s. It was eventually purchased by Hispano-Suiza for its airplane parts business in 1963.

Le Tracteur Austin, 1928
Charles Loupot (1892–1962)
46¾ x 62½ inches (118.7 x 158.7 cm)
Les Belles Affiches, Paris

Farming equipment, an unquestionable necessity for hardworking farmers, is not an inherently sexy item in the advertising world. But in Loupot's capable hands this tractor promotion turns from laborious to expressive. One gets the sense from the design that the diminutive Austin tractor, relegated to the background, is responsible for tilling the vast expanse set before it. It is a clever concept, one that relies on angles and deep, vibrant colors rather than on draftsmanship or photographic-style rendering to create an impression. The tractor advertised here was produced by the Austin Motor Company, a British automobile manufacturer founded by Herbert Austin (1866–1941) in Longbridge, Birmingham. Between 1919 and 1939, the firm also produced tractors. The Austin tractor was so well received in France that Austin bought a factory in Liancourt and imported tractors back into Great Britain in order to get around the costly French import tariffs. The production of Austin tractors ceased with the German occupation of France, when the factory was taken over by Krupp, the German armaments and munitions manufacturer.

Laffly, ca. 1930
Roggero (n.d.)
91½ x 60 inches (232.4 x 152.4 cm)
Les Affiches Roger Roy, Paris

Laffly truly came into its own as a company after World War I. It had always been a manufacturer of utility vehicles and fire trucks, but during the period between the wars it expanded its production of off-road vehicles and all-terrain military trucks, which would prove so vital during World War II. In this poster, a towering monolith of a locomotive, depicted in exaggerated proportions, barrels down the tracks. Beside it, a Laffly S15—painted an uncharacteristic flashy red—not only keeps pace with the train but appears to be overtaking it as well. Although this trope—a car holding its own against a train—is as old as the automobile poster itself, here the sense of man's ability to use technology to his advantage seems less important than the power of raw machine versus raw machine. The message is that technology across the board has reached a new level of sophistication.

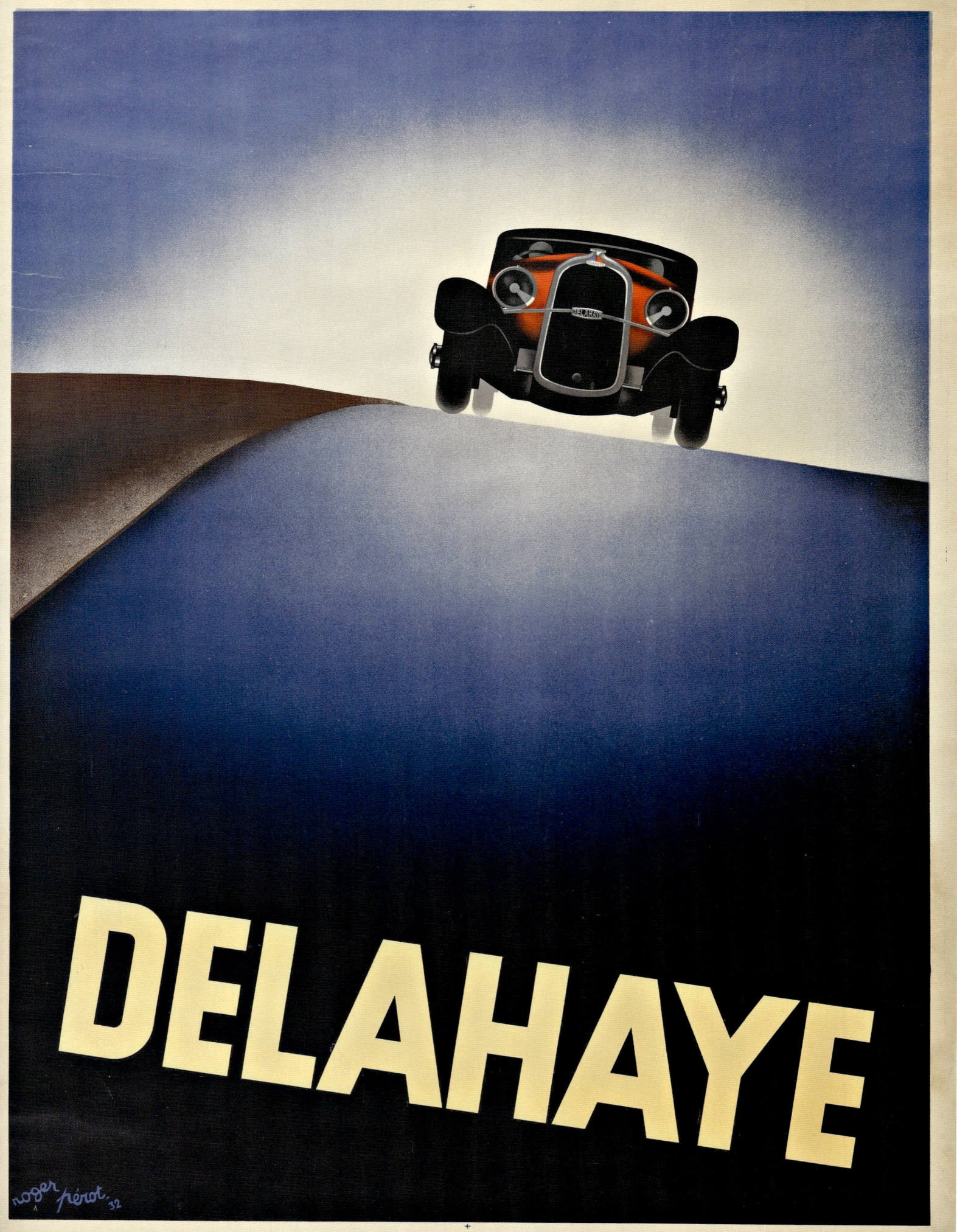

Delahaye, 1932
Roger Pérot (1908–1976)
62⅛ x 46¼ inches (157.8 x 117.5 cm)
Les Ateliers A.B.C., Paris

Fixated on a need for speed, Émile Delahaye founded his eponymous car company in 1894 and produced a handful of award-winning belt-driven racing vehicles over the next few years. By the 1910s, the company manufactured a host of luxury cars as well, but the crux of its business was trucks. This all changed in the early 1930s, when the company was restructured to incorporate the assembly-line procedures made famous by Ford. To mark the dawning of this new automotive age, artist Roger Pérot created an exceptionally enticing image. Gliding over a hill with the sun rising up behind it, a new Delahaye—or what little we see of it—fills the viewer with all manner of anticipation. Like a hero coming home after a long journey, this car acts almost as a beacon of hope for the future. Having the text run parallel to the slight banking of the hill adds a natural sense of lift to the design and draws one's eye back to the grille of the car. This poster would prove so popular that three years later it would be reissued in a slightly different color palette, with the sky and road in exuberant yellow rather than calming blue. Delahaye was acquired by Hotchkiss et Cie. in 1954.

Peugeot: La Grande Marque Nationale, 1926
Charles Loupot (1892–1962)
46½ x 62⅞ inches (118.1 x 159.7 cm)
Les Belles Affiches, Paris

Blurred with speed and captured in a manner somewhat suggestive of a hastily snapped photograph, the front of a Peugeot Type 177B surges forward in an uphill direction, the iconic *lion rampant* hood ornament aggressively pointing the way. A French tricolor roundel situated in the spare tire's traditional spot clearly indicates the vehicle's country of origin. Designed to replace the Type 163 in the midprice market, the 177B would compete admirably with the Citroën B12 and the Renault KZ. It is interesting to compare this poster to Loupot's Austin tractor advertisement (page 56). While not identical in design (the tractor is seen from a distance; the Peugeot is seen in a partial close-up, devoid of surroundings), both concepts use emphatic diagonals and rich colors to create an immediate and enduring impact. This Loupot poster is one of his best and is extraordinarily rare. Today, Peugeot is part of PSA Peugeot Citroën, the second-largest European carmaker.

Monet Goyon, 1933
Roger Pérot (1908–1976)
47⅛ x 31⅛ inches (119.7 x 79 cm)
Havas, Mâcon

It outpaces an automobile. It easily outruns a locomotive. Clearly the Monet-Goyon motorcycle is the vehicle to use if you need to get somewhere in a hurry. Roger Pérot does an excellent job of playing up the speed element in his design. The soft yellow and orange background colors make the blackness of the Monet-Goyon and its rider stand out while creating the illusion that the roaring machine is on the verge of surging off the page. Joseph Monet and Adrien Goyon founded their motorcycle company in 1917 in the commune of Mâcon, in the Burgundy region of France. When Joseph died in 1926, his brother, Marcel, replaced him. Monet-Goyon halted production during World War II, but the brand was relaunched in the post-war years with a focus on smaller motorcycles and scooters. Although well known in sporting circles, the company suffered from numerous commercial setbacks during the 1950s and ceased operations entirely by the end of the decade.

Motosacoche, 1927
Marcello Nizzoli (1887–1969)
51 x 35½ inches (129.5 x 90.2 cm)
Maga, Genève

More impressive than the mountain over which it soars or the winding road that leads up to it—a byway that might intimidate lesser vehicles—a 346cc Motosacoche 304 Tourisme motorcycle takes to the lemon-yellow sky, freed from the shackles of gravity, taking chunks of the mountain with it as it rises to new heights. It is a stunning and rare Nizzoli design that uses primary colors and an unusual off-kilter vantage point to lead the viewer's eye directly to the advertised product. In 1899, brothers Henri and Armand Dufaux designed a little four-stroke engine that could be bolted to the frame of any ordinary bicycle, thus converting it into a motorized conveyance. It was from these humble beginnings that Geneva-based Motosacoche was born (the company's name roughly translates as "motor in a bag"). The practicality and quality of the product soon earned a reputation far beyond Switzerland. Although the Dufaux brothers would leave the company in 1905 to concentrate on building airplanes, the company would continue to produce increasingly bigger and more powerful engines. In time, Motosacoche became the largest Swiss motorcycle manufacturer; it was also known for its MAG (Motosacoche Acacias Genève) engines, which were used by other manufacturers throughout Europe. The company began to decline during the 1930s, a result of the global economic crisis and a lack of success on the racetrack, where the company had hoped to promote its products. Motosacoche attempted several comebacks following World War II, but there was very little response from the public, which was more interested in cars and scooters. By 1958, Motosacoche had ceased motorcycle production, although it continued to manufacture MAG engines.

Styl'son: La Moto de Grand Style, ca. 1930
F. J. Martin (n.d.)
46 x 31 inches (116.8 x 78.7 cm)
Publicité F. J. Martin, Saint-Étienne

Beneath the diagonally placed flags of France, the United States, and Great Britain—all of which appear as mirror images of themselves—a shadowy rider streaks over the globe on his Styl'son motorcycle. The name of the game here is speed, and Martin clearly wants to get across the idea that Styl'son is the brand that dominates the world in that department. Although this claim constitutes a bit of promotional overstatement, it is true that Styl'son racing models did have a considerable amount of success. Manufactured in the capital of France's Loire *département*, Saint-Étienne, by a company known as S.A.D. Motorcycles, Styl'son bikes were in production from 1919 until 1938. The three flags in this poster featured heavily in the company's promotional material during the late 1920s and early 1930s, leading one to believe that these were the major Styl'son markets, although there is no specific documentation to that effect. This rare poster was acquired from the estate of movie icon Steve McQueen.

Automoto, ca. 1930
Max Ponty (1904–1972)
47⅛ x 31⅝ inches (119.7 x 80.3 cm)
Hachard et Cie., Paris

This rare design by Max Ponty is a futuristic photomontage for the French motorcycle manufacturer Automoto. It contrasts the appeal of the photographed bike against the angular, oversize art deco face of the biker, whose goggles perfectly reflect an expanse of open road (suspiciously similar to the tree-lined thoroughfare in Cassandre's *La Route Bleue*, page 305). Ponty creates a biking fantasia, capturing both the thrill and speed of the ride without ever placing the Automoto in simulated motion. The company, which was founded in Paris in 1901, was a pioneer in motorcycle manufacturing and had a reputation for building powerful machines. Automoto merged with Peugeot in 1931 before ceasing operations altogether in 1962.

FN (Fabrique Nationale), 1925
Marcello Nizzoli (1887–1969)
47¼ x 31⅞ inches (120 x 81 cm)
Publivox, Genève

This rare Marcello Nizzoli design for Fabrique Nationale motorcycles is a striking combination of strength and sly humor—the masculine, pitch-black phantom at the controls easily conveys the power-packed ride of the FN bike, whereas the lipstick-applying passenger, dressed completely in red, signals a smooth, comfortable journey. Additionally, the shadowy driver, without the assistance of a single feature or detail, imparts the bad-boy aura typically associated with motorcycles. It is not surprising in the least that he gets the girl. The bottom portion of the poster was left blank to allow FN dealerships to print their name and particulars for consumer identification. Here we see the information for Leon Houard, an FN agent in Ghent, Belgium. Nizzoli simplifies the company logo in his design, creating a much more linear representation than the one typically seen in FN advertising (right), which contains a central symbol that combines a rifle and a pair of pedals, both essential elements in the history of Fabrique Nationale. Founded in 1889 in the Liège suburb of Herstal, Belgium, FN originally manufactured bicycles, motorcycles, automobiles, and firearms. Production of motorcycles continued until 1965, and trucks were produced until 1970. Today, the company is a subsidiary of the Herstal Group and manufactures only firearms, both in Europe and in the United States.

FN (Fabrique Nationale), 1928
Albert Chavepeyer (1899–1986)
46⅝ x 31¼ inches (118.4 x 79.4 cm)
Imprimerie Bénard, Liège

In this intense Albert Chavepeyer design, the sheer mechanical prowess of FN motorcycles is celebrated by a speeding rider, purposefully focused and incognito, atop a 350cc FN M70 Sahara. In 1927, in order to prove the M70's reliability, two French army officers and a Belgian mechanic were commissioned to cross the Sahara Desert on these motorcycles. The feat covered nearly four thousand miles and was accomplished between April and June without a single breakdown. The much-lauded crossing brought a great deal of attention to Fabrique Nationale and led to the cycle being dubbed the Sahara. It was a very successful vehicle for FN, known for its easy starting,

3º Salone Internazionale dell'Automobile, 1930
Giacinto Mondaini (1902–1979)
79 x 55 inches (200.7 x 139.7 cm)
Gros-Monti & C., Torino

For the third Milan International Auto Show, Giacinto Mondaini creates a sparse, powerful art deco collage composed of three interconnected elements: bold text, an extremely appreciative colossus, and an elegantly simple vehicle. The artist utilizes the flat white of the paper to create a featureless background, which immediately draws the viewer's attention to the composition in the foreground. It's a wonderful combination of subtle artistry—especially the use of foreshortening, which thrusts the car toward the viewer—and humor: not only does the stylized embodiment of automotive appreciation hold the sedan (obviously a Fiat) aloft, he unabashedly sings its praises as well. The 1930 Milan Expo featured eighty-three parts and accessories makers as well as fifteen automotive manufacturers who exhibited forty-two different models and thirty-four makes of industrial vehicles.

VI Salón del Automóvil, 1928
A. Pombo and **J. Bolales** (n.d.)
45½ x 29¾ inches (115.6 x 75.6 cm)
Printer unknown

The universality of art deco style is perhaps best expressed through the posters that come from the most unexpected places. Here we have an image for a rather obscure automobile show in Uruguay. Although elements of art deco are still evident in the country's historic architecture, one does not necessarily think of Uruguay as a center for deco graphic design (see page 114). And yet this poster rivals the compositional quality of some of the best European images of that era, giving us the seductive essence of the event rather than a depiction of an absolute object. Were it not for the presence of the wheel, one would not even be able to tell that these waves and acute angles are meant to represent a car; yet once the shape of an automobile is inferred, we know instantly that it embodies the apex of style and fills the vast halls of the Parque Hotel with inimitable luxury. The show itself is still held today as the Montevideo Motor Show, sponsored by the Automobile Club of Uruguay, founded in 1918. The club would achieve international recognition in 1920, when it became a member of the International Automobile Federation, thus giving it the means to commission lavish posters such as this one for its annual event.

RAI: Amsterdam, 1929
A. M. Cassandre (Adolphe Mouron, 1901–1968)
44⅜ x 31½ inches (112.7 x 80 cm)
Nijgh & Van Ditmar, Rotterdam

The annual auto show sponsored by the Amsterdam RAI (De Rijwiel-Automobile Industrie, or bicycle and automobile industry) began when it was common for bicycles and automobiles to be manufactured by the same company and sold side by side. However, the last year that bicycles appeared at the RAI show was 1906, and in 1929 the name of the sponsor on this poster was simply the relic of a bygone era—a coupling made obsolete by technology. To promote the exhibition, though, Cassandre does give us an image that is two things at once. First, he depicts the grille of a luxurious new car, its details distilled down to a grayscale outline of its essential parts. In addition, the car's headlight acts as a monocle for the blue-eyed male depicted in profile who keenly observes the latest cars coming fresh off the assembly line. We are seeing him and seeing what he sees—a design that references itself in an endless loop. Rather than promote the show the traditional way—by tantalizing the viewer with a flashy car surrounded by stylish women—Cassandre's poster acts as a didactic emblem: one is here to observe the finest vehicles in the world, nothing less. The message is no-frills sincerity, while the composition adds an unmistakable splash of cool.

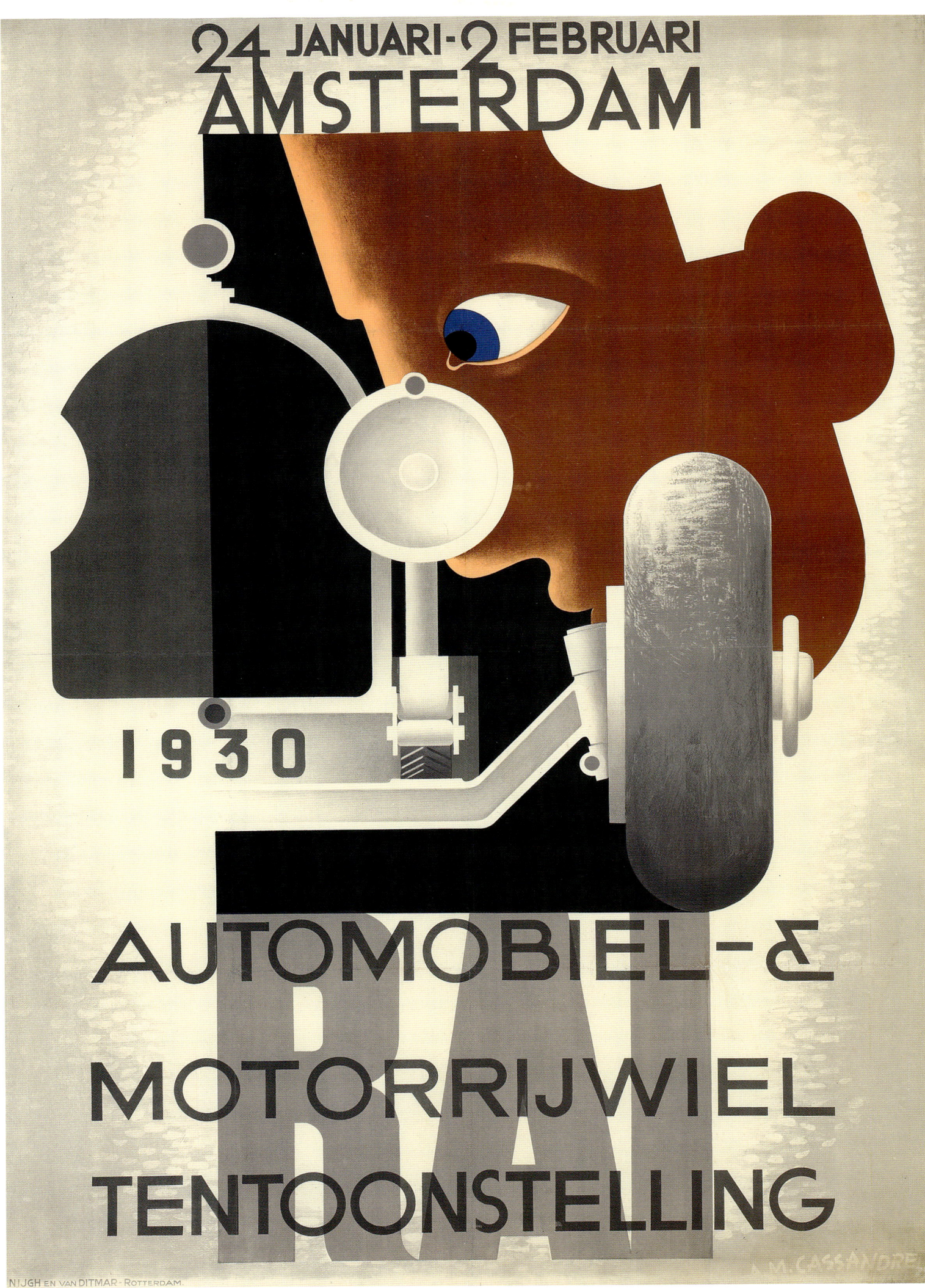

MOTOR COMPTOIR ZÜRICH 1932
AUTOHALLE 4.–7.
LETZIGRABEN MÄRZ

Motor Comptoir: Zürich, 1932
Otto Baumberger (1889–1961)
49¼ x 35⅞ inches (125.1 x 91.1 cm)
Gebrüder Fretz, Zürich

In this poster for a four-day Zurich trade show focusing on motorized transport, artist Otto Baumberger opts for simplicity, allowing the earth-tone silhouettes of airplane, automobile, and motorcycle to convey the exposition's thematic thrust to the public. Granted, the advertisement does not go into great detail, but it provides the essentials, with just the right amount of information to attract the curiosity of those with a need to go farther faster.

International Automobile and Motor-Cycle Exhibition: Berlin, 1939
Anton Klotz and **Eugen Kienast** (n.d.)
39¾ x 24¾ inches (101 x 62.9 cm)
Elsnerdruck, Berlin

The Third Reich's predisposition for monumentalism is fully displayed in this Klotz and Kienast poster for the 1939 Berlin International Automobile and Motorcycle Exhibition. The glowing *Ausstellungshalle* (exhibition hall), its searchlights beaming, towers above the globe, dominated by a Mercedes-Benz W154 (on the left) and an Auto Union Type D V16 (on the right)—the symbols of German automotive superiority. In fact, these two automobiles totally dominated Grand Prix motor racing from May of 1934 until September of 1939, winning fifty-two races between them. Ironically, the streak ended when Hitler invaded Poland and auto racing was suspended until after World War II. While the artwork may indulge in a bit of artistic overstatement, the 1939 show was actually rather massive, filling not one but nine enormous exhibition halls located near the Witzleben train station. Opened by none other than *der Führer* himself, Adolf Hitler, the show attracted more than one hundred thousand visitors from around the world eager to view the output of the German automotive industry at its peak. In addition to displaying a multitude of trucks, motorcycles, and cars—including Mercedes-Benz, Auto Union, Stoewer, BMW, and Opel, to name but a few—the exhibition also showcased the autobahn system, the first limited-access, high-speed road network in the world. Also exhibiting were the German state railway and makers of automotive replacement parts, such as Continental tires and Philips headlamps.

Right: Joseph Goebbels, Hermann Goering, and Adolf Hitler look at new innovations in automobile engines at the 1939 International Automobile and Motor-Cycle Exhibition in Berlin.

CONSUMER AND INDUSTRIAL PRODUCTS

CONTINUOUS IMPROVEMENT in manufacturing technologies during the early twentieth century resulted in easy public access to a large variety of consumer products, ranging from household goods such as razor blades and toothpaste to essential resources such as petroleum, water, and electricity. The development and broad use of commodities produced chemically, such as aluminum, nylon, vinyl, acrylic, and saran, increased the diversity of goods coming to market. With an ever-expanding choice of products at affordable prices, consumer demand grew at an unprecedented rate.

Product design, ease of use, accessibility, and affordability drove expanding revenues for manufacturers and sellers. Posters, which combined image and word into simple, eye-catching messages, served as an ideal way to grab consumers' attention and were crucial to a product's success. There was no such thing as a graphic designer at the start of the twentieth century, but by 1925 thousands of them were employed as the consumer advertising industry exploded.

This chapter contains exceptional examples of posters for consumer and industrial products by the top art deco graphic designers of the period—artists such as A. M. Cassandre, Charles Loupot, Jean Carlu, Lester Beall, Niklaus Stoecklin, Theodoro, Orsi, and Edward McKnight Kauffer—who produced some of the most beautiful and iconic posters ever made.

Gold Starry, 1930
Theodoro (Theodore Pfeifer, 1896–1973)
62¼ x 46⅛ inches (158.1 x 117.1 cm)
Imprimerie Kaplan, Paris

In the first decade of the twentieth century, France was importing a remarkable number of British-made pens—so many that producing them domestically seemed like a more-than-intelligent business idea. After a brief collaboration with the newly formed English company Conway Stewart, an entrepreneur named Maurice Jandelle broke off on his own and began to manufacture the pens domestically. By 1921, the name Gold Starry—after the gold star that appeared on the company's logo— was official, along with the tagline "Le stylo qui marche" ("the pen that works"). But *marche* means "to walk" as well as "to work," leading an array of poster artists to produce designs in which said pens are engaged in a combination of the two. Theodoro rises beautifully to the occasion, giving us an Asian man who uses the pens as stilts and dances across the page like a traditional circus performer. This rare image serves to show off the brand's handsome construction as well as to delight the viewer with a bit of humor—a key way of standing out amid the hundreds of posters lining the city streets at the time. Although it never really found a market outside of France, the company survived up through the 1980s, at which point it dissolved as a result of financial problems.

Gold Starry, 1932
Orsi (1889–1947)
62¾ x 47⅜ inches (159.4 x 120.3 cm)
Publicité Phogor, Paris

Playing off the idea expressed in Theodoro's design for Gold Starry (left), Orsi elevates the concept to a somewhat more sophisticated sphere. Rather than the pedestrian notion of a circus performer using the "pen that walks" as stilts, here we have a paper man perfectly balancing on the ink levers of the fountain pens, smoothly striding forward. Each poster attracts a slightly different audience: while the acrobat appeals to everyone as cute and funny, this notebook gentleman targets a more posh, masculine demographic. His bow tie and hat imply a white-collar lifestyle—and his walking on pen-stilts is less comical than it is merely amusing. Even the style of pen speaks to a more affluent clientele: the Theodoro poster presents the most bare-bones model, whereas this image showcases pens in a slightly higher price range. Seen side by side, each is an excellent example of fine art deco graphics; but while one is charming, the other is aspirational. It is interesting to note that the levers upon which the unofficial mascots stand were a unique element of the Gold Starry design, as they allowed one to draw in ink without removing the top of the pen.

le stylo qui marche

GOLD STARRY

Monsavon, 1925
Jean Carlu (1900–1997)
62 x 45¾ inches (157.5 x 116.2 cm)
Éditions d'Art Robert Lang, Paris

Generally considered to be the design that launched Carlu's career into poster superstardom, this image for Monsavon was reproduced in every important graphic-arts magazine of the time. The composition was a profound break from the style Carlu had been honing in the early portion of his career. It combines elements of his newfound love of cubism with traditional art deco angles, resulting in something particularly modern. This essence of the supermodern was all the more shocking when compared to posters in the style of Leonetto Cappiello, which were still decorating the streets of Paris. Luckily for Carlu, the two men in charge of green-lighting this project—Philippe de Rothschild and André Wismer—were of a younger generation than many of their colleagues and were open to a poster that pushed the graphic envelope. The design itself is all about implied information rather than revealed facts. The viewer only sees a pie slice of checkered wall, the hint of a sink rim, and a bare-chested figure leaning to the left; yet we know he is peering out from behind a shower curtain in a bathroom. The blocky coloring outside the lines of the man's form may make him appear more triangular and thereby more deco; however, it also turns his body into a giant arrow pointing toward the singular bar of soap. It is a design that constantly draws one's attention to the product in hand. The text, "My soap is Monsavon," also serves to reinforce the brand name.

Dentifrices Gellé Frères, 1927
Jean Carlu (1900–1997)
58⅞ x 39⅛ inches (147 x 99.4 cm)
Les Imprimeries Françaises Réunies, Paris

Still in operation today, Gellé Frères began in the seventeenth century as a private *parfumeur* to the French royal court. Over time, the company expanded into other cosmetics and toiletries, and in 1927 it released its first glycerin-based toothpaste. Always eager to tap into the most popular talents of the day, the brand had already used the famous art of Alphonse Mucha to promote its perfumes and had hired Mistinguett as the company's spokesperson in 1925. For the launch of its toothpaste, Jean Carlu—one of the most celebrated advertising artists in France at the time—was chosen to bring visual excitement to the product. What resulted is one of the most visually arresting and rare art deco compositions of the era. Not only is it simply a wonderful, eye-catching image, but every element of the design is deliberately placed to best show off the product. No other feature on the figure's face is visible except its bright white teeth, yet with the red-to-black shading we do not feel as if the face is empty or without texture. The palette, intentionally dark, allows the mouth to appear whiter than it really is, even when compared to the pale blue text; one is instantly drawn toward the teeth before one even knows what is being advertised—as one is drawn to the eyes in Paul Colin's poster for Leroy opticians (page 134).

DENTIFRICES
GELLÉ FRÈRES

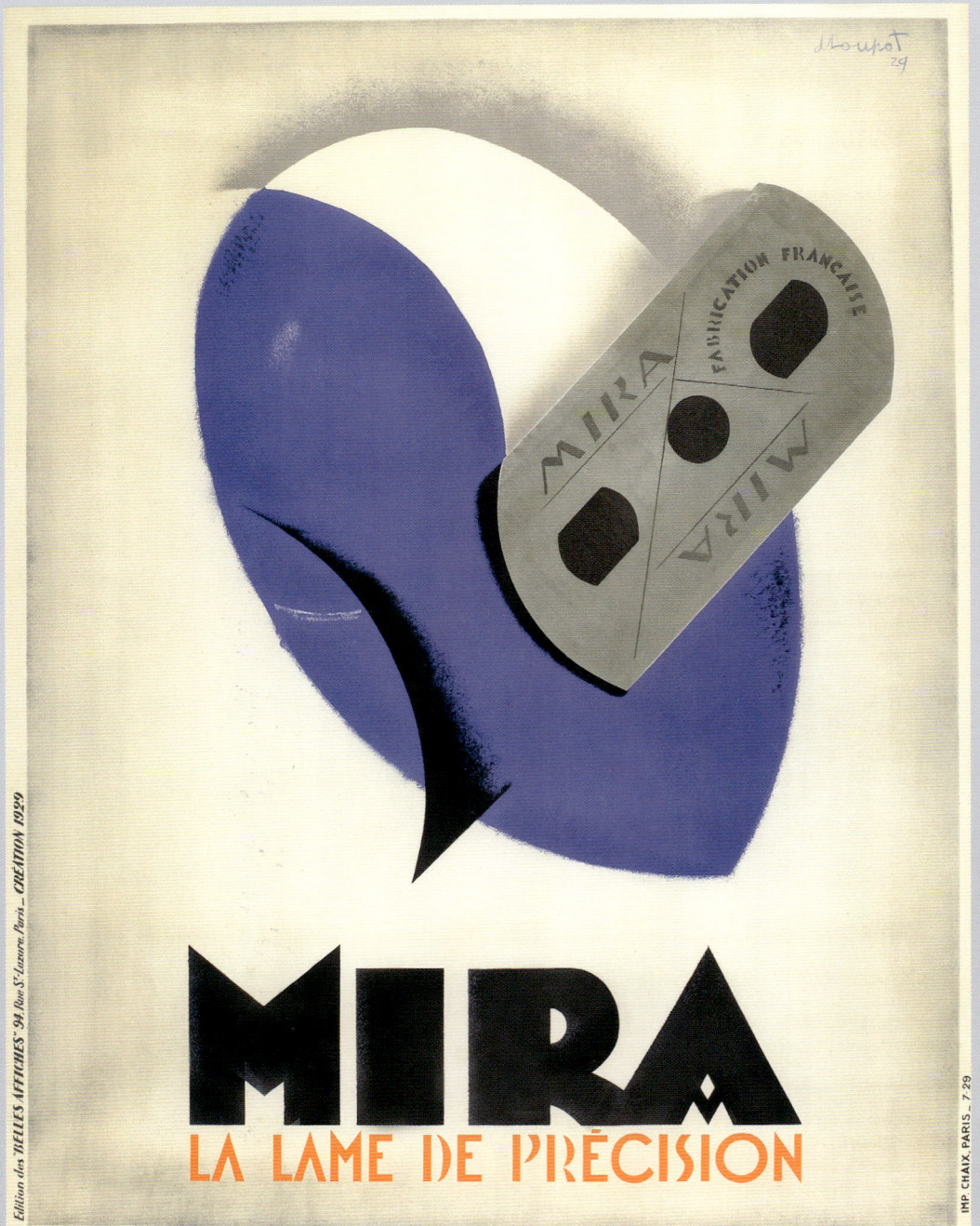

Mira, 1929
Charles Loupot (1892–1962)
63⅛ x 47¾ inches (160.3 x 121.3 cm)
Imprimerie Chaix, Paris

While it is perhaps not the most visually intelligible advertisement, this poster for Mira razor blades is without a doubt one of Loupot's most interesting. The product itself is shown in a straightforward, realistic manner, but the object being "shaved" is slightly confusing. It is perhaps Loupot's most cubist rendering of the human form, with no indication of it being a head save for the sharp curve of an implied ear. Even that one detail, though, requires trust and intuition on the part of the viewer. As the blade glides over the curved upper plane of the figure, a surface of solid white is left in its wake—presumably indicating the precision touted in the text below. Of course, if this were an actual face, it is unlikely that the forehead would be shaved; however, because the blade comes to rest halfway down the football-shaped form, the holes in the razor suddenly become eyes and a nose, subtly reinforcing the suggestion of a visage. In essence, Loupot has anthropomorphized the most inanimate of objects with as few visual indicators as possible—we know what it is, but we can't quite explain how we know. A further unusual element of the poster is that the razor blade is executed entirely in metallic silver—a unique touch, as Loupot was one of the only artists to use metallic paper in his work at that time (Robert Louis's *Pierce-Arrow,* page 48, and Aladár Richter's *Megnyílt Hirdető,* page 104, also use metallic paper).

Internationale Hygiene Ausstellung, 1930
Willy Petzold (1885–1978)
35½ x 23½ inches (90.2 x 59.7 cm)
Dr. Güntzchen Stiftung, Dresden

Originally appearing in the famous 1911 design by Franz von Stuck for Dresden's annual International Hygiene Exposition, the all-seeing eye in this poster, which announces the same event nearly twenty years later, has been updated and modernized. No longer gussied up in the trappings of Secessionist aesthetics, the eye here is simply a bold, stylized interpretation of a human orb as seen through an art deco lens. It becomes godlike in its singular stare, its radiating gold beams hypnotically drawing in the viewer. The exhibition itself, a kind of "world's fair" of health in which more than thirty countries participated, was intensely popular, allowing all five million visitors the chance to see lifelike models of the human anatomy in the context of informative panels and displays on the latest advances in health care, nutrition, and diet. This was at the height of the German cult of the body, a movement in which the athletic, healthy human form was valued above all else—a trend that Hitler would go on to exploit in his vision of a "perfect Aryan race." The eye design proved so effective that not only would it be used again on the following year's poster but the newly formed Deutsches Hygiene-Museum—founded by Odol mouthwash mogul Karl August Lingner—would also adopt it as its official logo. It is still in use to this day.

Gaba, 1927
Niklaus Stoecklin (1896–1982)
50⅛ x 35½ inches (127.3 x 90.2 cm)
Graphische Anstalt W. Wassermann, Basel

When Niklaus Stoecklin branched out from traditional painting into poster design, he borrowed elements of Neue Sachlichkeit (the "new objectivity")—a style made famous by the likes of Christian Schad and other Weimar-era artists—and brought them to advertising. The beauty and genius of the *Sachplakat*, or Object Poster, was that it placed its focus on a singular item and re-created it for the viewer with meticulous accuracy. In doing so, it elevated the ordinary—or, in some cases, the overlooked—to extraordinary status, creating high art out of the everyday. This particular image, though, stands out from the rest of Stoecklin's oeuvre, as it shares no graphic commonality with anything created by him before or after. We see a highly stylized human head, colored blue to indicate that the person is under the weather. He is craning his neck, like a child reaching for its mother's breast, in order to ingest a single Gaba lozenge. Below, the phrase "Protect yourself" is forcefully written underneath the product's name. For such a remarkably simple composition, it is extremely effective. This is perhaps why it continued to be reprinted years after its original appearance in 1927, and also why it was voted the popular favorite at Zurich's Graphische Fachausstellung (Printing Trades Exposition) in 1934.

Triplex, 1931
A. M. Cassandre (Adolphe Mouron, 1901–1968)
47 x 31⅜ inches (119.4 x 79.7 cm)
Alliance Graphique, Paris

The origins of Triplex safety glass can be traced back to the St Helens Crown Glass Company of England, a manufacturer of sheet glass (which would later become known as plate glass) founded by John William Bell in 1826 and renamed Pilkington Brothers in 1849. Triplex laminated automobile safety glass was invented in 1909, but it wasn't until 1929 that Triplex and Pilkington joined forces to form the Triplex Safety Glass Company, a result of increased demand and a need for specialized production. Their process was relatively simple: adhere a sheet of glass to both sides of a sheet of plastic. This interior polymer sheet wouldn't prevent the glass from shattering in the event of an accident,

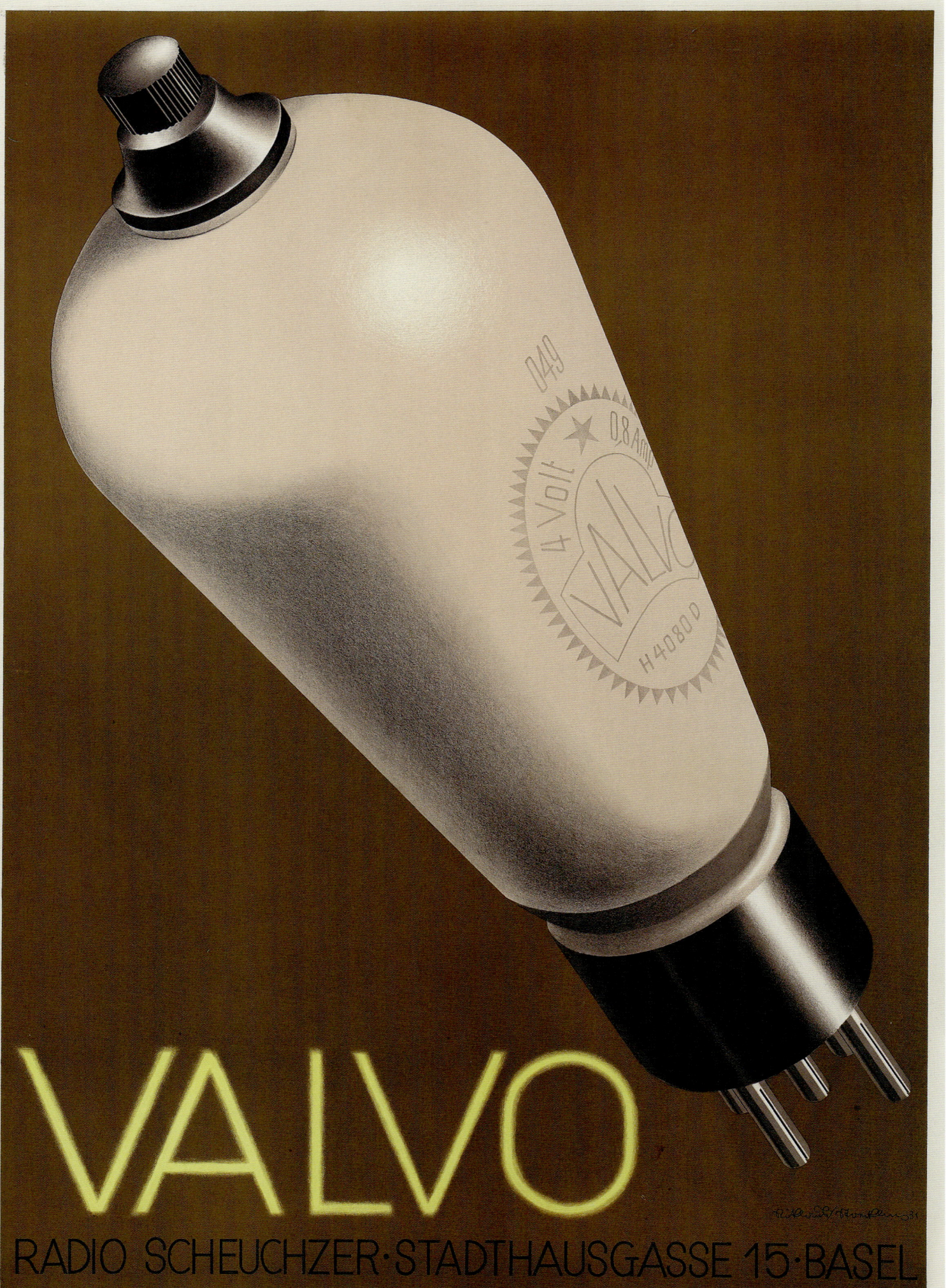

Valvo: Radio Scheuchzer, 1929
Niklaus Stoecklin (1896–1982)
50 x 35 inches (127 x 88.9 cm)
Graphische Anstalt W. Wassermann, Basel

Niklaus Stoecklin, the artist who made Clus Ironworks transmission components the singular focus of his promotional design (see page 98), employs the same strategy in this Object Poster for the Scheuchzer radio store and its inventory of Valvo vacuum tubes. Once again we see a rather ordinary, if overlooked, item elevated to extraordinary status—the tetrode tube, which was used in high-frequency radios. The approach is both grandiose and humorous, and Stoecklin executes the design masterfully. Interestingly, Stoecklin reverses the background color and the color of the tube—the majority of the Valvo products from this period were coated with a copper-colored sealant. However, the choice adds luster to the poster and certainly draws attention directly to the whitened tube. Valvo was a German subsidiary of Philips (see page 106), the multinational Dutch electronics corporation.

Tungsram Radio-Röhren, 1933
Anonymous
46¾ x 33½ inches (118.7 x 85.1 cm)
Meissner & Buch, Leipzig and Berlin

Although a Tungsram radio tube, rendered by an uncredited artist in a virtually photographic manner, appears front and center in this poster, it is the combination of the tube and the stylized bust behind it that gives the design its depth and resonance. It does not belabor the point, but the thoughtful profile of a head tilted forward in concentration adds a classic sense of portent to the design, making it instantly clear that choosing Tungsram is an informed decision. Even though vacuum tubes by themselves do not reproduce sound, the placement of the tube against the ear subtly informs the viewer that Tungsram is an integral element in the listening experience. Tungsram is a Hungarian company that has been manufacturing lightbulbs and vacuum tubes since 1896. Its name is an amalgamation of the word "tungsten" and its synonym, "wolfram"—the element used as a filament in vacuum tubes. Today, the company is a subsidiary of General Electric.

Right: A BBC technician performs maintenance work on the back of a control panel at London's Broadcasting House in October of 1932. In the early 1930s, engineers at General Electric made predictions that large vacuum tubes—technology originally used for radios—would one day replace motors.

LIGHT

RURAL ELECTRIFICATION ADMINISTRATION

Pages 82–87
Rural Electrification Administration, 1937
Lester T. Beall (1903–1969)
Series of 6
40 x 30 inches each (101.6 x 76.2 cm)
Rural Electrification Administration,
Washington, DC

As part of the New Deal, President Franklin Delano Roosevelt set up the Rural Electrification Administration (REA) on May 11, 1935, in order to better provide America's rural population with electricity and to create employment for a Depression-ravaged country. At the time, the United States lagged far behind Europe in its access to power: only 11 percent of American farms were electrified, as opposed to 90 percent of farms in western Europe. American companies generally refused to invest in the infrastructure necessary to provide access to electricity because they claimed it was not worth the cost, given that profits would be so limited in those areas. In the few rural areas where electricity was available, rates were often as much as four times higher than those in the city, making electricity a luxury most farm dwellers could not afford. In response, the REA supplied loans to co-ops that were established to lay power lines and distribute electricity to these communities. Even then, persuading farmers, most of whom were illiterate, to purchase power was a difficult problem, one that this very rare series of six visually efficient posters attempted to surmount. Each image depicts a simple day-to-day situation and shows in bold, crisp graphics how electricity can improve it. In one poster, a lightbulb and a warmly lit home on a prairie indicate that a productive day does not have to end at sundown. In another, the endless benefits of running water are symbolized by the image of arrows moving through a faucet. In one of Beall's most forceful designs, radio waves, drawn as sharp white arrows, pummel toward an isolated home. Farm work is modernized with the help of electrified machines. And with electricity, heat and cold become something controllable. Finally, electricity makes wash day as simple as dropping one's dirty laundry into a machine. These posters helped the Rural Electrification Administration achieve such success that by 1940, an impressive 33 percent of farming communities were supplied with electricity. It revolutionized the way Middle America operated and improved the standard of living exponentially.

Right: In an August 11, 1938, speech at the dedication of a Rural Electrification Administration project in Georgia, President Franklin D. Roosevelt said: "Electricity is a modern necessity of life, not a luxury. That necessity ought to be found in every village, in every home, and on every farm in every part of the wide United States."

HEAT

COLD

RURAL ELECTRIFICATION ADMINISTRATION

Spidoléine, 1932
A. M. Cassandre (Adolphe Mouron, 1901–1968)
62¾ x 47⅛ inches (159.4 x 119.7 cm)
Alliance Graphique, Paris

Cassandre goes for extreme simplicity in this very rare and important poster for Spidoléine motor oil and the security it provides. His straightforward execution, however, doesn't mean that he did away with playfulness. As Robert K. Brown and Susan Reinhold observe in *The Poster Art of A. M. Cassandre*, "The natural inclination would have been to take a relatively small object . . . and make it life size or larger. Here Cassandre makes a more effective advertisement by taking the completely opposite approach of shrinking the oilcan's size. Instead of re-creating the lettering on the oilcan, he turns to a typographic exercise by extending the letters beyond the limits of the object and progressively diminishing the size of the characters while switching their color from yellow to black as they intrude on the yellow band." The line of golden oil trickling from the can has a magnetic appeal for the eye, a classic example of less being more.

Magicians Prefer Shell, 1934
Edward McKnight Kauffer (1890–1954)
30 x 44¾ inches (76.2 x 113.7 cm)
Waterlow & Sons, Limited, London and Dunstable

In terms of advertising, the British branch of Shell Oil was one of the largest and most progressive companies in Great Britain in the period between the two world wars. The firm gave artists a tremendous amount of creative freedom and allowed their imaginations free rein. Shell's approach was to pick a theme and then create a series around it. One of the best-known and most successful featured the people in various professions who preferred to use Shell. Some of the choices, such as everyday motorists (page 90) and race car drivers, are obvious. Other choices, such as magicians, are less obvious. In the end, the implication is that everyone prefers Shell, and the notion is conveyed with a refreshing, low-key sense of humor. Edward McKnight Kauffer's magnificent art deco sleight of hand also produces an intriguing yin and yang—drivers cannot function without Shell, and Shell cannot function without drivers. It is a nifty trick—singling out a rather small demographic in order to address the public at large—and Kauffer pulls it off with mastery and style.

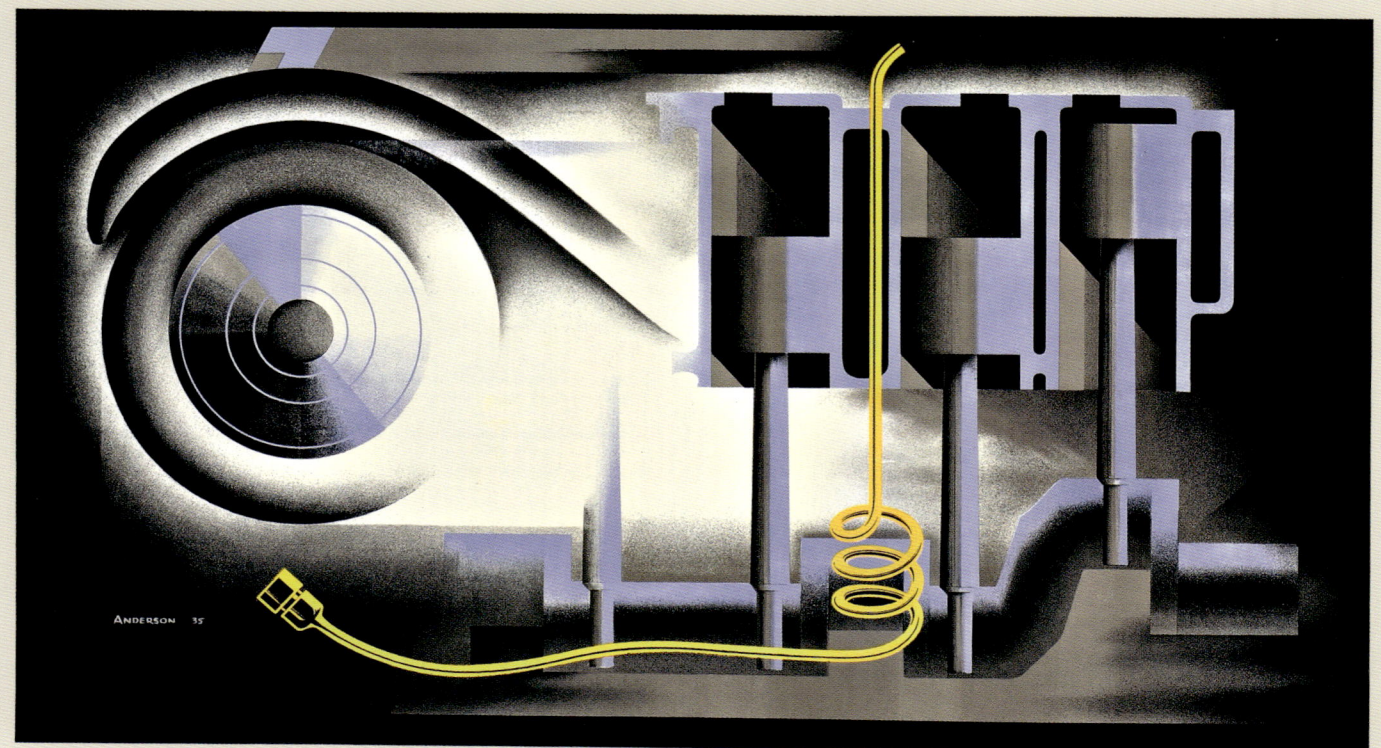

Motorists Prefer Shell, 1936
John Stewart Anderson (n.d.)
30 x 45 inches (76.2 x 114.3 cm)
Waterlow & Sons, Limited, London and Dunstable

In one of the finest designs in the distinguished series of posters created to show that persons in many different professions use Shell motor oil (see page 89), artist John Stewart Anderson poses pistons and a fuel line against an automobile seen in profile. The cool composition gives us the mechanical essence of the auto inside and out, which is, after all, the goal of a deconstructionist work—to provide a better understanding of the whole by taking it apart. It is not a typical approach for promoting the driving experience, but surprisingly, although the image contains essentially static components, Anderson conveys a wonderful sense of implied motion.

Shell for Anti-Knock, 1930
Yunge (n.d.)
30 x 44⅞ inches (76.2 x 114 cm)
Printer unknown

The relatively unknown artist Yunge creates a memorable, exciting design for Shell gasoline by relying on just three elements: speed, geometric precision, and the atypical use of lemon yellow as a dominant color. In today's recessionary economic climate, when the most important factor in purchasing gasoline is its cost, it is refreshing and more than a bit nostalgic to come across an advertisement that relies on artistry rather than price per gallon to attract our attention.

Time to Change to Winter Shell, 1938
Tom Eckersley (1914–1997) and
Eric Lombers (1914–1978)
30 x 45 inches (76.2 x 114.3 cm)
Waterlow & Sons, Limited, London and Dunstable

During the period when posters served as the company's primary promotional tool, Shell commissioned a "summer" and "winter" poster yearly from a variety of artists to remind the public that the blend of gasoline sold at the pumps was about to change. Since motorists were aware of the practice and accepted it, there was no need to include depictions of cars or gas pumps in the designs, which freed the artists to express themselves with whatever imagery they felt best conveyed the season in question. Eckersley and Lombers serve up this timely mixed-media photomontage reminder—composed of stencils and a glove knitted by Eckersley's wife—set against a background that modulates from flat black to beige, forcefully getting the message across.

BP Ethyl, 1934
Paolo Federico Garretto (1903–1991)
29 x 44¾ inches (73.7 x 113.7 cm)
Printer unknown

Paolo Federico Garretto's modernist graphic shorthand resembles an airbrushed pictograph—an ancient painting or drawing done on a rock wall, such as a cave or a cliff, that was used to convey a specific meaning through simple pictures. In this design, Garretto artfully depicts man's control of raw horsepower. The shadowed repetition of text in the poster's middle ground nicely cements the product's name in the mind of the viewer, while the central image of a man exerting command over a rearing stallion clearly conveys the concept of "controlling horse power."

Concentrum and Hydrogazo, ca. 1935
Gaston Gorde (1908–1995)
46½ x 31⅛ inches (118.1 x 79 cm)
Éditions Gaston Gorde, Grenoble

According to this poster, power, energy, and economy are what drivers can expect from Concentrum and Hydrogazo. To back up this boast, these two specialty gasolines are personified as gargantuan marksmen towering above their mountainous surroundings, powerful enough to propel any vehicle of any size to new performance heights. This masterful art deco composition is amazingly energetic—a high-caliber design executed with a superior economy of means, a repetition of strong forms, and a trio of vibrant colors.

There were twelve different types of gasoline available at this filling station in Berlin, Germany, in 1930.

Bergougnan: Pneus Motos Velos, 1930
Georges Favre (n.d.)
61⅝ x 46¾ inches (156.2 x 118.7 cm)
Affiches Gaillard, Paris

Pneu Bergougnan, 1935
Georges Favre (n.d.)
61¾ x 45⅜ inches (156.8 x 115.2 cm)
Affiches Gaillard, Paris

Georges Favre designed several promotional posters for Bergougnan tires, creating a good-natured orange fellow dressed in blue—influenced a bit by the Michelin Man, a.k.a. Bibendum—as an ambassador for the company. In one poster, the tire-peddling creature hops aboard an airy vehicle composed entirely of motorcycle and bicycle tires, accompanied as he streams along with a text that roughly translates as "Whiz along with Bergougnan!" In another, Favre communicates the strength of Bergougnan tires by showing how well they support the Jolly Blue Giant as he heads out for a stroll—or a roll, if you prefer. Originally a Belgian-owned company that began production in 1921, Bergougnan earned an immediate reputation as a leading tire manufacturer; the company merged with Sweden's Trelleborg (right) in 1988. Today, Bergougnan offers an extensive line of tires under the product names Elite and Expert. Despite a hefty body of work produced between 1927 and 1935, very little is known about the artist; some sources even claim that Favre is a Gabrielle, not a Georges.

Trelleborg, 1933
Olle Svanlund (1909–1994)
39⅜ x 27½ inches (100 x 69.8 cm)
J. Olséns Litografiska Anstalt, Stockholm

Tires are the focus in this rare Olle Svanlund design for Trelleborg, the Swedish rubber company based in the town of the same name. With the realistically rendered motorcycle and car tires placed front and center, the vehicles and rider become secondary elements, near phantoms relegated to the soft pastel background. But what truly creates the impression in this poster is the slant of the images—the acute angles that powerfully evoke motion, a secure grip, and speed. Trelleborg AB began as Trellborgs Gummifabriks in 1905. Under the direction of industrialist and philanthropist Henry Dunker (1870–1962), the company rapidly became Scandinavia's leading producer of rubber goods, principally tires and raincoats. Whereas the Great Depression and the global economic crisis it generated brought about the demise of a great number of companies, it had surprisingly little effect on Trelleborg, primarily because of an ever-increasing demand for cars. In the period between 1931 and 1935, the company doubled its sales of automobile tires. It produced the world's first winter tire (the Wittmer) and Europe's first tubeless tire (the Safe-T) in 1953. Today, the Trelleborg Group is a global industrial conglomerate specializing in advanced polymer technology.

Heemaf, 1930
A. M. Cassandre (Adolphe Mouron, 1901–1968)
11¾ x 7⅞ inches (29.8 x 20 cm)
Nijgh & Van Ditmar, Rotterdam

As the largest private energy company in the Netherlands since 1908, Heemaf (originally an acronym for Hengelosche Electrische en Mechanische Apparaten Fabriek) was not really in need of a strong advertising campaign at the time this poster was commissioned; however, Cassandre used the occasion to create one of the finest corporate images of the twentieth century. It is a composition primarily of circles—the positive and negative poles; the voltmeter; the gears cranking together. Some scholars have compared this design to the mechanical paintings of Francis Picabia; however, this was the Machine Age, and hundreds of artists were exploring the graphic purity of gears and levers in their work, from Diego Rivera to Wassily Kandinsky. The use of that motif is not what sets this poster apart; rather, it is the clear means by which it expresses that era's mantra of speed, precision, and power. It is not just a glorified image of mechanical parts but a concise abstraction of what the company stands for—the electricity to make your machines run. So clear is that message that the text—"for electric power," which runs diagonally across the design—is almost unnecessary. In addition to being an electrical supplier, Heemaf pioneered the vacuum-tube industry in the Netherlands and provided the country's first electric traffic lights.

Thomson, 1931
A. M. Cassandre (Adolphe Mouron, 1901–1968)
46¾ x 31⅜ inches (118.7 x 79.7 cm)
Alliance Graphique, Paris

The advent of widespread, reliable electricity reinvented the way a home operated. Suddenly almost anything one previously had to do manually could now be done by a machine. In Cassandre's rare and famous poster for Thomson, an electricity provider, the artist presents the viewer with a visual pun. The phrase *la main-d'oeuvre* literally translates as "hand labor," but in common usage means something closer to "workforce," or "hired hand." And any sort of home appliance can fall under the umbrella of an *electro-domestique*. So to promote the idea of Thomson bringing infinite power to your home, Cassandre gives us a hand being lassoed by an electrical cord as it shoots diagonally across the page. This human feature, rather than an appliance, is simultaneously plugged into Thomson's service, becoming a hand that is "powered" to do any sort of labor. The company could bring power straight to your fingertips—an idea made even more graphically whimsical by the presence of five shiny stars teetering above the pad of each blue digit. It is one of Cassandre's most literal compositions, borrowing more from the Dadaist tradition than from that of the Object Poster or the symbolists. The Thomson-Houston Electric Company merged with the Edison General Electric Company in 1892 to form General Electric. This advertisement was for GE's sister company in France, Thomson Electric.

Eisenwerk Clus, 1925
Niklaus Stoecklin (1896–1982)
50 x 35¼ inches (127 x 89.5 cm)
Graphische Anstalt W. Wassermann, Basel

This poster is considered to be Stoecklin's best image, a true masterpiece of design. Perhaps even more so than the mechanism depicted in Stoecklin's other automotive Object Poster (above right), this iron transmission wheel, seen here before the addition of text, makes a bold graphic statement and allows its precisely re-created subject to make an impression on the viewer without a single distraction. It also hints at what was artistically to come for Stoecklin—the near-photographic hyperrealism that would dominate his output during the 1940s.

Eisenwerk Clus: Transmissionen, 1925
Niklaus Stoecklin (1896–1982)
50½ x 35½ inches (128.3 x 90.2 cm)
Graphische Anstalt W. Wassermann, Basel

This Object Poster for Basel's Petitjean supply house and its selection of Clus Ironworks transmission parts carries an educational benefit: although most people might not have been able to identify transmission parts prior to viewing this poster, Stoecklin's unembellished artwork gives them a bit of new knowledge. The Clus (or Klus) Ironworks was located in the north-central Swiss municipality of Balsthal. It manufactured not only transmissions for mills and railways but also an array of products for the military. Although it is no longer in business today, at the time of the poster's production the Clus enterprise was the largest employer in the Thal district.

Giornata del Prodotto Italiano, 1930
Giuseppe Riccobaldi del Baza (1887–1976)
52¼ x 38 inches (132.7 x 96.5 cm)
Barabino & Graeve, Genova

Nationalistic sparks fly in this Riccobaldi promotion for Italian Product Day, giving the viewer a powerful, muscular portrayal of pride and virility. Although the dramatic use of the hammer and anvil is unquestionably the poster's central motif, note the fasces (a bundle of reeds wrapped around an ax, an ancient Roman symbol of authority co-opted by the Italian Fascists as their emblem) at the bottom of the poster. Used in this official capacity, it becomes an ideal companion to the VIII, which denotes Mussolini's eighth year in power.

Giornata del Prodotto Italiano

27 Aprile 1930 VIII

Rifobaldi

BARABINO & GRAEVE

Affissione autorizzata dalla Questura di Milano 20-4-1930 VIII ai sensi dell'Art. 217 Regolamento Legge di P. S.

ESENTE DA BOLLO

SERIE BALZA-RICC

Confederazione Nazionale Fascista dei Commercianti

LEISURE

LEISURE TIME, defined as the hours spent away from work, chores, and life-sustaining activities such as eating and sleeping, has increased since the Industrial Revolution and the advent of mass production. As machines replaced or reduced the amount of human labor required in factories, on farms, and in homes, people found time to engage in enjoyable, non-income-generating pursuits.

Fueled by a rapidly expanding economy and the desire to enjoy life following the hardships and sacrifices of World War I, the Roaring Twenties saw a dramatic increase in the demand for leisure-time activities. People had time to relax, read a newspaper or magazine, listen to the radio, or even speak with friends and family over the telephone.

By the late 1930s, television was offering regularly scheduled programming. Fairs, carnivals, art and consumer-product exhibitions, and sporting events sprung up everywhere as attendance grew rapidly. World's Fairs were held in Barcelona in 1929, Chicago in 1933, and New York in 1939, each proclaiming a brighter future despite the worst economic depression in history.

Sporting events were a popular way to spend nonworking hours, and consumers had a plethora of competitions to choose from at the local, regional, national, and international level. During the interwar years, nine Olympiads were held—five Summer Olympics and four Winter Olympics—in Belgium, France, the Netherlands, Switzerland, Germany, and the United States.

Johnny Weissmuller won five gold medals in swimming in the 1924 and 1928 Olympics and later famously played the role of Tarzan on film. Jim Thorpe, Jesse Owens, and Babe Didrikson Zaharias were also famous Olympians in the 1920s and 1930s. Their stellar performances in their respective disciplines drew the world's attention to playing fields and sports arenas worldwide.

Championships in soccer, tennis, ice hockey, cycling, skiing, basketball, fencing, motor racing, and many other sports were promoted to the public via advertising displays. In addition to being outstanding examples of graphic design, these posters serve as a historical record of the many leisure activities that were pursued during the period.

Daily Herald: Soaring to Success, 1919
Edward McKnight Kauffer (1890–1954)
79 x 63 inches (200.7 x 160 cm)
T. B. Lawrence Ltd, London

Le Progrès, 1927
A. M. Cassandre (Adolphe Mouron, 1901–1968)
31⅝ x 41 inches (80.3 x 104.1 cm)
Hachard et Cie., Paris

This soaring Kauffer design began its artistic journey as a black-and-white woodcut in 1916 and in time found its way to being used for the relaunching of the British Labour Party newspaper, the *Daily Herald*. It is also one of the most rare art deco posters ever created and is the design that transformed Kauffer from an artist struggling to gain recognition into one of the most distinguished graphic designers of the period and the most outstanding poster artist in Great Britain. There are only three other known copies of this famous poster—a longer, three-sheet copy, housed in London's Victoria and Albert Museum, that shows a bigger area of yellow background in the middle, and two one-sheet copies, featuring the stylized flock of birds only (without the yellow middle portion or the text at the bottom). One of the one-sheet copies resides in the collection of the Museum of Modern Art in New York. The two-sheet copy (missing only the larger yellow background area in the middle) is seen here. This poster, considered by many critics to be the finest of Kauffer's career, was most likely inspired by the work the artist viewed at the 1916 exhibition of the vorticists, members of a short-lived British avant-garde artistic movement that combined cubism and futurism to explore an obsession with speed as a metaphor for the Machine Age. Shortly thereafter, and after an intense period of observing birds in flight, Kauffer created the initial version of this artwork, entitled *Flight*. It may never have become an icon of advertising art had Kauffer not submitted it to *Colour* magazine in 1919. This magazine regularly included a Poster Page, where unpublished poster artwork was reproduced free of charge in order to encourage the business community to employ underused, talented artists as a way of breathing life back into the British consumer sector after World War I. Francis Meynell (1891–1975), a well-known book publisher, who was also in charge of organizing the poster campaign for the *Daily Herald,* saw *Flight* in *Colour* and purchased it to use in the promotional material for the Labour Party paper. Meynell believed that the ascending birds in Kauffer's artwork represented hope, and that they suggested renewal after the bloody conflict of war. Whether or not Meynell's interpretation is accurate, the public adored the image, and Kauffer's career— much like his geometric flock of birds—took flight. The poster even caught the eye of Winston Churchill, at that point the Secretary of State for War, who approached Kauffer to design a flag for the Royal Air Force. Churchill withdrew the commission, however, when he discovered that Kauffer had been born in the United States and was unwilling to change his citizenship.

Le Progrès is an exceptionally rare, innovative design from Cassandre's early period, a beautifully coordinated combination of geometry and humanity. The poster leaves little doubt that *Le Progrès* is a newspaper on the leading edge of guiding civilization in the right direction. While the black-and-white arrow pointedly gives off the impression that the daily paper may be leading its readership to the left, that isn't actually the case. Founded in 1859, the Lyon-based *Le Progrès* is fairly nonpolitical, primarily covering local news, sports, business, and community events. The poster is a mesmerizing creation whose concise geometry and strong lines ultimately reveal a journey from darkness into light, a journey made possible by *Le Progrès*.

Megnyílt Hirdető, 1933
Aladár Richter (1898–?)
49¾ x 37⅜ inches (126.4 x 94.9 cm)
Pogány Zsigmond, Budapest

Mercury—the fleet-footed Roman god of trade and communication, whose name derives from a Latin root word that applies to merchandise and wages—gets a cubist makeover in this Aladár Richter promotion announcing the opening of Budapest's Vállalatának public relations firm. Modern art freely intermingles with the classical motif as the artist relies on strict geometry and stark color contrast to create a Mondrian-like centerpiece. Like Robert Louis's *Pierce-Arrow*, page 48, and Charles Loupot's *Mira*, page 76, this is one of the few posters of the era to use silver paper. It relays a pointed message that clever public relations can be used to creatively call attention to any product. The resulting artwork is smart and sophisticated yet easily understood and stylish.

Le Petit Dauphinois, 1933
Leonetto Cappiello (1875–1942)
47⅛ x 63¼ inches (119.7 x 160.6 cm)
Devambez, Paris

Leonetto Cappiello was a versatile graphic artist, frequently referred to as the father of the modern advertising poster in large part because of his willingness to promote products in a nonliteral manner. It wasn't vital for Cappiello that his artwork identically match what was being advertised—what mattered was that he attract attention to the product. Once that attention had been secured, the image would stick with the viewer, associating itself with the name of the product and fixing it in his or her mind. Although he generated a tremendous body of work, very few of his designs were executed in an art deco style. One of two exceptions—the other being the bold Kub bouillon poster (pages 212–213)—is this poster for *Le Petit Dauphinois*, "the largest daily newspaper in the French Alps" and one of the best regional papers in France. Cappiello takes a literally global approach to stress *Le Petit Dauphinois*'s aim to keep an "eye" on the world for its readership. It is not difficult to recognize Cassandre's influence here—the prominent text, the elements of surrealism, the use of shadow to surround the central image (Cappiello almost always placed his figures against a flat background), and the use of geometry to lead the eye through the design.

Le Petit Dauphinois, ca. 1925
Pierre Andry-Farcy (1882–1950)
47⅜ x 63 inches (120.3 x 160 cm)
Imprimerie Générale, Grenoble

Compared to this "gripping" advertisement for *Le Petit Dauphinois*, Cappiello's professional, globally aware journalist (above right) is a soothing, utterly benign design. Pierre Andry-Farcy's strong graphic approach takes matters into its own "hand," showing that the publication has a firm grasp of every single bit of information that is worthy of being telegraphically transmitted. The poster implies this so assertively, in fact, that it gives off the distinct impression it may be controlling what's being disseminated. The monumental crimson hand and the exacting geometry of the converging transmission lines are strokes of genius, a rousing visual analogy for taking command of one's own informational destiny.

LEISURE

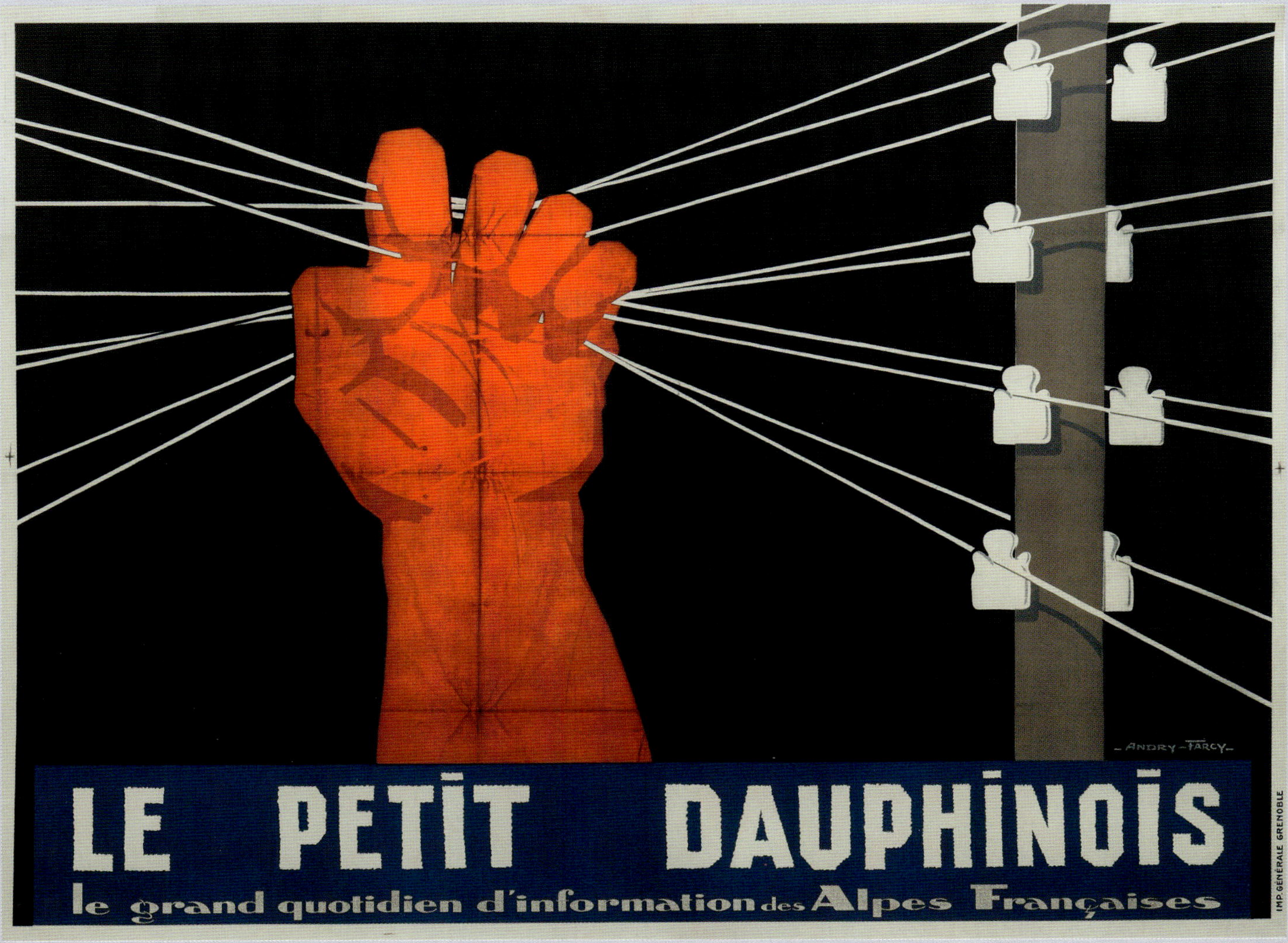

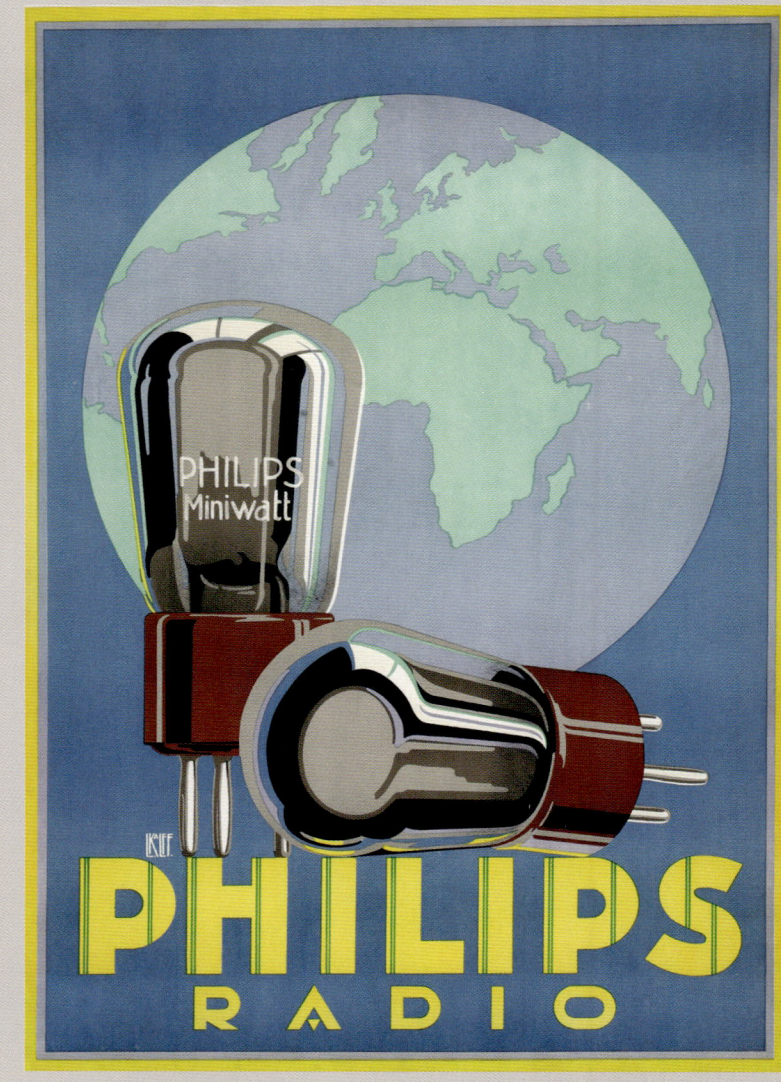

Use the Telephone, 1934
Edward McKnight Kauffer (1890–1954)
29 5/8 x 19 3/8 inches (75.2 x 49.2 cm)
General Post Office, London

In this interesting and rare poster, Edward McKnight Kauffer presents the notion that the telephone was making the world a smaller place to live in. To get this point across, he uses a photomontage of an E1 telephone handset with a "spit cup" held up to a lithographic image of the globe, much as one would hold a receiver to one's ear in order to make "contact with the world." When telephone communications technology came into existence at the turn of the twentieth century, Britain's General Post Office claimed monopoly rights to it in the UK on the basis that it essentially involved delivering information to both a "sender" and a "receiver," which were well-established components of their existing postal service business. So, in essence, all telegraph and telephone switching stations were viewed as electronic post offices. This postal control of telecommunications would remain in place until 1981, when the British Telecommunications Act transferred responsibility for phone service away from the post office to British Telecom. Alexander Graham Bell first demonstrated long-distance calling in the UK in 1878, when Queen Victoria called London from the Isle of Wight.

Philips Radio, 1928
Louis C. Kalff (1897–1976)
43 7/8 x 30 1/2 inches (111.4 x 77.5 cm)
Printer unknown

Philips started from humble beginnings in a small family-owned factory in Amsterdam in 1891. The corporation's first focus was on carbon filaments and small electric parts not dissimilar from the ones depicted in this poster. It is no surprise that the Dutch artist Louis Christian Kalff would produce this design during the late 1920s, as only a few years earlier Philips had started expanding its market outside of the Netherlands with the introduction of vacuum tubes and, most important, radios. The ability to produce reliable, affordable radio products would become the bread and butter of the business, and Kalff certainly gives these miniwatt tube amplifiers the respect they deserve in this handsome and rare design. Arranged in two tempting poses, the tubes have a sleek, sexy element to them normally reserved for studio nudes rather than common household objects. This goes one step beyond the traditional goal of the Object Poster as mastered by Lucian Bernhard: it brings the product out of the realm of matter-of-fact placement and into that of tempting fetish. The image of Earth behind the product emphasizes the global nature of the Philips corporation while implying that through the miracle of radio communication its connection with the rest of the world is at an all-time high.

Watt Radio: Torino, 1933
Nicolay Diulgheroff (1901–1982)
35 1/2 x 27 1/2 inches (90.2 x 69.8 cm)
Roggero & Tortia, Torino

Founded in 1924, Watt Radio is still a major Italian manufacturer of audiovisual equipment. Here, Nicolay Diulgheroff employs a bold art deco design that presents Watt Radio as a modern, innovative company. The strong black diagonal text melds perfectly with the face of the broadcaster while radio waves emanate from his mouth to inform the viewer of the power and reach of the firm's newest product. The bright red background serves to highlight the Watt Radio name.

**New York World's Fair:
The World of Tomorrow,** 1939
Joseph Binder (1898–1972)
30½ x 20 inches (77.5 x 50.8 cm)
Grinnell Lithographic Company, New York

The Trylon and Perisphere, universally recognizable symbols of the 1939 New York World's Fair, glow like celestial objects against a night sky. A stylized squadron of climbing airplanes and slashing searchlights provides an additional note of modernity to the poster while silhouetted skyscrapers and a converging ocean liner and locomotive create a specific sense of destination. It is a classic by any standard, and, not surprisingly, this art deco Joseph Binder design was the first-prize winner of the poster contest organized by the fair's sponsors. The 1939 World's Fair at Flushing Meadows Corona Park featured the theme of casting an eye toward the future—indeed, its slogan boasted that the event marked the "dawn of a new day." In the midst of the Great Depression and with World War II looming, the fair's organizers wanted to create a sense of optimism and hope as well as to increase business in New York City. RCA introduced the television to the U.S. market at the fair. All told, more than forty-four million people would come to see the "world of tomorrow" over the course of its two seasons (it was open from April to October in both 1939 and 1940). The spire-shaped Trylon was connected to the 180-foot-diameter Perisphere by what was at the time the world's longest escalator. Once inside the Perisphere, one would find a diorama depicting a utopian city of the future known as Democracity.

Railroads on Parade: New York World's Fair, 1939
Leslie Ragan (1897–1972)
40⅛ x 27⅛ inches (101.9 x 68.9 cm)
Printer unknown

Part of the 1939 World's Fair in New York, Railroads on Parade was a musical spectacle held in a three-thousand-seat theater that featured more than 250 performers and twenty real trains. It would be the last of many railroad exhibitions organized by noted journalist Edward Hungerford, who lived and breathed locomotives and traveled the country by rail to organize various large-scale train-themed shows. This particular presentation focused on the history of trains around the world, from the Tom Thumb and Stourbridge Lion of the mid-1820s up through the then-current Pullman passenger car. Although dominated by American-made trains, the show included steam, diesel, and electric specimens hailing from as far away as Canada, England, and Italy. Each segment appeared on stage as an interactive tableau, complete with narration and musical accompaniment. Hungerford's obsession is perhaps best expressed in the words of the program for the event itself: "Into every corner of our social and economic existence, the railroad is tightly interwoven. It is the backbone of the country, no, even more, it is its veritable lifeblood . . . If it were to die, then the nation would die." In this rare sunset-hued design, Ragan, the unparalleled master of American railway posters (see his *The New Twentieth Century Limited,* page 263), visually expresses the breadth of the performance, contrasting a nineteenth-century engine with the sleek power of an S1 locomotive operated by the Pennsylvania Railroad.

Right: The United States Navy blimp TC-14 took this aerial photograph of the Trylon, Perisphere, and surrounding buildings at the 1939 New York World's Fair.

Reklame Schau, 1929
Lucian Bernhard (1883–1972) and
Fritz Rosen (1890–1980)
32½ x 23¼ inches (82.5 x 59.1 cm)
Hans Pusch, Berlin

The primary goal of an advertising poster is to relay persuasive messages by means of appealing graphics and typography. Lucian Bernhard and Fritz Rosen joined forces to create this dynamic modernist tour de force to promote an exhibition in Berlin put together by the International Advertising Association. The artists' striking application of alternating blue and orange colors and strong art deco lettering convincingly conveys advertising's ability to engage the senses—in this case sight and hearing. The show was done as part of the IAA's twenty-fifth anniversary; a world advertising congress also took place during the nearly month-long event. The Bernhard and Rosen design was used as the cover for the show's exhibition catalog.

Internationale Tentoonstelling Klank en Beeld, 1932
Anonymous
41¾ x 30½ inches (106 x 77.5 cm)
Drukkerij Kotting, Amsterdam

This poster, created by an anonymous artist for a 1932 international sound and image exhibition in Amsterdam, captures the essence of the subject matter with a powerful, stylized, red art deco bust, which has sound waves and visual projections emanating from its ear and eye. The exhibition covered all the bases—radio, television, sound recordings, music, photography, and even the latest craze, talking pictures, even though the first Dutch-language sound film wouldn't be released until the following year. Because the design seems to hint at the possibility of constant sensory assault, one is left to wonder what the organizers of this event would think of the media-saturated world in which we presently live.

Muenchner Plakat Kunst, 1931
Hermann Keimel (1889–1948)
47 x 33½ inches (119.4 x 85.1 cm)
Chromolithographische Kunstanstalt AG, München

Set against a solid black background, alternating sheets of blue, red, and white in a variety of rectangular shapes and sizes unite to create a lithographic "face" in this outstanding poster for an exhibition of the works of the Neue Vereinigung Münchner Plakat Künstler (New Union of Munich Poster Artists). The image's suggestion of three-dimensionality not only implies the many layers of the creative process but also calls to mind the impermanence of the poster medium, with its tradition of covering old placards with new ones on city walls and billboards in a continual evolution of promotional art. This rather rare design is far and away one of the finest advertisements ever created for a poster exhibition.

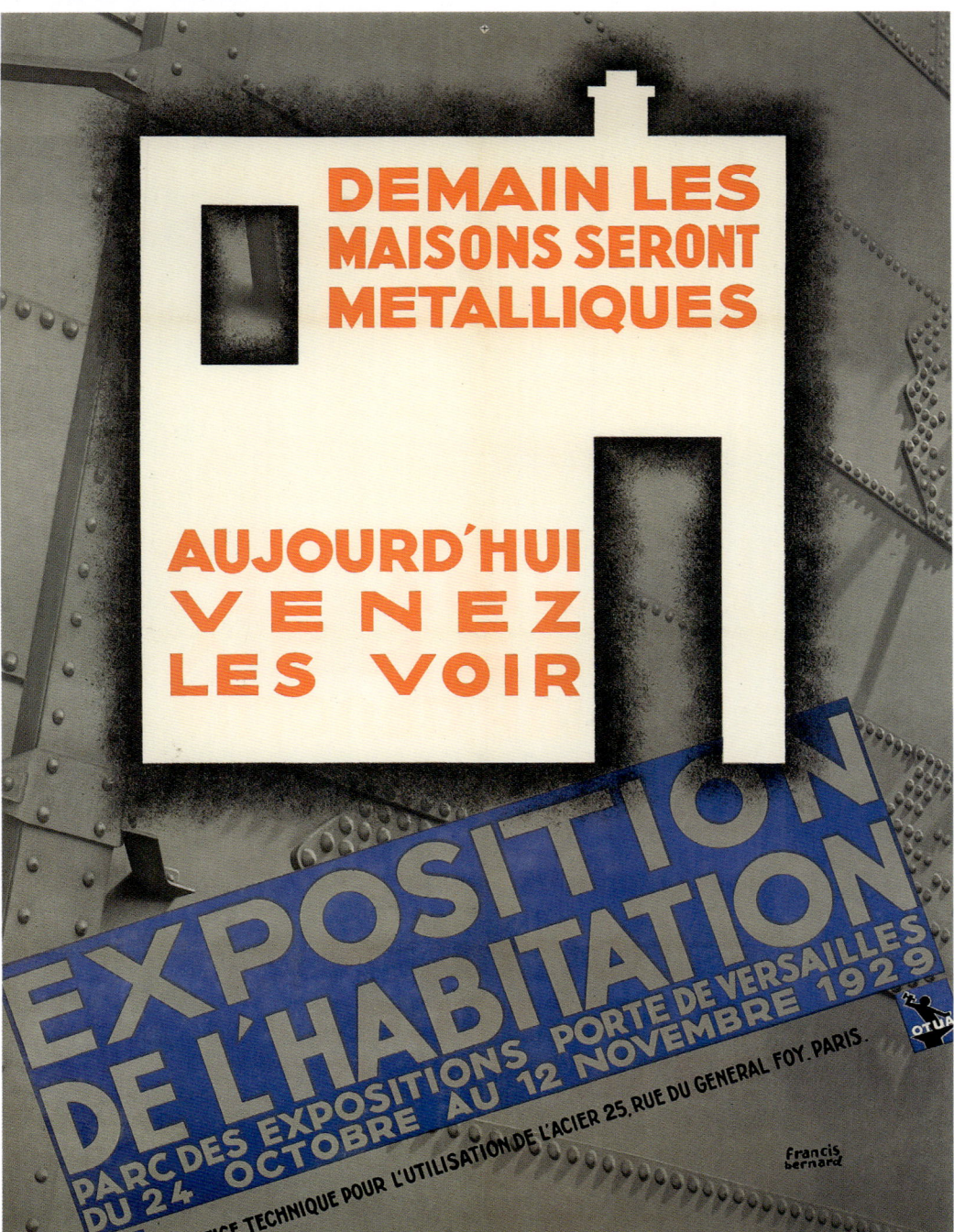

Exposition de l'Habitation, 1929
Francis Bernard (1900–1979)
62 x 45 inches (157.5 x 114.3 cm)
Éditions Paul-Martial, Paris

During World War I, Jules-Louis Breton was France's Undersecretary of State for Inventions. A trained chemist, Breton had a number of interesting passions, one of which was a desire to make the lives of women more comfortable through advancements in science and technology. Thus in 1923 he launched a home appliance competition, gathering inventions from around the world that promised to elevate objects in the domestic sphere to a new level of modernity. This show proved so popular that the following year it included an array of diverse exhibitions and panels that covered all imaginable aspects of home life. In this very rare poster by Francis Bernard, we are tempted with the assertion that "homes of the future will be made of metal; come view them today." Behind the bare-bones silhouette of a simple dwelling, we see a close-up of welded steel, its rivets providing photomontage-level texture to the background. This is the first of many designs Bernard would create for the Paris Home Exposition, as the event was called; indeed, he remained its primary artist up through the 1960s. Although it is not present in this poster, he eventually developed the figure of a mechanical maid—an ideal symbol of domestic advancement—who would appear repeatedly in subsequent posters.

Posters: Victoria and Albert Museum, 1931
Austin Cooper (1890–1964)
39¾ 24¾ inches (101 x 62.9 cm)
The Baynard Press, London

Of the many posters issued by the London Underground to promote museum shows, this fabulously art deco design, meant to advertise an exhibition of posters at the famed Victoria and Albert Museum, is possibly the finest. Shown in minimalist profile, Mercury, the god of swift communication and trade, perfectly embodies the bare-bones purpose behind every poster ever printed—the quick, easily understood dissemination of information. And this advertisement is as effective in communicating its point as some of the best political propaganda. The Victoria and Albert holds England's national collection of posters, with more than ten thousand images in its library. The show advertised here was the first time the museum publicly acknowledged and promoted its vast collection, putting nearly 650 posters on display. The tremendous public response resulted not only in myriad important posters being donated to the museum but also in the continuation of poster shows throughout the next several decades, most notably the London Transport poster exhibition of 1949 and the famous Mucha exhibition in 1963, which helped inspire the modern-day "poster craze." Austin Cooper, born in Canada, was one of England's top poster artists at the time. He created at least fifty-four images for the London Underground, including this one, which lets viewers know that the stop closest to their desination is South Kensington.

1ᵉʳ Campeonato Mundial de Football, 1930
Guillermo Laborde (1886–1940)
31 x 15 inches (78.7 x 38.1 cm)
Olivera y Fernández, Montevideo

This rare image, comprising sparse linear elements and geometric precision, tells its tale of an elastic goalkeeper and his magnificent save with little more than a circle, a hexagon, and a slightly raked, angular pair of goalposts. Its brevity is arresting. Add the text and you realize that this thrilling composition was created to promote the first-ever FIFA World Cup. FIFA, the Fédération Internationale de Football Association, had managed the Olympic football tournament from 1920 to 1928 as a championship for amateur soccer players. When the International Olympic Committee and FIFA couldn't agree on what constituted amateur status for the 1932 Los Angeles Summer Olympics, FIFA president Jules Rimet announced plans to stage an international tournament independent of the Olympics. Uruguay was chosen as the host country for the inaugural World Cup for a number of reasons: as the reigning Olympic champions, the Uruguayans were the de facto world champions; their bid included a new stadium; and the Uruguayan authorities offered to refund the expenses of all participating countries. Uruguay was also celebrating its centenary in 1930. Thirteen teams entered the tournament (only four of whom made the journey from Europe: Belgium, France, Romania, and Yugoslavia), and all the matches were played in the capital city of Montevideo. The majority were held at the newly constructed Estadio Centenario, which had a seating capacity of one hundred thousand. Uruguay emerged victorious in the first World Cup, defeating archrival Argentina by a score of 4–2.

Campeonato Abierto de Basket-Ball, 1934
Caroselli (n.d.)
43½ x 28⅝ inches (110.5 x 72.7 cm)
Printer unknown

Something in the human subconscious must find the forty-five-degree angle especially appealing for the depiction of athletes in action—especially in ball sports and especially if the figure leans from the lower left to the upper right. This is the model used by Guillermo Laborde to promote the 1930 World Cup Soccer competition (left). Four years later, Caroselli exchanges the pitch for the hardwood but keeps the angled competitor in place in this rare advertisement for the Open Basketball Championship in Buenos Aires, an event open to "clubs not affiliated with the Argentine Basketball Federation." The manner in which Caroselli has cocooned his player within a solid black airbrushed area is especially effective, giving the layup thrust and motion against the white-and-yellow background an implicit energy flowing directly through the player to the ball. The winners of this tournament were awarded the Estanislao S. Zeballos Prize, named after the Argentine lawyer, journalist, sociologist, politician, patriot, and man of letters (1854–1923). While it is not possible to say how many teams were not affiliated with the Argentine Basketball Federation in 1934 (the federation was founded in 1932), it is safe to say that nonparticipants would be far more difficult to find today—the Confederación Argentina de Básquetbol (as it is known in Spanish) is the governing body for the sport in Argentina. There are approximately 1,200 clubs registered with the association, which sanctions the national league and minor leagues and is also responsible for the national basketball team.

Coupe du Monde: FIFA, 1938
D. H. Desmé (n.d.)
62½ x 45½ inches (158.7 x 115.6 cm)
Imprimerie J. E. Goossens, Lille and Paris

Cast in bronze against a watercolor rainbow, this lithographic tribute to the sport of soccer makes it clear in a single glance that there is but one sporting event capable of dominating the globe. The placement of the ball under the colossus's foot leads the viewer's eye directly to the 1938 host country, France (FFFA stands for the Fédération Française de Football Association). Sixteen nations qualified for the 1938 World Cup, but Austria withdrew after its annexation by the Nazi regime in March of that year, bringing the total number of teams down to fifteen. The tournament was held in a knockout format, making it the last World Cup not to include a group stage. Brazil topped Sweden 4–2 to take third in the competition, while Italy topped Hungary at the Stade Olympique de Colombes in Paris with an identical 4–2 score for their second successive World Cup title. As a result of World War II and its aftermath, the tournament would not be held again until 1950. Legend has it that the Italian vice president of FIFA, Dr. Ottorino Barassi, hid the World Cup trophy in a shoe box under his bed throughout the war in order to keep it from falling into the clutches of occupying forces.

Coupe Davis, 1932
A. M. Cassandre (Adolphe Mouron, 1901–1968)
62½ x 47¼ inches (158.7 x 120 cm)
Alliance Graphique, Paris

In Cassandre's extraordinarily rare, iconic, and important poster for the Davis Cup, he seizes viewers' attention by placing them on court, with a volley rushing back in their direction. The perspective is perfect, from the commanding, rock-solid stance of the player on the far side of the net to the Dunlop tennis ball coming down the center-court line straight at the viewer. The implied motion is startling, the scale impeccable, and the graphic counterpoint of the close-up ball vis-à-vis the distant opponent is altogether transfixing. Perhaps the most ingenious aspect of this poster—and any number of Cassandre posters, for that matter—is the apparent ease with which he assembles the design's elements, an ease that produces maximum impact with seemingly minimal effort. The Davis Cup—the premier international team event in men's tennis—was conceived of in 1899 by four members of the Harvard University tennis team, one of whom was Dwight F. Davis (1879–1945), the future prominent U.S. politician who designed the tournament format and purchased the sterling silver trophy with his own funds. Though the original participants were limited to the United States and Great Britain, the field had expanded by 1905 to include Belgium, Austria, France, and a combined team from Australia and New Zealand. Whereas today's Davis Cup is run as a knockout tournament between competing countries, the "challenge round" noted on this poster alludes to the format the tournament followed until 1972, in which teams competed against one another for the privilege of facing the previous year's champion in the final round. In 1932, it was the French team who ultimately emerged victorious over the Americans at Stade Roland Garros (see page 31).

Count Henri de Baillet-Latour, president of the International Olympic Committee, congratulates American speed skater Jack Shea after he won his second gold medal at the 1932 Winter Olympics in Lake Placid, New York.

III Olympic Winter Games: Lake Placid, USA, 1932
Witold Gordon (1885–1968)
39½ x 24¾ inches (100.3 x 62.9 cm)
Printer unknown

National Championship: Brattleboro Vt., 1938
Gustav Nilson (1897–1988)
24¾ x 18¾ inches (62.9 x 47.6 cm)
Printer unknown

There is but one singular location that matters in this Witold Gordon design: Lake Placid, the village in the Adirondack Mountains of upstate New York that hosted the 1932 Winter Olympics. With the focus of the globe decidedly turned to the United States, the artist's high-flying ski jumper serves to indicate that the Olympiad is a matter of interest from coast to coast and around the world while at the same time providing an iconic silhouette of winter sports in action. The Lake Placid games in 1932 were the first Winter Olympics to be hosted in North America. As a result of the worldwide econmic depression, only seventeen nations participated that year, down from the twenty-five nations that competed at the 1928 games in Saint Moritz, Switzerland. The Lake Placid games were opened by the governor of New York at the time, Franklin Delano Roosevelt, who later that year would be elected president of the United States. The U.S. team won the medal tally in 1932 with a total of twelve, marking the only time Team USA would accomplish this feat until the 2010 games in Vancouver, when they would garner thirty-seven medals. Sonja Henie of Norway, who was also the 1928 and 1936 champion, won the figure skating gold while Americans Jack Shea and Irving Jaffee each won two gold medals, all in speed skating. Shea, who was the oldest living gold medal winner at the time of his death, was killed by a drunk driver at the age of ninety-one. Shea's son and grandson also competed in the Winter Olympics, in 1964 and 2002 respectively.

Suspended for eternity as he stretches out to achieve maximum flight distance, a black-and-blue ski jumper emblazoned with a shield of stars and stripes takes to the skies above Brattleboro, Vermont, to announce the 1938 U.S. ski jumping national championship. That year, the event was won by the reigning world champion at the time, Birger Ruud of Norway. Tucked into the southeast corner of the state in the foothills of the Green Mountains, the oldest town in Vermont has been hosting championship ski jumping events during February since 1923 at its Harris Hill venue, built in 1922 by Fred Harris, himself a ski jumper and sportsman. The Harris Hill jump was deemed unsafe in 2005, but thanks to a community-subsidized renovation, it reopened for enthusiasts and international competition once again in 2009.

Dartmouth Winter Carnival, 1938
Armsheimer (n.d.)
34¼ x 21⅝ inches (87 x 54.9 cm)
Printer unknown

Dubbed the Mardi Gras of the North by *National Geographic* magazine in 1919, the Dartmouth Winter Carnival is the oldest collegiate winter festival in the United States. Founded in 1910 by members of the Dartmouth Outing Club who wanted to promote the then-fledgling pastime of recreational skiing, the inaugural event attracted participants from nearby colleges, who trekked to Hanover, New Hampshire, to challenge Dartmouth students at skiing and snowshoeing events. It did not take long for the carnival to develop into the most celebrated college weekend in the nation. Although competition is the name of the game, this first-rate Armsheimer American art deco image conveys nothing but conviviality—with just a touch of romance thrown in for good measure. The simply portrayed, exclamatory pair are hale, hearty, and more than ready to take on whatever the DWC weekend might bring their way.

Dartmouth Winter Carnival, 1938
T. H. Joanethis (n.d.)
34 x 22 inches (86.4 x 55.9 cm)
Printer unknown

While the airborne skier in T. H. Joanethis's promotion for the 1938 Dartmouth Winter Carnival shares the same welcoming smile as his counterparts in the Armsheimer poster (above left), this individual is all about competition. Viewed from below, he clearly dominates the proceedings, fairly exploding off the poster into the face of the viewer. He is propelled onward not only by his competitive spirit but by the background snowburst as well.

Eastern Ski Championships, 1937
Joe Leibow (n.d.)
34½ x 21½ inches (87.6 x 54.6 cm)
Printer unknown

High-flying athleticism couples with sunny optimism in this Joe Leibow promotion for the U.S. Eastern Ski Championships at New Hampshire's Belknap Mountain ski area. Leibow cleverly plays with the perspective, giving us an over-the-shoulder shot of a ski jumper whose diminutive size turns the female spectator's sweater into the snow-covered terrain over which he soars. The 1937 Belknap championships marked the debut of the venue's sixty-meter jump, which had been completed a few weeks before (construction had begun in 1935). The text of the poster also provides us with an interesting tidbit: copies of Leibow's poster could be purchased from the Eastern Ski Championships office in nearby Laconia for one dollar—ten cents less than admission to the competition.

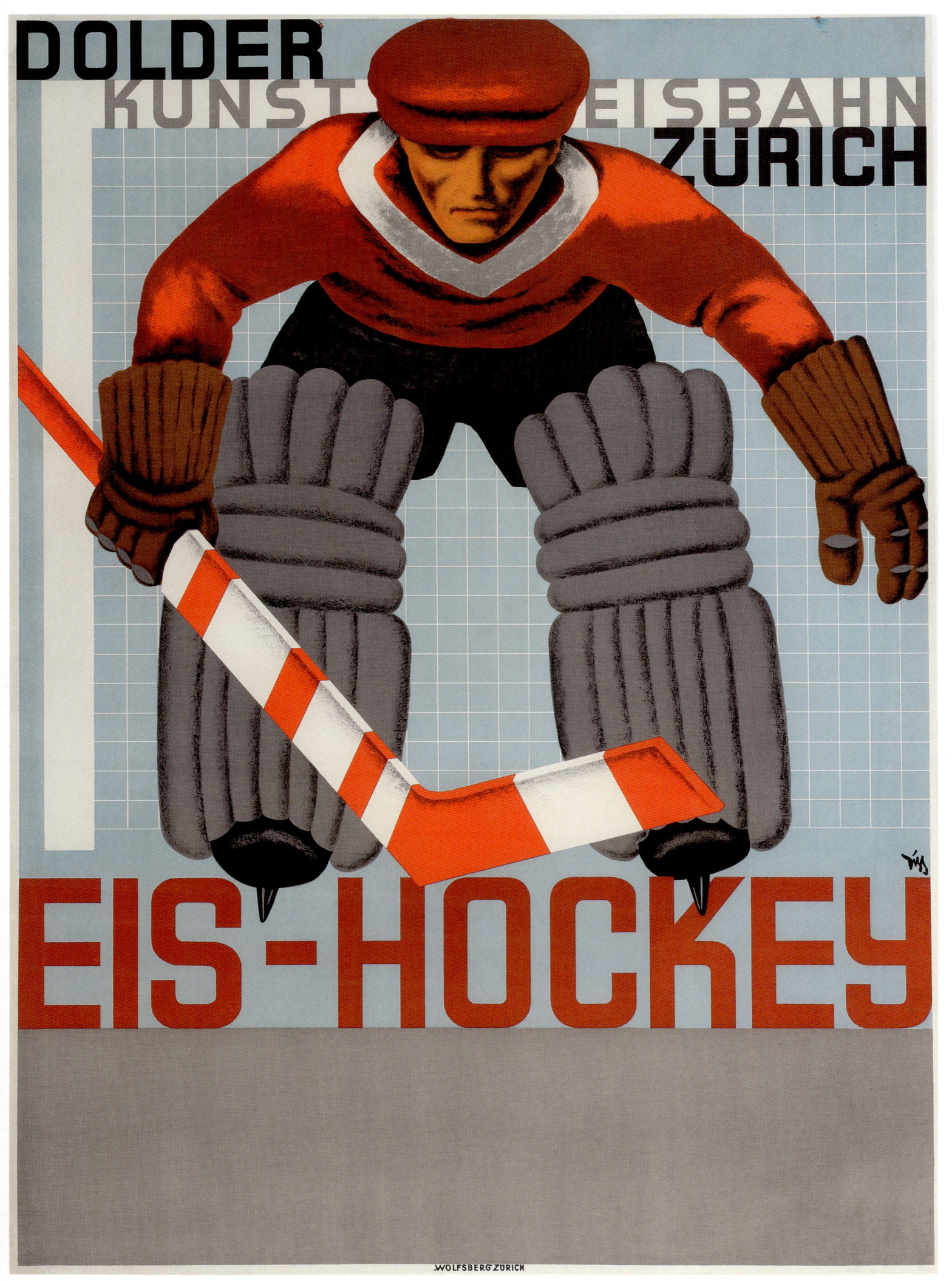

Eis-Hockey: Dolder Kunsteisbahn, 1935
Alex Diggelmann (1902–1987)
50 3/8 x 35 1/2 inches (127.9 x 90.2 cm)
Wolfsberg, Zürich

Hottingen is a neighborhood in Zurich's District 7, and the northern part of Hottingen is known as Dolder, a residential area on the southern side of Adlisberg, a wooded mountain overlooking Lake Zurich. Within Dolder one will find the Dolder Kunsteisbahn, the largest artificial ice rink in all of Europe, built in 1930 and featuring a six-thousand-square-foot surface. Alex Diggelmann's promotion for ice hockey at the facility (the blank text panel at bottom would have been imprinted with details regarding tournament or league play) puts the viewer in the unexpected position of facing off with an extremely large and intense goalkeeper. The lithographic one-on-one, while somewhat intimidating, directly involves passersby, converting them, at least temporarily, into active participants rather than spectators.

Eiropas Meistarsacīkstēs: Ātrslidošanā, 1939
Anonymous
39 3/4 x 28 inches (101 x 71.1 cm)
P. Mantnieka Kartografijas Instituta, Riga

Not to be confused with the World Speed Skating Championships, the European Speed Skating Championships have been held annually since 1893. At the time this poster was printed, four specific distances had to be raced by each competitor: 500 meters, 1,000 meters, 3,000 meters, and 5,000 meters. This was basically half the distance required prior to 1936. For this final race before the outbreak of World War II, the event was held in Riga, Latvia's capital city, indicated by a bull's-eye in the poster. The skater, wearing the Latvian team uniform, is more detailed and far more realistic than Corrado Mancioli's cyclist (page 130). It is interesting to compare the way in which the unknown artist has rendered the figure versus the style of typography announcing the race—the former is really a bridge between art deco and modern realism, while the latter is heavily steeped in the deco tradition. This would be the first year in the competition's history in which Latvia would take home the gold (its own Alfons Bērziņš came in first). A few months after this event, the Soviet Union would invade Latvia; it occupied the country until 1991.

Mistrzostwo Świata: Krynica, 1930
Stefan Osiecki (1902–1977) and
Jerzy Skolimowski (1907–1985)
38¾ x 27¼ inches (98.4 x 69.2 cm)
Litografja Artystyczna W. Główczewski, Warszawa

Even though the array of international flags and text on the bottom form something of a barrier between the passerby and the ice-skating adversaries in this promotion for the 1931 Ice Hockey World Championships in Krynica, Poland, it appears as if the action is about to surge right off the paper at any moment. The flattened perspective works marvelously, transforming the region's Beskids mountain range into an icy playing surface in one single, even flow, while the intertwined angularity and featureless intensity of the players serve to remind the viewer of the combative, team-oriented nature of the sport. The Ice Hockey World Championships, an annual event, was first held at the 1920 Summer Olympics. Interestingly, the flags at the bottom of this design lead the viewer to believe that a total of fourteen nations participated in the 1931 event, but the truth is that there were only ten participating countries (Belgium, Germany, Japan, and Switzerland were not in attendance, even though their flags are shown here). The competitors played a series of qualifying rounds to determine which teams would participate in the medal round. In 1931, Austria took bronze, the United States took silver, and Canada, represented by the University of Manitoba Grads hockey team, took the gold. Canada would become the tournament's first dominating presence, winning twelve times between 1931 and 1952.

Mistrzostwa Szermiercze Europy: Championnats D'Europe D'Escrime, 1933
Andrzej Stypiński (1907–1975) and
Jerzy Skolimowski (1907–1985)
39½ x 27¾ inches (100.3 x 70.5 cm)
K. Kozianskich, Warszawa

This dynamic poster announces the 1934 European fencing championships, held for the first time in Poland. Sponsored by the Fédération Internationale d'Escrime, or FIE (International Fencing Federation), this competition has been held annually with few exceptions since 1921 and has gradually grown to encompass all three divisions of the sport—épée, sabre, and foil. Despite being a joint work, the composition itself is perfectly balanced and harmonious. The fencer, donning the flag of the host country on his left bicep, exaggeratedly leans back, ready to lunge toward his opponent. In fact, his rapier is already slightly bent, implying that it is currently making contact with another fencer, which adds an additional level of drama to the image. The artists did a wonderful job of making the white fencing costume stand out against the background: they simply surrounded it with black, a solution as practical as it is handsome. Moreover, by creating a diagonal "ticker tape" of the participating countries' flags, the eye is forced to constantly move around the page—there is no logical resting place, keeping the viewer continuously interested and entertained.

Wioślarskie Mistrzostwa Europy, 1929
Stefan Osiecki (1902–1977) and
Jerzy Skolimowski (1907–1985)
51 x 39½ inches (129.5 x 100.3 cm)
Litografja Artystyczna W. Główczewski,
Warszawa

Broken down into fields of flat colors and basic shapes, the constructivist-style design for the 1929 European Rowing Championships is purposeful and done without a shred of extraneous artwork—yet it doesn't come across as utilitarian in the least. Rather, its seemingly simple composition and saturated hues result in a promotion that is vibrant and exceptionally inviting. The event was held on the Vistula River in Bydgoszcz, a major Polish city, originally a fishing settlement located northwest of Warsaw. The races were conducted under the auspices of FISA, the Fédération Internationale des Sociétés d'Aviron (the International Rowing Federation). Founded in response to the growing popularity of rowing and the need for uniform regulations, FISA came into being in Turin, Italy, in 1892. Composed of representatives from Italy, Adriatica (now part of Italy), Belgium, France, and Switzerland, whose flags appear at the upper left in the poster (see the artists' treatment of flags on page 124), it was the first international sports federation to join the modern Olympic movement and has been on the Olympic program since the 1896 Athens games.

XI Coppa di Ferro del Duce: Regata Universitaria, 1939
Franco Chelini (n.d.)
40 x 28 inches (101.6 x 71.1 cm)
Litografia Tacchi, Pisa

In this brilliant Franco Chelini design, an eight-man crew and their coxswain propel themselves silently forward in a scull, their oars dipping gracefully yet powerfully into the serpentine wake left by their boat. They are competing in a university regatta whose name roughly translates as the Eleventh Commander's Iron Cup. This early June collegiate rowing competition took place in the Tuscan city of Pisa in the seventeenth year after Mussolini's rise to power—1939 (the Roman numerals XVII at the lower right were required by the leader himself). The symmetry and tonal depth of the poster are remarkable, and the artist's capacity to simultaneously express strength and serenity is breathtaking. The races were run on the Arno River by teams representing two of Europe's oldest institutions of higher learning, the University of Pisa (founded by edict of Pope Clement VI in 1343) and the University of Pavia (founded in 1361). The schools' coats of arms appear in the poster's lower right corner.

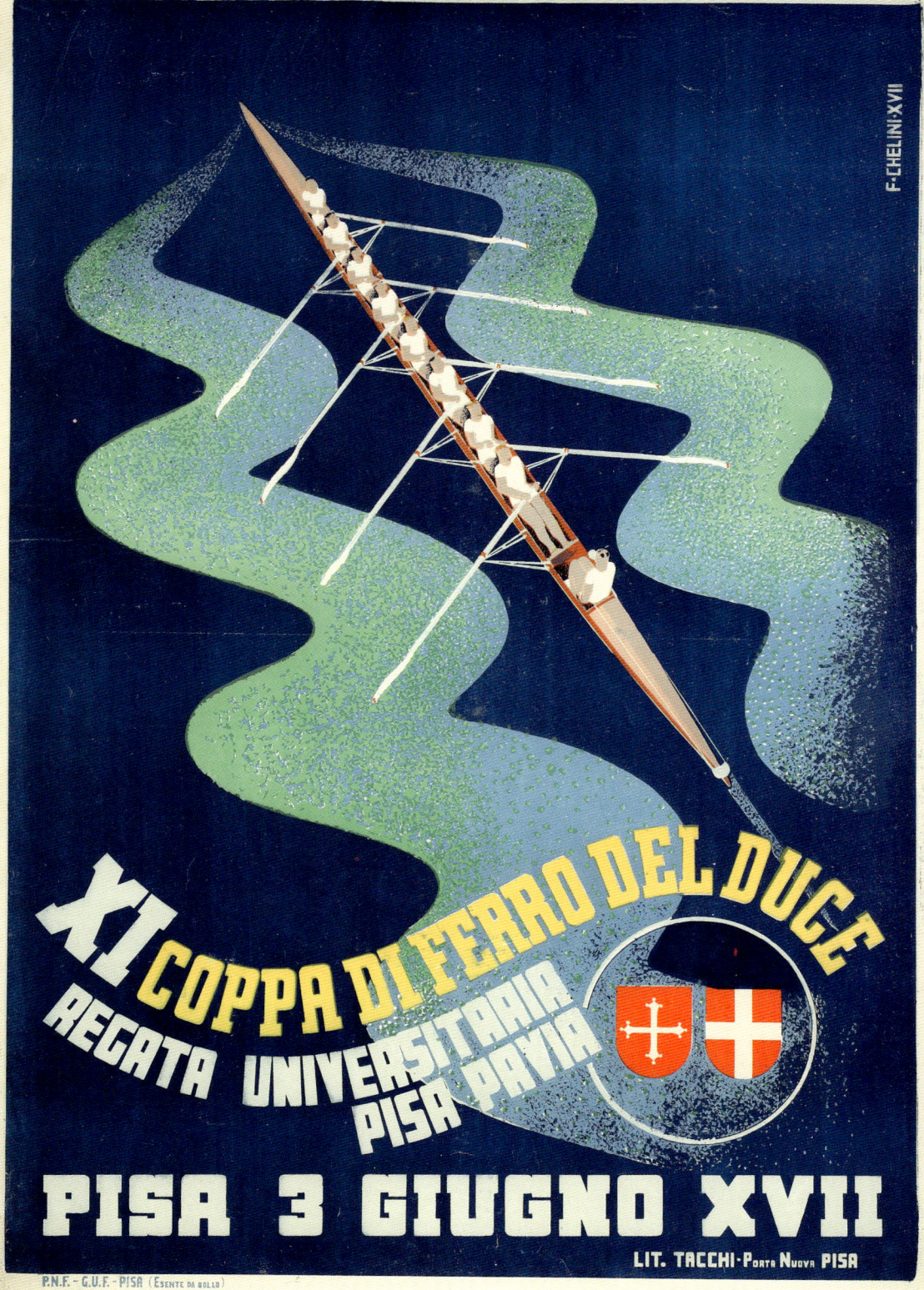

Cycles Brillant, 1925
A. M. Cassandre (Adolphe Mouron, 1901–1968)
46½ x 30¼ inches (118.1 x 76.8 cm)
Hachard et Cie., Paris

In addition to being a rare poster, this is one of Cassandre's most economically realized images, with every contour, curve, and shape serving a well-defined function. Its adherence to specificity and minimalism is truly brilliant, from the subdued use of colors to the fusion of bike with rider to the unified slant of image and text. Graphically, the poster is a sophisticated construction composed of circles—the cyclist's eyes, head, and shoulders; his hands; the handlebars; the curve of the velodrome. The end result, of course, instantly generates an aesthetic interest in the Brillant bicycle. The most astonishing element of all, however, is that Cassandre does all this without conveying any specifics about the product being advertised. This was one of the first posters ever created by Cassandre, who at the time had yet to earn his well-deserved reputation as a master.

Bicicletas Orbea, 1933
Anibal Tejada (1897–?)
39¼ x 27½ inches (99.7 x 69.8 cm)
Gráficas Laborde y Labayen, Tolosa

Orbea entered the bicycle manufacturing business much later than its competitors, launching its first model in the early 1930s. Prior to that, the Spanish company's main products were rifles. While the two may seem completely unrelated, in fact they are not unheard-of bedfellows; corporations such as Belgium's Fabrique Nationale (see pages 64–65) followed a similar path, producing both items in support of the war effort. This rare poster by Anibal Tejada presents the bicycle in an almost dreamy manner, spotlighting it in cobalt against a pastel-hued background. One could almost miss the fact that the strong, masculine figure riding the bike is holding a trophy, presumably implying the award-winning status of the brand. Indeed, the bike's color and positioning cause the eye to narrow in on the bright orange label identifying it as an Orbea—a clever artistic decision as that will be the one thing the viewer walks away remembering. It seems worthwhile to note the compositional similarities between this and Cassandre's famous *Cycles Brillant* (left) from a few years earlier, proving that the signature of one art deco masterpiece can trickle down into other important designs.

Cycles Dilecta, ca. 1928
Georges Favre (n.d.)
45¾ x 31½ inches (116.2 x 80 cm)
Affiches Gaillard, Paris and Amiens

Born out of a true passion for racing, Cycles Dilecta was founded by bicycle enthusiast Albert Chichery in 1912. Profits from this enterprise allowed him to form his own cycling team for the Tour de France in the 1920s. Each member of the team rode a Dilecta and sported the company's signature red, yellow, and blue colors. The fame brought on by both the team and the product then bankrolled his purchase of De Dion-Bouton, producers of bicycles, motorbikes, and even some automobiles. Only a handful of posters exist for Dilecta, and this is the only one that branches away from traditional realism into the world of the abstract (compare with Favre's posters on page 94). The human form is distilled into a series of sharp geometric curves and angles, echoing the original logo for the manufacturer, which consisted of a capital *A* laid on top of a stretched, ovoid *C*. It is, however, the use of the body as part of the lightning bolt that merges man, machine, and nature into a single symbol of speed and power and also leads the viewer's eye to the Dilecta name.

Campionati del Mondo di Ciclismo, 1939
Corrado Mancioli (1904–1958)
54 x 39 inches (137.2 x 99.1 inches)
Grafiche I.G.A.P. (Impresa Generale Affissioni e Pubblicità), Milano

Held annually, the UCI World Championships are sponsored by the Union Cycliste Internationale, or International Cycling Union. Each year, a different country is chosen to host the events, which range from traditional velodrome sprints to cross-country endurance races. The year 1939 marked the beginning of an eight-year hiatus the competition would take as a result of World War II. In fact, the races were already under way when Germany invaded Poland on September 1, halting the competition in Italy before it could be completed. It would resume in Zurich in 1946. Corrado Mancioli was a master of the athletic poster: the majority of his output features muscular youths engaged in their sports of choice, usually deep in concentration. This design is without a doubt his finest. The toned body of the cyclist combines the classical Roman ideal of the human figure with the angular, almost robotic notion of the man of the future. Caught just as he rounds a corner, leaning in ever so slightly to the gentle bend of the course, the cyclist is the perfect depiction of man as machine. In fact, there is nothing organic in the poster at all. It acts not just as a promotion for a bike race but also—and this was more important—as a reflection of the way Mussolini demanded the human body be represented in art. The Roman numerals at the bottom of the poster give a nod to the Fascist ruler's seventeenth year in power.

Maccabiah, 1932
De Soto (n.d.)
39⅜ x 27¼ inches (100 x 69.2 cm)
Printer unknown

Inspired by the Olympics, the Maccabiah games are an international, Israeli-based sporting event presided over by the Maccabi World Union. All Israeli citizens and all Jewish non-Israelis are eligible to participate. This poster was commissioned for the inaugural year of the games, held in the British Mandate of Palestine. More than four hundred athletes took part in the competitions, which included track and field, swimming, and soccer events. It took more than fourteen years to plan this first series of games: teams of motorcycle-riding ambassadors traveled throughout the Middle East and Europe to drum up support and collect donations. With these funds, an official stadium was built in Tel Aviv; a hint of the stadium can be seen amid the city skyline on the lower left. The design itself is remarkably simple for the power it evokes. Israel was more than a decade away from being an officially recognized state, and in just a few years' time the Arab revolt against the Jews and the British would reach a new intensity. Yet here all we see is the emblem of a united people, not just proud of their heritage but also enthusiastically propelling their culture into a new era. That flag is brandished in celebration of the games, but it is also used to stake a claim to the land upon which they are played.

FASHION AND ENTERTAINMENT

AS THE ECONOMIES of Europe and the United States expanded after World War I and more time was available for leisure pursuits, the demand for fashionable clothes, accessories, and cutting-edge entertainment grew rapidly. Radical changes in fashion were ushered in along with the Jazz Age in the Roaring Twenties. The flapper style (called the garçonne look in France)—short hair, above-the-knee dresses, feather boas, and flashy accessories—became popular among young women. Sportswear came into vogue for both sexes as social and cultural trends shifted toward casual styles.

Department stores, furniture galleries, and specialty shops were quick to capitalize on these trends, always eager to provide the newest fashions and accessories for their growing clientele. Likewise, bars, restaurants, nightclubs, and theaters offered the latest and hottest entertainment available. To lure new customers, well-executed advertising was essential. As with other products, such as cars, European advertisers preferred posters for promoting fashion and entertainment, whereas magazine ads were the method most often used in the United States.

Campaigns for Beristain, a department store in Barcelona; Leroy, a Parisian optician; PKZ, a Swiss haberdasher; and Austin Reed, a British clothier, stand out as superlative examples of fashion advertising. Paul Colin's posters promoting *La Revue Black Birds* and the dancer Lisa Duncan are simply iconic graphic designs in the entertainment field.

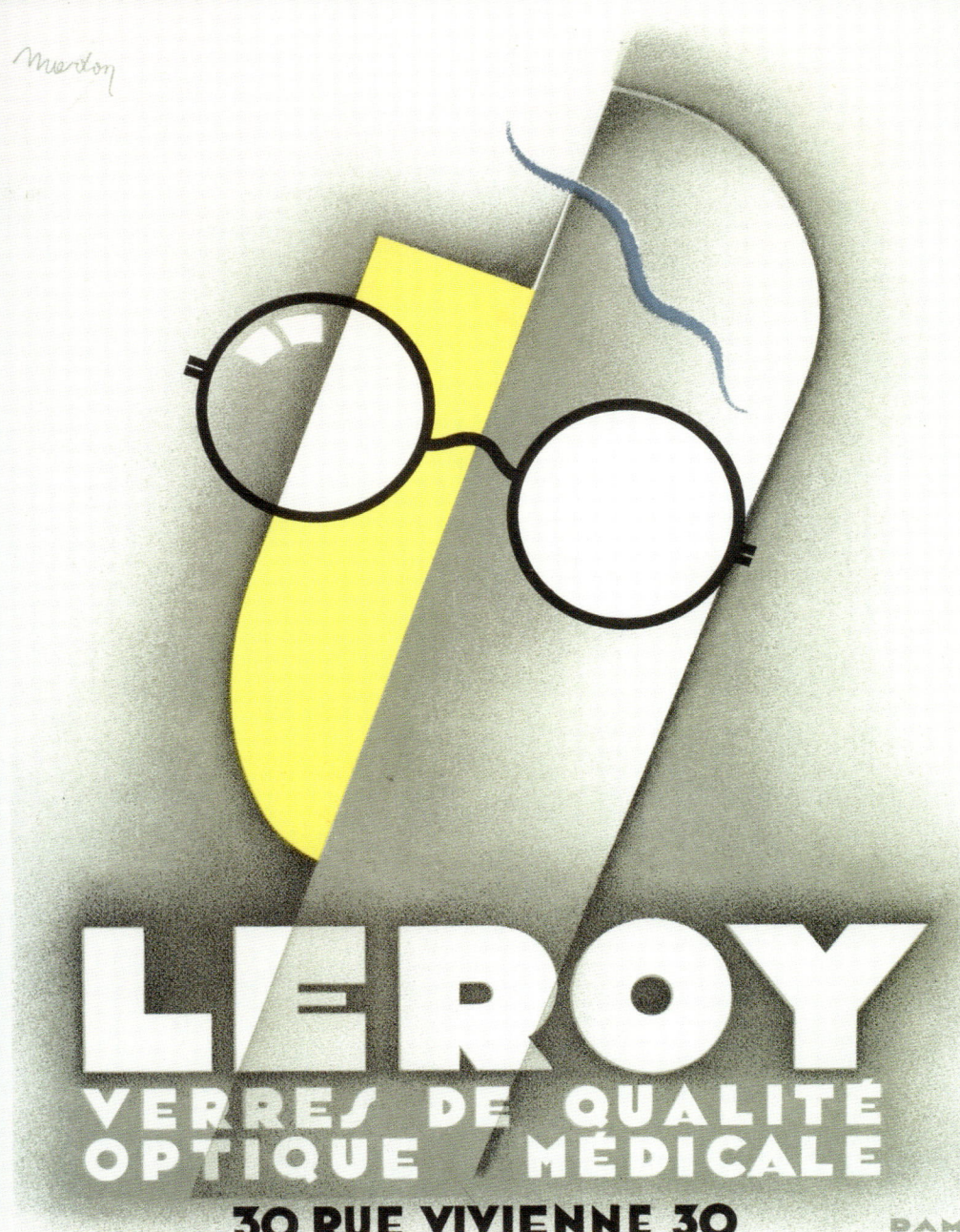

Leroy: Premier Opticien de Paris, 1938
Paul Colin (1892–1985)
62½ x 45½ inches (158.7 x 115.6 cm)
Publicitas, Paris

In this very rare and exemplary promotion for Leroy opticians, we get the distinct impression that this tuxedoed theatergoer, emerging from the flat black background darkness, may well have been featureless until mere seconds ago. However, when he brought out his Leroy glasses to better see the onstage action, his eyes revealed themselves—a necessity in service of his fashionable new spectacles. The restrained use of airbrushed white on the lenses, across the eyes, and onto the gloves solidly delivers the message that Leroy glasses produce an entirely illuminating visual experience. In 1988, Leroy and its ten Parisian outlets were acquired by Alain Afflelou, SA, making them part of one of France's leading optical retailers. Following the acquisition, the Leroy store on the Champs-

Leroy: Verres de Qualité, 1930
Lajos Marton (1891–1952)
12 x 9 inches (30.5 x 22.9 cm)
DAM Publicité, Paris

Predating Paul Colin's classic advertisement for Leroy (left) by nearly a decade, this smaller Marton design for the eyewear firm is executed with an even greater devotion to stylized art deco modernism. With the glasses firmly planted in the center of the poster—which creates a lithographic staring contest of sorts with the viewer—the Leroy product is the only realistic artistic element in the design. Behind it, a face composed of two disparate geometric halves implies that the eyewear is well suited to any personality, head size, or situation. The addition of a flyaway eyebrow adds an unexpected touch of levity to the image.

Galeries Barbès, 1927
Charles Loupot (1892–1962)
79 x 50 inches (200.7 x 127 cm)
Les Belles Affiches, Paris

Monsieur Toutenbois (Mr. All in Wood), a character created by artist Charles Loupot in 1927, became the official mascot of Galeries Barbès, the Grenoble-based furniture store, and would appear in myriad advertisements for the company up through the 1950s. The brand was known for its humor, allowing Loupot to put M. Toutenbois in a variety of amusing situations, from carrying a wardrobe on his head to relaxing in a club chair while smoking a cigar—all the time reinforcing the idea that the furniture being advertised was of the highest quality and crafted from solid wood. Such brilliant marketing allowed the brand to evolve into an international chain, which still operates today—albeit on a much smaller scale and only in Paris. Loupot's figure even managed to survive World War II, when many of the store's French locations were shuttered because they were owned and operated by Jews. The variety of poses M. Toutenbois took on lessened after the war, when he evolved into more of a logo that appeared in print advertising next to the company's name rather than the main character in a full-scale poster. This, however, is his first and greatest appearance, perfectly showcasing the strength and beauty of the furniture he was created to promote. This image is most likely the rarest of all Loupot's posters.

Palais de la Nouveauté, 1928
Sepo (Severo Pozzati, 1895–1983)
46¼ x 63 inches (117.5 x 160 cm)
Imprimerie de L'Affichage National Dufayel, Paris

As one of France's most famous department stores—the largest in the world in the early 1900s—the Palais de la Nouveauté commissioned a treasure trove of eye-catching posters to advertise its seasonal sales and latest collections. This rare art deco design by Sepo, though, stands out as perhaps its most intriguing. Rather than focus on the products for sale, the poster instead presents us with a sleek, powerful locomotive rushing toward the viewer. Although it predates Pierre Fix-Masseau's masterful *Exactitude* (see page 259) by a year, the similarities are notable and striking. However, rather than glide mightily down the track, as the train in *Exactitude* does, this train barrels with all its force over the hills of the French countryside toward the rolling sea. The composition makes travel appear not only enticing but also adventurous and bold—and what calls for a new wardrobe better than a holiday in a different climate? The destination of this train is unknown—the consumer gets to pick in her mind where she is going, be it a ritzy seaside spa or a remote pastoral village, and subsequently imagine her ideal ensemble for such adventures. It becomes an advertisement suggesting limitless options, appealing to both sexes and all classes and tastes. The store closed in 1930, but after World War II, the building became the headquarters for the Banque Nationale de Paris.

Au Bûcheron, 1926
A. M. Cassandre (Adolphe Mouron, 1901–1968)
59 x 161 inches (149.9 x 408.9 cm)
Hachard et Cie., Paris

This extremely rare, epic design is actually a reworking of what is considered to be the artist's very first poster in his signature style. In 1923, he created a golden-hued image for the Parisian furniture store Au Bûcheron in which a lumberjack is seen taking a final, far-reaching swing in his task of felling a tree. It is a cinematic composition, backlit by a sunset that casts long shadows and exaggerates the man's glowing muscles. Here, though, the details of that original image have been simplified; the artist focuses on the powerful, radiating geometry behind the figure and letters rather than on narrative content. The typography has also been updated in this later design to further intensify the visual dynamism of the composition. It is no longer heroic but modern; no longer a legend but a harbinger of the future. And in both cases, it is remarkable that such masterful images are meant to promote nothing more than a furniture store. Cassandre would be commissioned to create a third and final poster for the company in 1934, in which he pushed the silhouette of the lumberjack into the colorful domain of a cartoon; however, this 1926 version is without a doubt the finest of his efforts for the brand.

Beristain: Dunhill, 1932
Jacint Bofarull (1903–1977)
38⅞ x 27⅜ inches (98.7 x 69.5 cm)
Printer unknown

Based in Barcelona, Beristain was a shop specializing in a variety of typically masculine products, such as sporting equipment, cigarette lighters, and leather goods, all sold at moderate prices. Artist Jacint Bofarull created four posters for the brand, each portraying a specific type of object—a series that visually documents a progression in the way Beristain thought about its customers and its products. In 1932—two years after his designs that advertised the Beristain department store's dedication to the sporting life and travel (see pages 142–143)—Bofarull created this brilliant poster for the Barcelona emporium's selection of Dunhill lighters, touted in the poster as the "greatest stock in Barcelona." British-based Alfred Dunhill, Ltd., specializes in men's luxury items, including clothing, leather goods, fragrances, timepieces, writing implements, and lighters. In 1927, the company introduced its revolutionary Unique Lighter—the first that could be operated using just one hand. (According to legend, Alfred Dunhill invented the item after losing an arm in an accident.) Bofarull's elegant geometric arrangement of a couple lighting up in parallel stances is classic. Of the works that Bofarull created for Beristain, this is by far the finest.

Beristain: Escopetas Búfalo, 1932
Jacint Bofarull (1903–1977)
39¼ x 27½ inches (99.7 x 69.8 cm)
T. G. Llauger, Barcelona

This striking art deco design promotes the Beristain store's extensive shotgun offerings, with a focus on their standard Buffalo rifle. Unlike London's exceptionally expensive James Purdey & Sons and other such firearms purveyors, Beristain focused on affordable sporting guns for the middle-class consumer, personified here as a tanned and chiseled fellow in shirtsleeves rather than a traditional country gentleman. As a communist activist and artist during the Spanish Civil War, Jacint Bofarull was attracted to the company's appeal to the average man. This is Everyman—a universal character using a universally available product—skillfully mastering his task in an anonymous but hospitable landscape. As in all Bofarull's Beristain posters, the popularity of the brand is highlighted by the fact that the text appears partially cut off—the average person is so familiar with it that he automatically inserts the missing information. Beristain went out of business in 1995.

Beristain: Todo para Deportes, 1930
Jacint Bofarull (1903–1977)
38½ x 26⅞ inches (97.8 x 68.3 cm)
Gráfica Moderna L. Cortina, Barcelona

Jacint Bofarull earned a reputation as a politically outspoken artist from the many caricatures he drew for a number of satirical political magazines, including *La Esquella de la Torratxa* and *Papitu*. None of his leftward political leanings is to be found, however, in this snazzy promotion for Beristain, the Barcelona department store, and its line of sporting goods and apparel. While these sharp-as-tacks art deco triplets appear timeless, in large part because of their angular construction, it is unlikely that you will find pipe smoking touted as a necessity for either golf or mountain climbing in today's health-conscious age.

Beristain: Artículos para Viaje, 1932
Jacint Bofarull (1903–1977)
39½ x 27 inches (100.3 x 68.6 cm)
Printer unknown

This design, in which Bofarull focuses on Beristain's leather goods, is noticeably busier than previous posters he created for the brand. It also removes the interactive human element from the image and instead showcases the products and their various uses. Instead of illustrating a single moment, it tells the story of a purchase that leads to exotic travel. The luggage is poised on the diagonal, its lines working against those of the airplane and the ship, thereby creating a kinetic sense of movement that would have been lacking had the trunk and bag been situated on a flat plane. Moreover, the objects are stacked and therefore partially hidden, suggesting that intimation is more important than full disclosure. This is perhaps a result of Bofarull's interest in cubism, which Picasso had explored in the same city thirty years earlier. Bofarull's left-wing beliefs would force him to flee Spain in 1939, when Franco's regime made it impossible for artists like him to remain both safe and employed. He would continue to live abroad, stirring up the political-artistic landscape in Paris, Buenos Aires, and Caracas, until he returned to his native soil in 1959.

Preceding pages
PKZ: Jedermann, 1928
PKZ: Vestiti, 1928
PKZ: Vêtements, 1928
Otto Morach (1887–1973)
50½ x 36 inches each (128.3 x 91.4 cm)
Wolfsberg, Zürich

Otto Morach's design for PKZ, a Swiss clothier, exhibits an exceptional and cunning interplay of pattern and color. Moss green, rust, and blue contrast boldly, one off the other, while stripes play off plaids. Combined with the fashionable cant of the two men, each reading a newspaper bearing a PKZ ad on the back page, they transform an ordinary situation into a real eye-catcher. When seen individually, each poster is wondrous; when the three are placed next to each other in a single display, as they would have been when they first appeared on the streets of Europe, the effect is startling—a lithographic reflection of an ordinary urban situation executed in an extraordinary manner. The poster was printed in three languages: German (*jedermann* means "everyone"), Italian, and French (*vestiti* and *vêtements* mean "clothes"). PKZ stands for Paul Kehl of Zurich, who in 1881 founded Switzerland's first large-scale men's clothing retailer. (Some customers at the time noted wryly that in Swiss German, the initials PKZ also stand for *Papa kann zahlen,* or "Papa can pay.") Though the firm subsequently became Berger-Kehl & Company, the name PKZ remained on its menswear labels and storefronts. In the world of advertising, these letters stand for a remarkable body of outstanding posters commissioned by the firm over an eighty-year period. It employed the finest Swiss graphic artists and allowed their individual styles to express the seasonal differences in the clothing available at PKZ. It was an innovative strategy, one that resulted in a diverse promotional output based on artistic vision rather than corporate vision.

Right: Before the advent of mobile devices, newspapers absorbed the attention of businessmen on the streets of London, circa 1929.

Page 148
PKZ, 1928
Herbert Matter (1907–1984)
50¼ x 35¾ inches (127.6 x 90.8 cm)
Wolfsberg, Zürich

Herbert Matter is most recognized for his pioneering use of photomontage in commercial art. However, before he became a master of this technique, he studied with a broad range of instructors in a variety of disciplines. One of his instructors was A. M. Cassandre, who taught poster design in Paris in the late 1920s. It was during this period that the young Matter created this authoritative yet lighthearted design for PKZ in a cubist-inspired mode. Composed of little more than a series of background rectangles and simplified forms in predominantly subdued colors accentuated with airbrushed shadows, the poster tells the story of PKZ quality through the eyes of a porter, who is unable to disguise his pleasant surprise upon viewing PKZ outerwear, even though he has undoubtedly seen more than his share of overcoats during his time on the job.

Page 149
PKZ, 1934
Niklaus Stoecklin (1896–1982)
56 x 35 inches (142.2 x 88.9 cm)
Wolfsberg, Zürich

While Niklaus Stoecklin's poster for PKZ doesn't possess the singular focus of his posters for Valvo radio tubes and Clus transmission parts (see pages 80 and 98), there's an understated surrealism at work that makes it difficult to look away—somewhat reminiscent of the work of the Belgian artist René Magritte, who focused on challenging observers' preconceived opinions of reality. There's something just slightly off in the design: the shoulders are a bit too broad, the head is a touch too small, and the hat is somewhat too big. It is as if we are being shown a boy dressed in his father's outdoor apparel. If that's the case, then why include the cane and the newspaper? The elements don't quite add up, and it is these irregularities, along with the beautifully rendered overcoat, that make this rare and powerful Stoecklin design unforgettable.

FASHION AND ENTERTAINMENT

149

Grand-Sport, 1925
A. M. Cassandre (Adolphe Mouron, 1901–1968)
31¾ x 23 inches (80.6 x 58.4 cm)
Hachard et Cie., Paris

Created at the onset of his career, Cassandre's poster for Grand-Sport caps—"the champions' choice"—is one in which we can clearly see his trademark style beginning to take shape: a simple geometric abstraction (in this case, a face) contrasted with the realistic rendering of a product (a yellow driving cap) presented in a flattened perspective. It is a textbook example of the way in which a bold, direct image can command our attention. Noting the influence of Oskar Schlemmer and Picasso on this design, Robert K. Brown and Susan Reinhold, writing in The Poster Art of A. M. Cassandre, find that "what is most subtle and interesting about the poster is the suggestion of a multiple perspective, which gives a simultaneous straight-on and cocked-to-the-right viewpoint of the face."

Grand-Sport, 1931
A. M. Cassandre (Adolphe Mouron, 1901–1968)
31¾ x 23 inches (80.6 x 58.4 cm)
Alliance Graphique, Paris

Six years after his previous Grand-Sport poster (left) appeared on the hoardings of Paris, Cassandre—by then in possession of his own advertising firm—revisited his design for the "champions'" cap. In the end, the artist changed very little, emerging with a pared-down, simplified version of the original. The genius of this tactic reveals just how little a master like Cassandre needed to change the original elements in order to create an entirely new, memorable poster. Essentially, he made only two significant changes. First, he reduced and tilted the outline of the face, leaving only the eye-nose schematic and the pipe, while using the text to create borders and further define the head. Second, he softened the color scheme, making the Grand-Sport product appear even more realistic. It's a positively brilliant, confident rethinking of the original, one that yields a design equal to, if not more impressive than, its inspiration.

Savo, 1930
A. M. Cassandre (Adolphe Mouron, 1901–1968)
15⅝ x 11¾ inches (39.7 x 29.8 cm)
Compagnie Artistique de Publicité, Paris

In this poster for Savo work clothes, geometry once again proves to be the primary implement in Cassandre's artistic toolbox. He composes a body from a series of right angles, a head and hands from three simple circles, and a background from rectangular bricks. While the hammer is fairly lifelike, it is the Savo clothes that come across as the most realistic items in the poster, much like the caps in the Grand-Sport promotions (left and above left). The understated strength of the design is perfectly suited to the product it promotes—sturdy, strong, and reliable—and its background not only sets the scene for the work being done by the man in the poster but also suggests the factory where the clothes were manufactured. Innovative in its simplicity, this Savo graphic is one of Cassandre's rarest posters. It also served as the model for an eight-foot-high metal-and-wood sign that stood in the display window of the Savo headquarters in Montmartre for sixty years.

Austin Reed: 13 Fenchurch St., ca. 1927
Tom Purvis (1888–1959)
59½ x 39¾ inches (151.1 x 101 cm)
Printer unknown

Vibrant bands of color offset the somber sophistication of evening wear and provide a sense of motion to this poster advertising Austin Reed's very first store, at 13 Fenchurch Street in London. The retailer of upmarket clothing, known for its menswear, was founded in 1900 and had seventy outlets throughout Britain; it also operated concessions on the RMS *Aquitania* and the RMS *Queen Mary*. Winston Churchill was a patron of the firm. With superb simplicity and just two colors—black and white—Purvis creates a classic vision of formal wear: gloves, top hat, overcoat, striped scarf, bow tie, trousers, and vest. His choice to not completely place his man-about-town within the frame of the poster works to perfection, instantly cementing our attention on the featureless gent, whose lack of facial detailing allows the viewer to focus entirely on the couture. Purvis, along with Edward McKnight Kauffer, was the top poster designer in England in this time period, and this is considered to be his best poster for Austin Reed.

Candee, 1929
Franco Barberis (1905–1992)
51 x 35⅜ inches (129.5 x 89.8 cm)
A. Trüb & Cie., Aarau

This image of a pristine, leggy flapper and her pert terrier breezily making their way through a patch of inclement weather provides some stylish zip to a product not necessarily associated with high fashion: rubber rain boots. The advertisement also reflects a Roaring Twenties optimism: unlike in olden days, when seeing a bit of stocking was—as the song says—"something shocking," boots now had to look good with an ensemble that included a short skirt. Here they look fabulous—the cool background colors make certain that the red boots, which match the elegant woman's lipstick, stand out, completely in tune with 1920s high style. Leverett Candee, having licensed Goodyear's vulcanization process, was the first to market rubber footwear in 1852.

Trage Schmuck du Gewinnst, 1932
N. Weber, n.d.
35⅜ x 23½ inches (89.8 x 59.7 cm)
J. J. Weber, Leipzig and Berlin

"Wear jewelry—you win" was the slogan for an event called Jewelry Week, which took place in Berlin in 1932. Couple the striking typography with the opulent decadence of Weber's masterful image on this poster and it becomes difficult to find fault with the credo. The after-dark color scheme is sexy and enticing, as is the partially seen model upon whom the jewelry is draped. She could be a mannequin or a statue, with her flawless skin, exaggerated facial features, and complete lack of clothing. All of this serves to display the jewelry exquisitely, from the string of pearls to the serpentine bracelet slithering three-quarters of the way down her arm to the oval ring to the abstract miniature sculpture that hangs from her earlobe.

Noveltex: Pour le Soir, ca. 1935
Sepo (Severo Pozzati, 1895–1983)
59 x 38 inches (149.9 x 96.5 cm)
Sepo, Saint-Ouen

In this poster, Sepo (see his *Palais de la Nouveauté,* page 137) sets the scene with stylish art deco finesse in order to bring to mind the unspoken masquerade inherent in certain nocturnal engagements. While the artist makes it clear that a Noveltex tuxedo shirt can stand on its own with sleek flair and razor-sharp elegance, it is the essentially featureless face that provides the visual hook: broken down into geometric patterns and bisected by the brand's trademark colors, it cunningly suggests the mask of polite society. Teasingly, Sepo tilts the *s* in "soir" to give the impression that things are just slightly awry and not quite as they may appear. Shirt maker Noveltex was one of Sepo's first clients, and he would provide the company with a steady stream of promotional material for more than twenty-five years, from 1925 through 1951. The company made shirts and collars that were sold in only the finest haberdashers.

155

Le Bal Fleuri: des Fêtes du Printemps, 1927
Paul Colin (1892–1985)
62 x 46¼ inches (157.5 x 117.5 cm)
H. Chachoin, Paris

Paul Colin's use of a lithographic "triple exposure"—three virtual snapshots of an elegant couple making their way around a packed dance floor, layered one on top of the other and drawn from three different points of view—creates a wonderful, sweeping sense of stop-motion sequencing to promote a 1927 springtime "floral ball" at the Théâtre des Champs-Élysées, held to benefit French orphans. Although Colin doesn't include a single flower, he does manage to wedge three additional couples into the prismatic angularity of the design, hinting at the event's romantic sensuality and allowing the triple-exposed foreground couple to lead the way with their nimble sophistication. Colin makes his artistry look easy, but it's the precision and complexity of the design, with a splash of pink included as an additional attention-getter, that breathes style into this advertisement.

La Revue Black Birds: Moulin Rouge, 1929
Paul Colin (1892–1985)
62 x 45 inches (157.5 x 114.3 cm)
Hachard et Cie., Paris

While this poster (the only known copy) for *The Blackbird Revue*'s appearance at the Moulin Rouge is something of a return to the African-American caricature Colin used in the 1925 *La Revue Nègre* poster, which created a sensation with Parisian passersby, here he shows artistic growth beyond the exaggerated showmanship of the 1925 work. Whereas the earlier poster relied almost exclusively on minstrel-show motifs, this Jazz Age masterwork incorporates elements of cubism and abstraction. Its characters—Bill "Bojangles" Robinson (1878–1949), unsung diva Adelaide Hall (1901–1993), and celebrated vaudevillian Tim Moore (1887–1958)—create a memorable art deco trio. The poster's stunning combination of hot color and extreme angularity is remarkable, and while the name of the venue (which means "red windmill" in English) is written at the top, Colin takes it one step further by placing the Moulin Rouge at the "heart" of the matter. The show's three-month-long engagement in Paris followed its successful run on Broadway at New York's Liberty Theatre, where it played a total of 518 performances under the title *Blackbirds of 1928*. The show was conceived and directed by impresario Lew Leslie (1888–1963). Although Leslie was Caucasian, he was the first Broadway producer to present African-American performers onstage without blackface. He is most famous for these *Blackbird* revues and for mounting stage shows at Harlem's Cotton Club.

Singer Adelaide Hall is mobbed by fans at the Gare du Nord in Paris, 1929.

André Renaud, 1929
Paul Colin (1892-1985)
60½ x 45⅛ inches (153.7 x 114.6 cm)
H. Chachoin, Paris

At first glance, one might get the impression that Colin was making a monumental overstatement with regard to André Renaud's musical ability in this quintessential art deco poster. But Renaud was a virtuoso who played two pianos simultaneously during his performances—for a while he even did this blindfolded, for no apparent reason other than to demonstrate his superior showmanship. The poster's two overlapping pianos—one a grand, the other a horizontally extended upright—look like a double exposure, which was a technique Colin used frequently to create maximum visual impact (see his poster of dancer Lisa Duncan, at right, and the Bal Fleuri, page 156). Renaud would eventually give up his pianos to become a bandleader.

Lisa Duncan, 1927
Paul Colin (1892-1985)
47 x 31½ inches (119.4 x 80 cm)
H. Chachoin, Paris

This very rare and absolutely gorgeous Paul Colin poster promoting the dancer Lisa Duncan is intended to shock the viewer, much as Duncan's performances were intended to shock audiences. In many ways, it is the ideal pairing of a graphic designer and an artist: both Colin and Duncan rejected the traditional in favor of the alternative in their respective mediums. Colin's artwork is magnetic—a stunning combination of hot pinks and oranges, aggressive geometry, and sex appeal. His portrayal of Duncan is phenomenal, uniting the dancer's movements and the grand piano in a single art deco image. Lisa Duncan (1898-1976), born Elisabeth Milker in Dresden, Germany, was one of a group of six young women who came to be known as the Isadorables. These women studied with the legendary modern dance pioneer Isadora Duncan (1877-1927) at her school in Grünewald, Germany, during their childhoods. The Isadorables went on to perform with Duncan, who legally adopted the six dancers in 1919, allowing them to share her surname.

Oxford Blag's, 1929
Marc Fernand Severin (1906–1987)
25 x 19 inches (63.5 x 48.3 cm)
Éditions J. Hoste SA, Bruxelles

This awesome and very rare cubist poster by Marc Fernand Severin remains enigmatic despite extensive efforts to uncover its origins. The reason for the mystery is that there appears to be no record of precisely what Oxford Blag's was. All we know is what we can discern from the poster itself, and that information is minimal. It was a ten-day event, and the rest is pure speculation. The word "Oxford," as is commonly known, refers both to the city and the university named for it in southeast England. "Blag" is a British slang term with an array of meanings, ranging from "obtaining through deception" to "bluffing" to "joking around." Combining the two words doesn't clarify matters. What is clear in the art deco design is a wonderful sense of joyous motion combined with an inventive modernist typography. My best guess would be that this poster was designed to promote a British dance troupe or theatrical company—one whose performances were loaded with ironic humor—during an extended appearance on the Continent.

Regina Palast Hotel, 1932
Walter Schnackenberg (1880–1961)
34¼ x 22¾ inches (87 x 57.8 cm)
Kunst im Druck, München

Two frequent Walter Schnackenberg motifs were seduction and decadence. He portrayed late-night pleasures in an attractively seedy manner that didn't moralize. His art deco design for the "dance bar" at Munich's Regina Palast Hotel features slashing bands of text and color that surround a dancing couple so into one another that they can't be bothered to notice such promotional intrusions. Also mentioned on the poster is Billy Bartholomew (1901–1972), a British saxophone player who worked as a sideman in England, Scotland, and France before relocating to Germany in 1924. There, he would play with several big bands before founding his own dance orchestra.

Disques Odéon, 1929
Jean Carlu (1900–1997)
78⅜ x 51½ inches (199 x 130.8 cm)
Les Imprimeries Françaises Réunies, Paris

In 1903, Max Straus and Heinrich Zuntz purchased a handful of smaller record companies to form Odeon Records. Although based in Berlin, the company took its name from the famous Parisian theater and used the image of its classical dome on the label. Odeon was the first to introduce the double-sided record as well as what is considered to be the first "album"—the four-disc version of Tchaikovsky's *The Nutcracker*—in 1909. By the 1920s it was truly a global concern, exporting more than 70 percent of its output. Here, Carlu has created what is arguably the brand's most celebrated image, masterfully using elements of cubism to elevate a trademark into the realm of high art. As one of the leading poster artists of the day, along with Paul Colin and A. M. Cassandre, he understood how to make a masterpiece out of the mundane, which is exactly what he does in this very rare design. The red stylus of the tone arm takes on an anthropomorphic quality as it gazes out at the viewer through its single black "eye," while the record itself, poised at an impossible angle and appearing in a disproportional size, becomes both an image of the product and a means of introducing the brand's name, which runs at an angle off of the round label in the center.

MOTOR RACING

THE SPORT OF MOTOR RACING began soon after the development of gasoline-powered automobiles. The first organized race is believed to have been held in Paris in 1887, but unfortunately, only one participant entered the event! In 1894, the first truly competitive race was run from Paris to Rouen. Sixty-nine vehicles pulled up to the starting line for the thirty-one-mile contest. In the United States, the first motor racing event was held on Thanksgiving Day, 1895. It was a fifty-four-mile trip from Chicago to Evanston, Illinois, and back; the winner took nearly ten and one-half hours to complete the circuit.

Grand Prix automobile races began in Le Mans, France, in 1906. In the United States, the first Grand Prix race was held in Savannah, Georgia, in 1908. But it was not until the early 1920s that these contests were held in other countries—namely, Italy, Spain, Belgium, Great Britain, and Germany. The interwar years were known as the Golden Age of motor sports: airplane, motorboat, and car races were contested regularly, but automobile racing was clearly the king. Initially, races were run in high-priced road cars, enthusiastically supported by the manufacturers who used racing to promote their brands.

By the 1930s, specially designed and built race cars were used in competition. The leading marques were Bugatti, Delahaye, Alfa Romeo, Fiat, Mercedes, and Auto Union (see chapter 2, Automobiles and Motorcycles). Taking a lead from Mussolini, the Nazis encouraged German manufactures to build better, faster cars to promote the supremacy of the Third Reich, and from mid-1934 to the fall of 1939, Mercedes and Auto Union won fifty-two of fifty-five Grand Prix races. Ironically, Hitler brought about the end to this string of victories when he invaded Poland and World War II began. Automobile racing did not resume again until after the war ended, in 1945.

The outstanding motor racing posters in this chapter are some of the most iconic and rare designs ever made. They were typically printed in small quantities, displayed only locally, and routinely destroyed after the race ended. Many important graphic artists of the period were hired to design these posters, including Robert Falcucci, Raymond Savignac, Federico Seneca, Ernst Ruprecht, Noël Fontanet, and Percy Trompf. Not only did these beautifully illustrated works of art serve to promote each race as it happened, they also provide a graphic historical record of the splendor and aura of glamour surrounding motor racing.

10ème Rallye Automobile Monte Carlo: Janvier, 1931
Robert Falcucci (1900–1989)
46⅞ x 31⅛ inches (119.1 x 79 cm)
Imprimerie Monégasque, Monte-Carlo

Rally racing—as opposed to Grand Prix racing—is run not on a designated racing circuit but rather from geographic point A to geographic point B. Participating cars depart in stages, at regular controlled intervals. The Monte Carlo Rally was the brainchild of Prince Albert I of Monaco, who inaugurated the race in 1911 in an effort to increase winter tourism to the area, though it would also come to serve as an important means of testing automotive improvements and innovations. Organized by the Automobile Club de Monaco, the rally required its competitors to start from various sites throughout Europe and follow a precise itinerary that concluded with a dramatic automotive entrance into Monte Carlo. Falcucci's imaginative design makes it clear that no matter where on the globe the contestants started, all roads lead to Monte Carlo and its famous bay, which here is silhouetted in the rising sun. Although French drivers had dominated the rally since its inception, it was Englishman Donald Healey (1898–1988) who won the 1931 rally behind the wheel of an Invicta.

Monaco: 19 Avril, 1931
Robert Falcucci (1900–1989)
47¼ x 31¼ inches (120 x 79.4 cm)
Imprimerie Monégasque, Monte-Carlo

The Grand Prix of Monaco is the most glamorous, prestigious, and famous auto race in the world. This classic art deco poster for the third running of the Monaco Grand Prix shows a red Bugatti racing uphill toward the viewer in the blazing Mediterranean sun, with Monte Carlo and the harbor in the far distance. In hot pursuit is a Mercedes SSK with the number 2 emblazoned on its grille, careening precariously as it comes. Falcucci uses white streaks and concentric circles to convey the rush of the wind along the length of the racer, giving this streamlined design a particular panache. The bright palette of red, yellow, and blue adds heat and drama to the scene. This is surely one of the great art deco images in the history of motor sports posters; it is also the rarest and most valuable of the Grand Prix de Monaco series. The race was broadcast live on radio (a first-time event) and was also carried by the French telegraph service in Nice, Cannes, and Juan-les-Pins. Midway through the contest, Achille Varzi was comfortably ahead of Louis Chiron and Luigi Fagioli, and appeared to have the race under control, when a punctured tire spoiled his chances to win. Chiron, a Monte Carlo resident piloting a Bugatti Type 51, thrilled the locals by being the first of their own to win the race. He finished in three hours and thirty-nine minutes and clocked an average speed of fifty-four miles per hour. This was the third straight win for Bugatti, which manufactured sixteen of the twenty-three cars entered in the race.

Grand Prix Automobile de Nice, 1935
Henri Delval (n.d.)
38⅞ x 24⅜ inches (98.7 x 61.9 cm)
A.D.I.A., Nice

The two-mile-long street circuit for the Grand Prix de Nice was similar to the course for the Grand Prix de Monaco (see page 165): a lovely seaside route mostly paralleling the beach promenade, with a hairpin turn at each end and a minor loop around the Jardin Albert Premier. This powerful Henri Delval design bears down on the passerby with a quartet of fierce competitors who appear to be as much a part of the race cars as the engines under the hoods. The inaugural Grand Prix de Nice was held in 1932. In 1935, the Ferrari-sponsored team took the top three spots behind the wheel of Alfa Romeos, while fourth place went to a privately sponsored entry—French racing legend Raymond Sommer (1906–1950), who also drove an Alfa Romeo.

Pau Grand Prix Automobile, 1937
Scot (n.d.)
63 x 46½ inches (160 x 118.1 cm)
Imprimé Spéciale de l'Automobile Club

As Henri Delval does in his poster for the Nice Grand Prix (left), the artist Scot also makes single-minded competition the centerpiece of his advertisement for the 1937 Pau Grand Prix, discarding, by and large, the beautiful street circuit upon which the race is run. Scot does include the Pyrenees mountains as a backdrop in his promotion, which not only geographically identifies the race's setting in southwestern France but also adds a touch of grandeur to the design. In 1901, the Pau Grand Prix was the first race to be called a Grand Prix. However, the 1901 competition was a one-off event, and the term "Grand Prix" didn't gain widespread usage until it was applied to the French Grand Prix held at Le Mans in 1906. The Pau race started running regularly in 1933 and has been held essentially every year since, except during World War II. French race-car driver Jean-Pierre Wimille (1908–1949) won the 1937 Pau Grand Prix in a Bugatti Type 57C Tank, the vehicle that he also drove to victory in that year's Le Mans twenty-four-hour endurance race. During the Second World War, Wimille joined Britain's Special Operations Executive (also known as Churchill's Secret Army) with fellow racers Robert Benoist and William Grover-Williams (the winner of the first Grand Prix de Monaco, in 1929) to aid the French Resistance. Of the three volunteers, Wimille was the sole survivor.

2e Grand Prix de l'Albigeois, 1934
F. Andrieu (n.d.)
49½ x 33½ inches (125.7 x 85.1 cm)
Imprimerie Chabrillac, Toulouse

4e Grand Prix Automobile Albi, 1936
F. Andrieu (n.d.)
40½ x 25 inches (102.9 x 63.5 cm)
Imprimerie Chabrillac, Toulouse

ACF: 31e Grand Prix, 1937
Raymond Savignac (1907–2002)
63 x 47½ inches (160 x 120.6 cm)
Alliance Graphique, Paris

In 1935, the graphic artist Raymond Savignac had the good fortune of meeting A. M. Cassandre, who took him on as an apprentice. This extremely bold—and extremely rare—poster for the Automobile Club de France's thirty-first Grand Prix is one of Savignac's first posters and clearly shows Cassandre's influence on his pupil (the poster was printed by Cassandre's advertising agency, Alliance Graphique). The results are spectacular—a warp-speed composition anchored at an uncommonly low angle that stunningly blurs the line between driving and flying. In fact, the image is rather reminiscent of Cassandre's *LMS: The Best Way* (page 251), which was created nearly a decade earlier. Neither artist included the entirety of what was being advertised: rather, a circular foreground object—Savignac uses a wheel, Cassandre a points lever, or manual switch—sets the scene and creates depth while a series of linear elements (Savignac's speed-elongated tire, Cassandre's rails) delivers perspective. Savignac's poster stands on its own merits, but it's impossible to overlook Cassandre's artistic "signature" on the work, especially in the design's geometry and the bold, succinct placement of text. The ACF was a men's club founded on November 12, 1895. In 1906, the organization sanctioned a race in the Sarthe *département* of northwestern France that would pave the way for such famous French races as the 24 Hours of Le Mans and the French Grand Prix. The 1937 race was won by Monaco-born driver Louis Chiron (1899–1979) in a Talbot T150C, making him the first driver in history to have won three French Grand Prix. All told, Chiron would win that prestigious race a total of five times, in addition to his win in the 1931 Grand Prix de Monaco (page 165).

In F. Andrieu's 1934 poster advertising the second Albi Grand Prix, the cars appear to be somewhat pliant, literally bending to their drivers' wills as they head into a turn on the Circuit d'Albi, the racetrack located near the city of Albi, northeast of Toulouse. The Circuit d'Albi has been hosting international racing events for nearly eighty years; however, it hosted a mere six Albi Grand Prix—the last one was held in 1949. The 1934 race was won by British driver Rupert "Buddy" Featherstonhaugh (1909–1976) in a Maserati 26M. Featherstonhaugh was actually only an occasional race-car driver—he is best known as a jazz saxophonist who played with the likes of Louis Armstrong and Benny Carter. In Andrieu's poster advertising the fourth running of the race, in 1936, a single blue car in front of a red background is depicted in typical art deco fashion. The winner of the race was the Thai driver B. Bira, a.k.a. Prince Birabongse Bhanudej Bhanubandh (1914–1985), driving an ERA Type B.

Course de Côte de la Baraque, 1931
Erma (n.d.)
45⅜ x 30 inches (115.2 x 76.2 cm)
Affiches Mon-Louis, Clermont-Ferrand

Hosted annually since 1926 by the Automobile Club d'Auvergne, the Course de Côte de la Baraque is an uphill automobile and motorcycle race held near the industrial city of Clermont-Ferrand. One of the region's signature volcanic domes—part of the Chaîne des Puys—is depicted in hazy blue on the horizon, cut ever so slightly at the top left by the implied continuation of the racecourse. Compared to such majestic scenery, the two drivers appear almost out of place, surprising and sudden ambassadors of the modern mechanical age in an otherwise tranquil setting. This forceful sense of rushing into untouched terrain is underscored by the juxtaposition of angles in the composition: while the organic elements of the image are undulating and soft, the road upon which these drivers race lies at an unnaturally sharp incline—a man-made "slice" into the land. Even the text appears aggressive, pushing emphatically up the slope, the horizontal lines trailing after it mimicking those on the vehicles and further emphasizing the overall sense of swiftness. And while today the public is concerned with preserving and, in many cases, restoring the wilderness, in the 1930s images of dominance over the earth's resources were highly celebrated. It is a visual dialogue between man and nature in which man proves the dominant power.

Budapest Grand Prix, 1936
Károly Gerster (1859–1940)
37¼ x 24¾ inches (94.6 x 62.9 cm)
Klösy, Budapest

This rare Gerster design for the 1936 Hungarian Grand Prix epitomizes classic art deco style. The determined driver who appears to be on the verge of breaking free from the confines of his Alfa Romeo 12C adds to the poster's magnetism and makes the passerby feel like part of the action. Also worthy of mention is the Széchenyi Chain Bridge, seen in the distance at the center left of the image—it's this bridge that spans the Danube River, connecting Buda on the west with Pest on the east to create the Hungarian capital of Budapest. The bridge takes its name from one of the greatest statesmen in Hungarian history, Count István Széchenyi (1791–1860). Budapest's famous thermal baths (see pages 286–287) also take their name from this politician, writer, and theorist. The year 1936 marks the first-ever running of the Hungarian Grand Prix, staged on a 3.1-mile track that had been laid out in Budapest's Népliget Park ("People's Park"). The race was sponsored by the Royal Hungarian Automobile Club, whose blue-crossed pennant is prominently displayed along with the Hungarian national flag. The race drew a large crowd, and Maserati, Mercedes-Benz, and Auto Union all sent teams to participate. However, it was Italian driver Tazio Nuvolari (1892–1953) who took the checkered flag behind the wheel of an Alfa Romeo 8C-35. Nuvolari raced both motorcycles and cars, and was known as il Mantovano Volante ("the Flying Mantuan"). Dr. Ferdinand Porsche—the legendary Austrian engineer who designed the Volkswagen Beetle, the Mercedes-Benz SSK, and, of course, the first Porsche—referred to Nuvolari as "the greatest driver of the past, the present, and the future." Nuvolari began his racing career on a motorcycle and is one of very few people to have attained Grand Prix victories in both forms of racing.

1ª· Gran Semana Internacional: Autódromo Nacional, 1923
Josep Segrelles (1885–1969)
34¼ x 46¾ inches (87 x 118.7 cm)
Rieusset, Barcelona

Artist Josep Segrelles celebrates speed and forward motion in this poster for the first International Race Week held at the Autódromo de Sitges-Terramar, a racing circuit located between Sant Pere de Ribes and Sitges near Barcelona, Spain. The unusual point of view places the viewer underneath the vehicles as they speed by, which makes the cars seem as though they're flying through midair, not touching the track at all. The message is clear: expect speed. It's interesting that the most historic feature of the race isn't even included in the poster—the Sitges-Terramar track itself. In 1922, the Autódromo Nacional organization was founded to oversee the construction of a concrete one-and-a-quarter-mile oval for car and motor-cycle racing in the Barcelona area. The facility was completed in slightly less than a year, and its inaugural event was the 1923 race week, which included the Spanish Grand Prix. French driver Albert Divo (1895–1966) won the race in a Sunbeam with an average speed of nearly ninety-seven miles per hour. Although the Segrelles poster promises "500,000 francs in prize money," not a single cent was given out—unpaid construction costs motivated the builders to seize the gate, leaving organizers unable to pay the drivers. As a result, the track was banned from ever hosting another international race. Nonetheless, a few minor races have been held at Sitges-Terramar over the years (the last one took place in 1953). The track and its surrounding land are currently being used as a chicken farm.

Gran Premio de España: San Sebastián, 1935
Javier Gómez Acebo and
Máximo Viejo Santamarta (n.d.)
39 x 27¼ inches (99.1 x 69.2 cm)
Gráficas Laborde y Labayen, Tolosa

The idyllic Bay of Biscay, in Spain's Basque Country, contrasts with the racer's determined stare to marvelous effect in this promotion for the eleventh Spanish Grand Prix, held on the Circuito Lasarte road course at Lasarte-Oria, in the province of Guipúzcoa, near the resort town of San Sebastián. The second half of the 1930s, in terms of motor racing, belonged to Mercedes-Benz: no matter the location or type of track, Mercedes seemed to dominate. The winner of the 1935 Spanish Grand Prix was the hugely successful German driver Rudolf Caracciola (1901–1959), remembered as one of the preeminent pre–World War II Grand Prix drivers. Caracciola was a perfectionist who excelled in wet-weather races, a skill for which he was nicknamed Regenmeister ("rainmaster"). The year 1935 marks Spain's descent into civil war, and the race promoted here was the final Spanish Grand Prix until the contest was resumed as a Formula One event in 1951.

FN: Le Raid au Cap, 1928
Auguste Mambour (1896–1968)
31 3/8 x 19 3/4 inches (79.7 x 50.2 cm)
Imprimerie Bénard, Liège

The 1928 Raid au Cap, or Trek to Cape Town, was the second in a series of three long-distance endurance races intended to demonstrate the feasibility of establishing an airmail route between Belgium and the colonial Belgian Congo in Africa. The notion of creating this route was put forward by Belgian aviator and adventurer Robert Fabry (1899–1987), who proposed the concept as a natural extension of the existing airmail route between Paris and Dakar. Fabry set off on the first of his endurance treks (see page 65) on December 26, 1926, departing solo from Liège on a motorcycle. The outbound journey to the Democratic Republic of the Congo covered more than 15,500 miles and lasted seven months, but Fabry managed to complete the difficult round trip and returned to Liège on October 17, 1927. His exploits attracted the attention of Fabrique Nationale, the Belgian manufacturer of armaments, motorcycles, and automobiles, and Englebert, a Belgian tire manufacturer. The companies proposed that Fabry make another endurance run, this time by car and this time going all the way to Cape Town, South Africa. Fabry put together a team of two officers from the Belgian army and a journalist. They would make the lengthy trip in a pair of FN sedans equipped with Englebert tires. They left Liège on May 13, 1928, and the arduous expedition came to an end in Cape Town on August 25. The Mambour poster commemorating the feat is fantastic and evocative, addressing both the automotive and the ethnic elements of the journey. It even manages to suggest the outline of continental Africa in the central facial silhouette. Fabry served as the copilot in 1930 for the third endurance race, a flight carried out on behalf of Belgium's Civil Aviation Administration in a Breguet XIX. In the end, the three voyages taken by Robert Fabry made it perfectly clear that an airmail route between Belgium and the Belgian Congo was a viable notion.

Le R.A.M.C.H. à Tournai, ca. 1937
M. Lenoble (n.d.)
43 x 24 1/2 inches (109.2 x 62.2 cm)
Imprimerie Rimbaut, Tournai

The Royal Auto Moto Club du Hainaut, or RAMCH, based in Tournai, Belgium, is still in existence today. This stock poster for the organization (the area in the center was left blank so that the club could imprint the details of individual events) is an engaging exercise in minimalism and angular symmetry, from the inclined quintet of stylized art deco heads that bear the club's initials to the vehicular and architectural schematic at the bottom that reduces Tournai's Cathédrale Notre-Dame to five precise spires. RAMCH was officially founded in 1912, but it was in the years following the First World War that RAMCH truly began to take shape. It became a tireless proponent of better road conditions and legislation to improve the safety of all motorists. In 1927, after twenty-five years in existence, the organization came under the patronage of the governor of the Hainaut province, officially making it the country's "royal" motoring club.

Copa Emilio Saint: Automovil Club Argentino, 1933
Pachelo (n.d.)
31½ x 23½ inches (80 x 59.7 cm)
Talleres Gráficos Saint Hermanos, Buenos Aires

Sand, sea, and speed, with a seagull thrown in for good measure, are the only elements the artist Pachelo needs to promote the Emilio Saint Cup, an approximately 250-mile coastal race run between Mar del Plata (an Argentine beach resort situated on the Atlantic Ocean; see page 301) and Florencio Varela (a suburb of greater Buenos Aires). Though no longer in existence, the race was named for Emilio Saint, president of the Automovil Club Argentino from 1931 to 1935. Founded in 1904 by Dalmiro Varela Castex, who had imported Argentina's first two registered automobiles during the 1890s (a Daimler and a De Dion-Bouton), the ACA oversaw the country's first automobile race in 1906. Although racing is an integral part of the club's history, the organization is also noteworthy for its national network of more than 230 service stations, which it began developing in 1936 after reaching an agreement with the Argentine state-owned oil company, YPF (Yacimientos Petroliferos Fiscales, or "reserve of petroleum fields"). Much as AAA does in the United States, ACA offers maps, roadside assistance, insurance, and other services to its membership.

3 Corsa Automobilistica Cuneo, 1927
Lucio Venna (1897–1974)
74⅜ x 53⅛ inches (188.9 x 134.9 cm)
Edizione Studio Venna Innocenti, Firenze

At first an active and enthusiastic member of the Italian futurist movement, Lucio Venna became frustrated with the ideas of his futurist colleagues after World War I and decided to turn away from painting and illustration. Starting in 1922, he fixed his attention almost exclusively on posters, hundreds of which he created up through the beginning of World War II. This is one such image from the height of his advertising career. The poster was commissioned to promote an automobile race in Cuneo, Italy, although the racecourse itself actually ran through the Maddalena Pass, which connects the Maritime Alps with the Cottian Alps and Cuneo with Barcelonnette, France. The design perfectly represents the varied topography of the Italian city, which is located in a tree-lined valley at the base of the mountains. The Stura di Demonte river is depicted at the left. This is not the only design Venna created for an automobile race, but it is perhaps the most graphically harmonious work in his oeuvre. It conveys a remarkable sense of depth through nothing more than simple, geometric planes of color. There is a collagelike feel to the shapes, as if they were layered pieces of paper and not printed ink—perhaps a subtle nod to the work of Hans Arp, with whom Venna was familiar, thanks to his earlier involvement with the Dadaists and futurists. Alfa Romeo dominated this particular running of the race, taking the top three places. The winner covered the hundred-mile distance at forty-nine miles per hour.

IIa. Coppa della Perugina, 1925
Federico Seneca (1891–1976)
78¾ x 55¼ inches (200 x 140.3 cm)
Grafiche Baroni, Milano

The Perugina Cup—the perfect marriage of fast cars and chocolate—came into existence when Italian chocolate tycoon Giovanni Buitoni (not to be confused with his great-grandmother Giulia Buitoni, who founded the Buitoni pasta company) recognized the promotional possibilities of motor-car racing. Thus the Coppa della Perugina arrived on the scene in 1924. The Coppa was run a mere four times: the candy company was the event's sole sponsor and lacked the funds to continue the race beyond 1927. Seneca's outstanding promotion for the second Perugina race is a unique depiction of speed, as are his promotional creations for the third and fourth races (below and right). Here, velocity-bowed telephone poles and insectlike vehicles disappearing over the horizon convey the rapidity one can expect to encounter at the Perugina Cup. Seneca is considered one of the top art deco graphic artists of the period.

IIIa. Coppa della Perugina, 1926
Federico Seneca (1891–1976)
78¾ x 55¼ inches (200 x 140.3 cm)
Grafiche Baroni, Milano

A stellar Seneca design brings the third running of the Coppa della Perugina to the public's attention by depicting a victorious red race car and driver bearing down on the viewer as they emerge from what best can be described as a pristine supernova to cross the finish line.

IVa. Coppa della Perugina, 1927
Federico Seneca (1891–1976)
76 x 53 inches (193 x 134.6 cm)
Printer unknown

The scene depicted by Seneca in this amazing poster for the final Perugina Cup is anything but stationary, with its two race cars passing by a row of bowed trees in a glorious blur of acceleration-distorted momentum. It is an electrifying image and one of the most dynamic racing posters ever produced. The Classic Car Club of Perugia revived the Perugina Cup in the mid-1980s, but unlike the original competition, it is not a race—it's an opportunity for enthusiasts to roll out their vintage automobiles and socialize with like-minded individuals. All Coppa della Perugina posters are extremely rare.

VIIIᵉ Course Internationale du Klausen, 1930
Ernst Ruprecht (1891–1954)
50 x 35½ inches (127 x 90.2 cm)
Wolfsberg, Zürich

In this rare poster for the 1930 running of the nearly fourteen-mile historic hill-climbing competition that took place in Switzerland's high-mountain Klausen Pass, Ernst Ruprecht's stylized car and driver are almost out of focus because they are moving so rapidly. The winding road through the pass was originally intended as a thoroughfare for pedestrians and carriages. As late as 1921, it was still closed to most vehicles except stagecoaches and haulers used to transport heavy lumber. However, the ever-increasing popularity of the car and the rise of racing in France, Italy, and England resulted in the road being opened to automobiles and the introduction of the Klausenrennen in 1922. Until the race was discontinued in 1934, the best male and female drivers from around the world assembled to compete—speeding, skidding, and screeching their way through the winding gravel roads and deep gorges to the finish line, at the peak of the Klausen Pass. In 1930, Monte Carlo–born driver Louis Chiron (1899–1979) won the hill climb behind the wheel of a Bugatti Type 37 in sixteen minutes and 24.6 seconds.

X.Internationales Klausenrennen, 1934
E. Schönholzer (1913–1995)
50⅜ x 35⅜ inches (127.9 x 89.8 cm)
J. C. Müller, Zürich

Whereas Ernst Ruprecht plays curved roads against spiked mountain peaks in his poster for the 1930 Klausenrennen (left), Schönholzer's design from four years later is composed with angular precision. The red-hot Bugatti is racing forward as the icy-blue Alps retreat: here the artist creates the illusion of speed by using the lower-right-hand vanishing point to its fullest extent. The 1934 race, the final running of the Klausenrennen, was won by German racing legend Rudolf Caracciola (1901–1959) in a Mercedes-Benz W25. He clocked a record-breaking time of fifteen minutes and 22.2 seconds with an average speed of fifty-two miles per hour.

**A.D.A.C. Winterfahrt:
Garmisch-Partenkirchen,** 1925
Hans von Römer (1896–1970) and
Botho von Römer (1896–1980)
48 x 34½ inches (121.9 x 87.6 cm)
Graphische Kunstanstalt Sonntag & Co., München

You'd think that the February chill would make competing in the winter race sponsored by the General German Automobile Club (or ADAC—the Allgemeiner Deutscher Automobil-Club) a fairly uninviting proposition. You certainly don't get that impression, however, looking at the cheerful faces of the intrepid drivers as they make their way through the frigid grandeur of the Bavarian Alps in their open-air Stoewer D series racer. The 1925 race was held on a course set up on frozen Lake Eibsee, situated on the outskirts of Garmisch-Partenkirchen at the base of the Zugspitze, Germany's highest mountain. In 1899, the Stoewer brothers—Bernhard, Jr., and Emil—recognized the automobile's promising future, even though at that time it was regarded as a plaything for the wealthy. The company they founded was trendsetting and unique in that it never concerned itself with volume but concentrated instead on technical innovation. The ADAC was founded on May 24, 1903; today, it's the largest automobile club in Europe. Of its more than seventeen million members, 1.5 million are motorcyclists, making it also the largest motorcycle association in the world.

Forstenriederpark-Rennen: Bayer Automobil Club, 1925
Julius Ussy Engelhard (1883–1964)
35¼ x 46½ inches (89.5 x 118.1 cm)
Oscar Consee AG Kunstanstalt, München

A superb design from a master of German art deco, this poster captures two roadsters zipping down the track, barreling neck and neck toward the finish line at the Forstenrieder Park automobile race in Munich. Engelhard knew how to convey a sense of space and depth with relatively flat panels of unoutlined color, a skill he shows off beautifully in this image. There is something painterly in the muted tones he uses to render the figures and their cars, almost as if he originally executed the design in watercolor. The vehicles seem ethereal in the way in which they swim around the course, the speed lines swirling like white smoke over their chassis. By taking away the hard edges and flashy colors inherent in the sport, Engelhard allows the viewer to see the race as a gentleman's activity. This high level of sophistication and glamour is further enhanced by the sponsors for the event: Batschari, a classic German cigarette manufacturer, and Arnhold and S. Bleichroeder, a New York–based German investment bank closely associated with the Rothschild family. Such an elegant and refined overall composition becomes even more understandable when one learns that Engelhard's primary professional occupation was fashion illustration. His work appeared in a variety of high-end German periodicals.

F PORTIER

7 JUIN 1931

GRAND PRIX AUTOMOBILE DE GENEVE

AUTOMOBILE CLUB SUISSE (SECTION DE GENEVE)

AFFICHES "SONOR" S.A GENEVE

Grand Prix Automobile de Genève, 1931
Francis Portier (1876–1961)
33¼ x 25½ inches (84.4 x 64.8 cm)
Affiches Sonor, Genève

While there are a number of ways to communicate the visceral thrill of racing to passersby and get their adrenaline flowing, the most frequently used approach is to place the viewer directly in the path of an oncoming vehicle—Federico Seneca's 1926 Perugina Cup poster (page 178), Henri Delval's Nice Grand Prix poster (page 166), and Károly Gerster's Budapest Grand Prix poster (page 171) immediately come to mind. Francis Portier, however, takes a far less aggressive but no less effective approach by allowing the spectator to simply watch in amazement as two racers streak by, blurred by speed and looking more like rocket ships or projectiles than race cars. Run on the Meyrin circuit, the 1931 Geneva Grand Prix was the first international automobile race ever held in Switzerland. The winner was French driver Marcel Lehoux (1888–1936) in his Bugatti Type 51.

Grand Prix de Suisse, 1938
Noël Fontanet (1898–1982)
39½ x 25½ inches (100.3 x 64.8 cm)
Affiches Sonor, Genève

Noël Fontanet was known for using slick, sharp colors and lines to make bold graphic statements, and this poster is among his finest creations in that style. While it matches the signature red-and-black color palette of his other two designs for the Swiss motorcycle Grand Prix, this poster strikes a more sophisticated note. Unlike those other designs, this composition isn't about rolling movement but rather comprises a single visual punch, a stamp in shallow relief meant to represent the race. It lacks the cartoonish nature of the other two posters and offers a more stern, mature image for the world of motorcycle racing. This is a direct result of the figure speeding straight toward the viewer at eye level, showing no intention of veering off to the side at the last moment. That unrelenting aggression is what gives this poster its power. First prize in the 1938 Geneva competition—which was not yet an official part of the Grand Prix motorcycle racing season, a status it would attain in 1949—went to Ewald Kluge of Nazi Germany in the 250cc category and to Harold Daniell of England in both the 350cc and 500cc categories.

World's Greatest Air Race: England to Australia, 1934
Percy Trompf (1902–1964)
39¾ x 29¾ inches (101 x 75.6 cm)
Moore-Young Lithography Co., Melbourne

The face of Trompf's intrepid airman clearly illustrates focus, determination, and an uncompromising will to win the "world's greatest air race," a grueling 11,300-mile journey from Mildenhall in Suffolk, England, to the Flemington Racecourse in Melbourne, Australia. The air race, organized by Britain's Royal Aero Club, took place in 1934 as part of the Melbourne centennial celebration. Sir Macpherson Robertson (1859–1945), the Australian entrepreneur, philanthropist, and founder of the MacRobertson's confectionery company, put up the seventy-five thousand dollars in prize money for the event on the condition that the race be named after his candy company and that it be organized in as safe a manner as possible. The basic rules for the MacRobertson Trophy were fairly clear-cut: no size limits, no power limits, no crew limits, and no new pilots once the planes left England. There were five compulsory stops along the route: Baghdad, Allahabad (in northern India), Singapore, Darwin, and Charlesville (the latter two in Australia). Other than that, the pilots could choose their own routes. Prizes would be awarded for the outright fastest aircraft and also for the best performance, based on a handicap system, by any plane that finished within sixteen days. A field of twenty planes started the competition on October 20, but it was Flight Lieutenant Charles William Anderson Scott (1903–1946) and Captain Tom Campbell Black (1899–1936) of England who would emerge victorious aboard their scarlet de Havilland DH.88 Comet, *Grosvenor House*, completing the flight in just under seventy-three hours at an average speed of 180 miles per hour. While this is undoubtedly an impressive accomplishment, the second- and third-place finishers—a Douglas DC-2 from the Netherlands (winners of the handicap race) and a Boeing 247-D from the United States, both finishing less than a day behind the winner—provided invaluable information that was subsequently used in the development of long-distance passenger air travel. The de Havilland DH.88 Comet later evolved into the World War II de Havilland DH.98 Mosquito fighter plane.

Auto Races: Bridgewater Grange Park, 1936
Anonymous
43 x 31 inches (109.2 x 78.7 cm)
Buck Printing Co., Boston

Sometimes a poster is the only surviving document from a moment in history. That is the case with this advertisement for the July 4, 1936, automobile race held at Bridgewater Grange Park in Massachusetts. The quarter-mile oval dirt track was used only on that day, and no surviving information indicates why the racing activity stopped. What remains is this single image promoting the glamour and thrill of the sport. Compared to its equivalents in Europe, this poster appears provincial—but it is a remarkable slice of Americana not without graphic merit. There is a bulk and power within the rendering of the cars, a sense of movement in the angle at which they approach the bend. Even the simple dot-and-line expressions on the drivers' faces impart a real feeling of determination. Such clean details and harmonious composition indicate an artist with a keen sense of art deco graphics, taking this poster beyond the mundane world of sleepy suburban amusements.

FOOD, BEVERAGE AND TOBACCO

ONCE WORLD WAR I ENDED and the Roaring Twenties began, the pent-up demand for pleasure, celebration, and relaxation captured the consumer psyche around the globe. Corporate advertising departments and independent advertising agencies hired graphic designers to develop logos and eye-catching promotions for their products to ensure brand leadership. In 1904, Campari, the Italian aperitif company, pioneered modern display advertising when it required all bars that bought its products to display the Campari bitters sign on the premises.

Aperitifs and digestives, including Dubonnet, St Raphaël, Pivolo, Sissa, and Vera Mint, employed poster advertisements to promote the consumption of their products. Similarly, beers, coffees, and teas (Bosio, Van Nelle, Twinings) used graphic designs to promote their brands. Diverse consumable products such as Perugina chocolate, Kub bouillon cubes, and Wrigley's spearmint gum also used posters to establish their brand names. Tobacco companies such as Modiano, Sato, and others developed memorable art deco posters to reaffirm their brand image in the minds of consumers.

Many of the best and most prominent graphic artists of the 1920s and 1930s were engaged to develop these rare and iconic posters. A. M. Cassandre, Charles Loupot, Marcello Nizzoli, Leonetto Cappiello, Noël Fontanet, Otis Shepard, Paul Colin, and Federico Seneca perfectly capture the collective consciousness of the era.

Campari l'Aperitivo, 1926
Marcello Nizzoli (1887–1960)
77⅛ x 55⅛ inches (195.9 x 140 cm)
Davide Campari & C., Milano

Generally considered to be one of the finest art deco designs ever created, this is one of at least three images Nizzoli produced for Campari, a brand of Italian bitters. Utilizing the dark, dramatic palette popular among German expressionists, the artist clearly draws from the more famous cubist table paintings by Pablo Picasso and Georges Braque for the composition. The café table is raked at an extreme angle, as is the white coaster, but the aperitif glass and bottle of Campari face the viewer head-on. There is the hint of a chair off to the right. Meanwhile, an invisible hand tilts the soda siphon so that a bubbling stream of carbonated water shoots into the glass, resulting in the brand's signature cocktail. The image is moody and tantalizing and presents the product in a mysterious setting, the brilliant colors of the bitters and the soda siphon reflecting like so many jewels off the shiny, nickel-finished tabletop. Moreover, unlike the bar still lifes of Picasso and Braque, this image has distinct movement, granting it a graphic energy usually not present in cubism. The image manages to be both stable and kinetic at the same time, resulting in an unprecedented boldness rarely seen in advertising art.

Cordial Campari, 1926
Marcello Nizzoli (1887–1960)
77⅛ x 55⅛ inches (195.9 x 140 cm)
Edizioni Star, Milano

No longer in production, Cordial Campari was a sweet aperitif meant to complement its bitter red cousin. And just as the one Campari contrasts harmoniously with the other, so does this poster form a dynamic graphic dialogue with Nizzoli's 1926 image for the brand (left). The precarious, nearly impossible angle of the bottle tempts the viewer to reach out and catch it before it topples to the floor. This moody nervousness is heightened by the oxblood-and-crimson background, its hues dancing around the bottle like ominous flames. Meanwhile, an undefined light source casts long, haunting shadows across the table, creating a black panel that forms the ideal background for the letters that spell out the brand's name. Red and black were favorite colors of the expressionists: they called to mind the dark carnage of World War I and its aftermath as well as the decadent nature of society at the time. And yet while there is a dark uncertainty about this design, it is sexy rather than smutty, elevating expressionist tropes out of the gutter and into the jazz lounge.

Vov, ca. 1926
Marcello Nizzoli (1887–1960)
39 x 27⅜ inches (99.1 x 69.5 cm)
Edizioni Star, Milano

This exceedingly rare promotion for Vov liqueur rushes the brand name's three letters—shadowed, to look like a fist—toward the viewer in an exceptionally aggressive manner, creating a virtual graphic punch. The three bold letters, like brass knuckles, hit the consumer just below the eye. After this visual assault, one's attention is drawn upward, toward the product itself. Unlike many other liqueurs, Vov does not come in a delicate glass bottle but rather in a weighty, opaque, milky-hued jug with a colorful label. The opacity is necessary, as Vov is basically a mixture of Marsala and egg, and a transparent container would shorten its shelf life dramatically. Yet despite such an unassuming bottle, the product takes on a dapper flair all its own. As the diminutive cup and saucer to the left imply, Vov is a thick yellow liquid typically served with espresso or cappuccino as a digestive aid or sweet after-dinner treat—a truly Italian creation meant to dress up the art of drinking coffee. When viewed in conjunction with the artist's Campari posters (above and far left), this design demonstrates why Nizzoli is a master of Italian art deco and, more important, a genius at creating impressive, high-impact images that turn products into iconic totems of the era.

St Raphaël, 1937
Charles Loupot (1892–1962)
45¾ x 61¾ inches (116.2 x 156.8 cm)
Imprimerie Joseph-Charles, Paris

St Raphaël, 1938
Charles Loupot (1892–1962)
63⅛ x 47⅜ inches (160.3 x 120.3 cm)
Société Anonyme Courbet, Paris

The energetic composition above is the first poster that Loupot created for St Raphaël, a quinine-based aperitif. It introduces to the world the two waiters who would come to symbolize the brand. Although they would undergo a multitude of tweaks and refinements over the years, the general concept of the "twins" always remained the same: a tall, slender, white fellow representing the *blanc* version of the beverage and a short, plump, red figure representing the *rouge*. It is the most elaborate of any poster created for St Raphaël; the style calls to mind the dreamlike cityscapes of Marc Chagall, in which figures float effortlessly over an indistinct landscape. If the presence of the Eiffel Tower were not enough to indicate the Frenchness of the brand, then the six French flags dotting the page certainly bring a nationalistic pride to the company's image. In later posters, such as the one seen at right, the waiters became more barrel-shaped and geometric, as if filtered through the mind of Fernand Léger. Their appearance would continue to evolve up through the 1950s, when they reached their final incarnation—reduced to the purest elements of the original concept born in this poster.

Sandeman, 1928
George Massiot Brown (n.d.)
63 x 46 inches (160 x 116.8 cm)
Imprimerie Draeger, Paris

Little did George Massiot Brown know when he was creating this image for Sandeman, makers of port and sherry, that his design would become one of the most frequently reproduced images in poster history. Nothing more than a seductive shadow in Portuguese attire, the figure attracts us almost as much as he is seemingly attracted to the beverage he holds in his hand. The success of the design lies in its mystery, in what it does not show. The silhouette dominates the page, but the focal point is the ruby red port. Though the artist doesn't use very much of it, the wine's intense pigment pops in contrast to the calming tones of pale yellow and green and is made even more bold against the black curve of the figure's cape. By doing away with details, Brown gives Sandeman a mascot that points only to the product and not to itself. That said, for a figure with so few physical details, the don, as he came to be known, is identified by some scholars as the first universally recognized logo for a wine product. His enduring popularity is perhaps most evident in the fact that the brand still uses him today on its bottle.

Fine Calvados, ca. 1930
Noël Fontanet (1898–1982)
50¾ x 36 inches (128.9 x 91.4 cm)
Affiches Sonor, Genève

Based in Geneva for most of his career, Noël Fontanet created caricatures for satirical magazines and newspapers before turning to poster design. His ability to visually exaggerate an idea while maintaining graphic boldness and simplicity shines through perfectly in this image for Calvados, a type of French apple brandy. Here, three identical magenta faces pucker their lips to sample the beverage; the extreme height of their top hats mimics the slender stems of the glasses, constantly drawing the eye upward. Combined with the figures' oversize monocles, these effects mark the trio as hyper-upper-class—a tongue-in-cheek representation of a social stratum into which this particular drink wouldn't necessarily fit. In reality, Fine is the lowest and least expensive grade of Calvados, in the same league as Trois étoiles or Trois pommes. Because it only has to be aged two years, it ranks below Vieux or Réserve and does not even come close to VSOP (which stands for "very special old pale") or the higher grades of the brandy. However, unless you were a connoisseur, this distinction would be meaningless, and the design would be enough to convince you that Fine Calvados is indeed the most posh variant of the drink and that the imbiber of such a beverage would have to be quite genteel and sophisticated indeed. Curiously, this poster does not mention a specific brand of Calvados—just the one particular grade.

Vera Mint de Ricqlès, 1930
A. M. Cassandre (Adolphe Mouron, 1901–1968)
80 x 52 inches (203.2 x 132.1 cm)
Société Anonyme Courbet, Paris

Even though it is one of Cassandre's rarest and most graphically simple designs, this poster for Vera Mint, a mint-flavored aperitif, embodies volumes of subtext—layers of meaning that calmly unfold before the viewer like a lazy Sunday afternoon. At first, the milky green glow of the beverage creates a haze that hovers around the glass, spilling out over a crisp white tablecloth, perhaps at a sidewalk café. The two sunshine-yellow straws jut out at a casual angle toward the clear blue sky, giving the drink a summery, if not downright tropical, feel. Vera Mint is apparently the ideal refreshing warm-weather beverage. And yet upon second glance, the tablecloth looks more like a snowcapped mountain, the minty burst surrounding the glass more akin to cloudy puffs of breath on a frigid, fresh winter morning. The artist has managed to suggest all seasons without actually giving the viewer any precise indicators regarding the time of year. Vera Mint is therefore perceived as timeless, the perfect refreshment for any occasion, time, or place. Despite the sparseness of the graphics, one is not bored looking at this poster. Stacking the brand's name at an angle and then placing the straws perpendicular to it creates a series of visual bumpers and flippers that leads the eye up toward the clouds, as if it were a pinball.

Pages 198–200
Dubo, Dubon, Dubonnet, 1932
A. M. Cassandre (Adolphe Mouron, 1901–1968)
79 x 54½ inches each (200.7 x 138.4 cm)
Alliance Graphique, Paris

Pages 201–202
Dubonnet: Vin Tonique au Quinquina, 1935
A. M. Cassandre (Adolphe Mouron, 1901–1968)
56⅞ x 77¼ inches (144.5 x 196.2 cm)
Alliance Graphique, Paris

Originally appearing as a triptych, Cassandre's iconic design for Dubonnet was issued in a variety of formats over the years, the examples on these pages being some of the finest and most rare. It all began with the concept of a somberly dressed man in a bowler hat gradually becoming more complete as he imbibes the beverage. The first in the series shows the man gazing at the drink, his head and arm the only parts of his body depicted in color. Below, the "Dubo" portion of the brand's name is highlighted—a word that translates roughly as "doubt," or "dubious." As the man emphatically tilts back the glass to get that last drop, the color of his body is about halfway complete, while below, "Dubon," which means "good," is filled in. Finally, as the product's name is fully colored in, we see the man reaching for the bottle to pour yet another glass. The quirky little image correlates perfectly with the wordplay on the name of the brand—one is first questionable, then happy, then enthusiastic when presented with a glass of Dubonnet. In addition to the very rare large-scale trio of posters, the design appeared as a much smaller banner, and, in 1956, was reissued as just the final panel in the Danish market. There were also myriad seasonal compositions featuring the same character—including the extraordinarily rare winter version, in which he is bundled at an outdoor café table, up to his knees in snow; yet a glass of Dubonnet and tonic drives away the cold. The series is without a doubt Cassandre's most popular creation, a fine dance between art deco sophistication and clever humor that takes the brand beyond the realm of the memorable into the truly enduring. Dubonnet was introduced in 1846 as a way to get members of the French Foreign Legion on assignment in North Africa to drink quinine, which combats malaria. Dubonnet and gin, a cocktail known as a zaza, is reportedly the preferred drink of Queen Elizabeth II, as it was for her mother, the Queen Mum.

Below: Patrons at Le Dôme, a popular café in Montparnasse, enjoy the atmosphere at the outdoor tables. In the 1930s, when this photograph was taken, the restaurant served as a gathering place for an international group of writers and artists—as it had since its opening in 1898.

Pi Volo, 1924
A. M. Cassandre (Adolphe Mouron, 1901–1968)
14 x 10 inches (35.6 x 25.4 cm)
Hachard et Cie., Paris

While trying to come up with an eye-catching poster for the aperitif Pivolo, Cassandre realized that the product's name sounded like *pie vole haute*—French for "magpie fly high." Thus the brand's iconic emblem of the magpie was born. This attraction to puns and plays on words would surface in a number of Cassandre's advertisements, most notably the Dubonnet series, which he created eight years after this one (see previous pages). Yet unlike that set of images, in which the pun unfolds as the composition evolves, this design is static—although it still provides a playful visual punch. It is a poster almost entirely comprising triangles and curves—the line of the beak is echoed in the way the light hits the glass, which is continued through the point of the bird's tail and in the V of the brand name. Meanwhile, the bird's head rolls into the bowl of the glass, which mimics the curve of its chest, and so on and so on. The design endlessly falls in upon itself, and the viewer's eye is led in a ski-slope pattern repeatedly over the page. It is also a stellar example of Cassandre's interest in typography: he would go on to use this particular font in many subsequent posters.

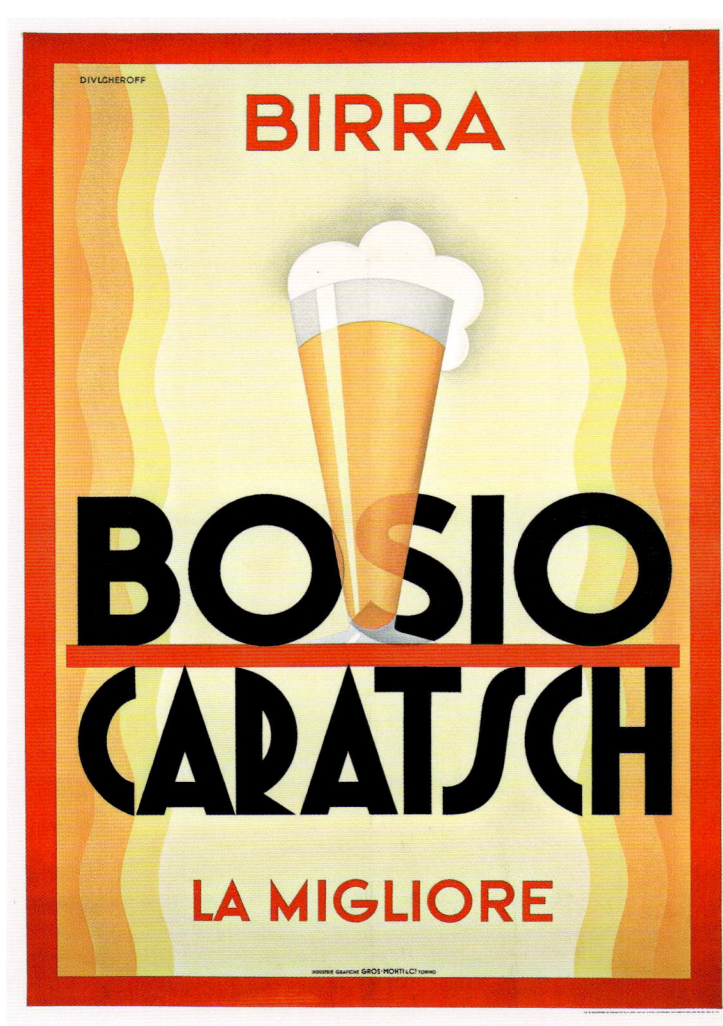

Bosio Caratsch, 1936
Nicolay Diulgheroff (1901–1982)
78 x 55 inches (198.1 x 139.7 cm)
Gros-Monti & C., Torino

Sissa, 1932
Hermann Alfred Koelliker (1894–1965)
50⅜ x 35½ inches (127.9 x 90.2 cm)
J. C. Müller, Zürich

Cora, 1930
Kräuss (n.d.)
78¼ x 54¾ inches (198.7 x 139.1 cm)
Gros-Monti & C., Torino

Founded in 1845, Bosio & Caratsch attempted to re-create the classic Bavarian methods of brewing in Italy. In 1885 they expanded their factory to include an elaborate and elegant beer garden, complete with medieval-style murals illustrating the historic roots of the beverage. The company even hosted an annual Oktoberfest. The quality of the product did not go unrecognized, as it was awarded the gold medal at the Esposizione dell'Industria Italiana (Exhibition of Italian Industry) in Turin in 1898. This popularity, however, did not make it a drink for the common man, as the heavy taxes levied upon it pushed it into the category of a luxury item. Nicolay Diulgheroff's design for the product reinforces this idea of class and sophistication, making the beer appear as chic as the finest Champagne. Coming from a strong background of European constructivism, Diulgheroff seamlessly merges his artistic roots with elements of Italian futurism, elevating a fairly pedestrian product to a cinematic level of beauty. Yet regardless of its demographic, this handsome image certainly befits the company's motto: "Good beer gladdens the hearts of men."

Less well known than its competitors Eptinger and Pepita, Sissa is a flavored carbonated mineral water sourced from the Swiss town of Sissach. Hermann Koelliker's straightforward central figure echoes the rotund gentlemen that Kräuss created for Cora vermouth (right). This particular fellow, however, is a bit sassier than the others, his hand on his hip and his leg akimbo as he swigs back a brightly flavored mouthful of Sissa. Perhaps the most interesting detail of the figure is the small protuberance meant to indicate his bottom lip—a simple but brilliant tweak that gives the character even more personality. Also adding to the graphic impact of the composition is the beam of hard-lined light that streaks down the center of the poster. The slight variance in the color of that plane both draws attention to the act of drinking Sissa and creates a depth of field otherwise lacking in this two-dimensional design. It is similar to the panels of light used by Sonia and Robert Delaunay in their color-panel paintings—with the addition of a simple block of lighter green, the whole image suddenly pops off the page.

In the latter part of the eighteenth century, sweet vermouth, an aromatic wine, was produced and sold exclusively by one manufacturer in Turin. In 1835, the Cora brothers purchased the business and soon became the first company to export "vermouth di Torino." Similar in concept to Charles Loupot's waiter duo for St Raphaël (pages 192–193), this trio of identical geometric gentlemen, holding aloft their glasses of Cora vermouth, are arranged as if in a chorus line. The rotund little caricatures appear bolder in color as they get closer to the viewer: like a locomotive racing down the tracks, they create a visual punch and sense of acceleration. Such a strong graphic impact works because of the simplicity of the design—if there were any additional elements, the power would be lost. It also helps that only the three primary colors (red, yellow, and blue) are used in the poster, a choice that stands out to the human eye more than any other combination of hues. This composition sets itself apart from other posters created for the brand. Kräuss boils down his image of the product to the very bare-bones elements of art deco.

Nicolas, 1935
A. M. Cassandre (Adolphe Mouron, 1901–1968)
13 x 14⅝ inches (33 x 37.1 cm)
Alliance Graphique, Paris

In 1922, the artist Jules Isnard Dransy created Nectar, an endearing, wide-eyed porter meant to convey the fact that the wine merchant Nicolas had begun offering home delivery of its vast stock. Nectar would become one of the most instantly recognized and beloved symbols in French advertising. Because Étienne Nicolas, the owner of the company, was enthusiastic about using inventive artists to promote his brand, it comes as no surprise that a little more than a decade later he would commission Cassandre, one of the most famous graphic artists in France at the time, to try his hand at the Nicolas emblem. What resulted is something distinctly apart from the rest of the Cassandre oeuvre. In a hypnotic, almost psychedelic graphic explosion, Nectar appears just off center, his signature bulging eyes in shadow—but the white N on his cap leaves no question as to who it is. His bottles of red and white wine have taken on prismatic hues beyond the typical burgundy and green, and even the figure's shadow takes on a life of its own in purple and blue. It is two-dimensional vertigo, distracting if not alarming, making it almost impossible for the viewer to look away. Cassandre would go on to create a variety of ephemeral materials for the company, including price lists and promotional pamphlets, as well as an additional poster the following year.

Van Nelle, 1931
A. M. Cassandre (Adolphe Mouron, 1901–1968)
46 x 62 inches (116.8 x 157.5 cm)
Nijgh & Van Ditmar, Rotterdam

Van Nelle was a major producer of coffee and tea in the Netherlands from the early 1900s until production ceased in the 1990s. In 1925, the owner, Kees van der Leeuw, commissioned a new factory building, a structure that was heavily influenced by Russian constructivism. Completed in 1931—the year this poster was created—it remains one of the most important industrial buildings of the twentieth century. But Van Nelle's passion for the constructivist aesthetic did not end with architecture. Many of the company's advertisements from 1925 onward fit within that genre, following the ethos of Vladimir Mayakovsky and Alexander Rodchenko, who formed their own constructivist advertising agency in Soviet Russia.

This unique work by Cassandre follows the same principles, its *tektonika* (spatial presence) creating depth of field both within and beyond the two-dimensional plane of the paper. The viewer is at once able to see into as well as outside of the unassuming brown box of packaged coffee. The single oversize bean conveys the nature of the product as boldly and simply as possible and creates an opportunity for texture and graphic complexity within the typography, which dominates the composition. Although Cassandre created a handful of similar designs for the Dutch advertising agency Nijgh & Van Ditmar, this is the finest example of his mastery of the prevailing style of the European avant-garde.

The Van Nelle factory in Rotterdam was designed by architects Leendert van der Vlugt and Johannes Andreas Brinkman. It is now a protected national monument in the Netherlands.

Victoria Tee, 1930
Otto Löbl (n.d.)
74 x 49⅝ inches (188 x 126 cm)
J. Weiner, Wien

Although it has little to do with tea, the image of an ostrich was first linked to the Victoria brand by the artist Hans Neumann around 1911, when he created a poster in which a baby ostrich inquisitively nods its wide-eyed head toward a steaming kettle of the hot beverage. Here, Otto Löbl takes that concept to a new level, merging the unofficial mascot with a depiction of the product. The result is both smart and witty, a humorous hybrid of teapot and bird that certainly sticks in any passerby's memory. It is interesting that Löbl manages to reduce both elements down to their most basic geometric shapes, so that neither loses its integrity as an object in the design—the viewer can see the kettle and the ostrich simultaneously, one neither detracting from nor perverting the other. As a whole, the image is an ostrich; yet if one focuses on the teapot, the tail becomes the handle, the legs an implied table, and the neck a column of steam emerging from the spout. Of course, Löbl was no stranger to intelligent poster design, as he ran one of the most popular and successful commercial advertising studios in Vienna from 1926 to 1938. This, however, may be one of the best images to come out of that venture—a stellar achievement both in terms of its economy of linear expression and its visual impact.

Twining, 1930
Charles Loupot (1892–1962)
63 x 47¼ inches (160 x 120 cm)
Les Belles Affiches, Paris

One of the world's oldest tea importers, Twinings (founded in 1706) has commissioned dozens of posters throughout its long history. This very rare design by Charles Loupot, however, may be the most elegant representation of the brand on the printed page. It appeared on the streets just around the time the company was releasing its signature Irish breakfast and Ceylon blends—types of tea we now consider classics but that at the time were curious and new. Such innovation is brought to the level of connoisseurship in this poster: the brand, represented handsomely by a two-color *T* (the world's oldest logo, dating to 1787), is identified as a purveyor of sophisticated hot beverages. No humorous mascot or lady with a low-cut neckline is necessary. All we need to be intrigued is the golden-hued contents of the cup, which releases undulating wisps of steam that waft elegantly off the poster into oblivion. It isn't just selling tea; it's selling a genteel lifestyle. Unlike quinine, port, and some alcoholic beverages, this drink cannot be consumed in a single shot. Because it's served hot, it takes time to drink, and, as time is something most available to the leisure class, there is an implied refinement and luxury about enjoying an unhurried cup of tea, a concept that Loupot masterfully expresses in this poster.

Wrigley's, ca. 1935
Otis Shepard (1894–1969)
41 x 27 inches (104.1 x 68.6 cm)
McCandlish Lithograph Corporation, Philadelphia

When William Wrigley, Jr., founded a soap company in 1891, he had no idea that the premium he placed within each package, a container of baking soda, would become more popular than the soap itself. So he switched to selling baking soda. Then the premium he packaged with the baking soda—two complimentary packages of chewing gum—became more popular than the baking soda. Finally, after some restructuring, Wrigley changed his business model and became a chewing-gum mogul, launching the famous trio still available for purchase today—Wrigley's Spearmint, Wrigley's Doublemint, and Juicy Fruit. As the artistic director of the company from 1932 to 1963, Otis Shepard was given multiple opportunities to promote all three varieties of gum, during which time he also developed the idea of the Doublemint twins. Each of his posters is distinguished by a clear, crisp felicity of graphic expression, bright, eye-catching colors, and an overall ease and sense of joy. This design is no exception: the cheery palette and light-hearted tagline give Wrigley's the aura of homegrown, girl-next-door goodness. The airbrushed black shadowing is actually the most important aspect of this composition, since it lifts the product off the page toward the viewer while the green arrow, or spear, emphasizes the spearmint flavor. It is not simply an inviting poster; it is one that jumps out in order to pull you in. Along with Doublemint and Juicy Fruit, the Spearmint flavor temporarily disappeared from the domestic market in 1944, when Wrigley's son and successor as CEO, Philip K. Wrigley, made the executive decision to ship the company's entire manufactured output to American soldiers serving abroad. Because the ingredients that went into the gum were subject to rationing, Wrigley couldn't manufacture enough to satisfy both the domestic and overseas markets. Rather than sacrifice the quality of the product by making more with less, he sent whatever he could make to the armed forces. The gum was reintroduced in the United States in 1946.

Cacao Perugina, ca. 1930
Federico Seneca (1891–1976)
77¾ x 55 inches (197.5 x 139.7 cm)
Grafiche Baroni, Milano

Formed in 1907, Perugina, which specializes in a variety of chocolates and confections, was named after the Italian town in which it was founded. Here, Federico Seneca gives us an art deco take on Perugina products' West African roots—two ebony-hued women carrying overflowing baskets of red cocoa beans back from a day's harvest. The simple lines of two tropical trees off in the distance add to the exotic nature of the image, placing it distinctly outside the world in which it is being advertised. In fact, this image is all about the concept of the Other: although Perugina chocolates are created on Italian soil, the poster wants to focus only on the candy's most far-off origins. It indelibly links the product to a land worlds away, where slender, dark-skinned women in revealing outfits labor under the unforgiving sun. It is a logical continuation of Europe's artistic obsession with Africa, which broke onto the scene around 1906, when artists such as Pablo Picasso began collecting African artifacts and incorporating them into their work and when ethnographic museums were popping up everywhere from Paris to Berlin. This poster celebrates that seductive fetish—the desire to procure and dominate something from a world unlike one's own. Perugina chocolates were exhibited at the 1939 World's Fair (see page 108), and the company was acquired by Nestlé in 1988. Seneca also designed the famous posters for the Coppa della Perugina (pages 178–179).

Following pages
Bouillon Kub, 1931
Leonetto Cappiello (1875–1942)
50¾ x 77⅞ inches (128.9 x 197.8 cm)
Devambez, Paris

When this poster first appeared on the streets of Paris in 1931, it had as much shock value as Édouard Manet's unapologetic *Olympia* or, to put it in a more contemporary context, the famous Brooke Shields advertisement for Calvin Klein jeans. Nothing so bold or graphically aggressive had ever been done in advertising. It was, and remains, a revolutionary poster, pushing the medium to a new level of compositional directness and intensity. At an almost uncomfortably close range, the stone-faced bull stares directly into the viewer's eye. At the same time, the Kub product, placed so that it appears to be sizing us up along with the bull, covers its other eye. It takes on the power and unrelenting gaze of the animal, drilling its message into the viewer's mind and hitting the "bull's-eye." Cappiello successfully reemployed the eye concept in his other equally rare art deco masterpiece, *Le Petit Dauphinois,* in 1933 (page 105).

BOUILLON KUB

Cappiello 1931

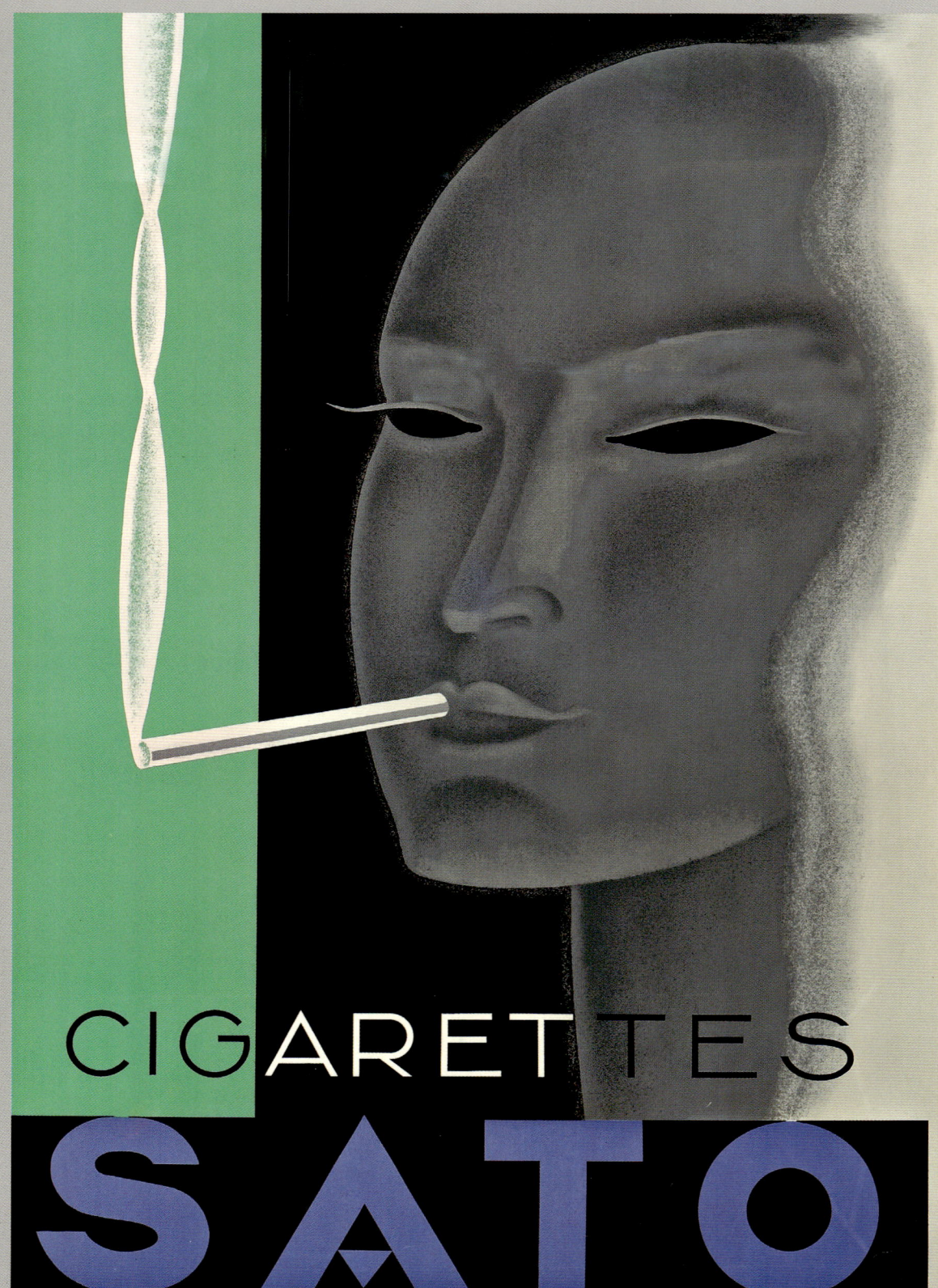

Sato Cigarettes, 1933
Anonymous
49½ x 34½ inches (125.7 x 87.6 cm)
Säuberlin & Pfeiffer, Vevey

In Japanese, sato literally means "home," or "village." Although this definition may not apply specifically to the brand name of this Swiss cigarette, it seems plausible that the unidentified artist may have been familiar with the word, since he created his poster with swank art deco Orientalism. The cool tones and exacting geometry of the background contrast wonderfully with the contours of the statuesque bust, itself an almost feline vision of pleasurable addiction. The airbrushed tendril of curlicued smoke pairs nicely with the smoker's flowing peroxide-blond hair, an artistic device that brackets the poster's central information and prevents the eye from wandering too far afield. Also, it's interesting that the "aret" in "cigarettes" is differentiated from the rest of the word by dropping out in white. A French-speaking viewer would definitely recognize "aret" as a homophone for the French word for "stop."

Lyra Extra, n.d.
Monogrammed JPB; artist unknown
39⅜ x 27¾ inches (100 x 70.5 cm)
F. Maas & Söhne, Saarbrücken

Pleasure. Indulgence. Enjoyment. Consumption. The German word genuss means all these things. In this case, genuss ist: can be translated to "pleasure is:"—a good thing. So right from the top you know that the unidentified artist (a cleverly conceived monogram, JPB, appears at the bottom right) is more than up to the task of promoting Lyra cigarettes. All this information is passed along to the viewer even before his or her eyes can wander down to the graphic portion of the design. Somewhat cubist, somewhat formalist, somewhat deconstructionist, and altogether spectacular and extremely rare, this vision of droopy-lidded, decadent sophistication makes you wonder exactly why it is you're not smoking. It is the flip side of healthful, yet its attraction is undeniable. From the murky jade of the background to the dismissive attitude of the art deco rogue at its center, this Lyra advertisement is nothing short of perfection. Lyra cigarettes are produced in Slovakia, but this poster was used to advertise the brand in Germany.

MODIANO

ATHENAEUM BUDAPEST

Modiano, 1929
Federico Seneca (1891–1976)
49¼ x 37¼ inches (125.1 x 94.6 cm)
Athenaeum, Budapest

For a number of years the Hungarian branch of Modiano, an Italian maker of cigarette papers, was one of the biggest buyers of poster advertising in Europe. As an article in the January 1994 issue of *Plakat Journal* explains, "Towards the end of the twenties, Hungary's most celebrated graphic artists were working for this company.... Smokers in Hungary came to know exactly what Modiano stood for.... It was largely thanks to this campaign that, between 1924 and 1930 ... Modiano acquired a market share of 80 percent." Fluorescent yet inviting, this glowing pasha, the Ottoman Empire's equivalent of a British lord, places his entire concentration on the rolling of the cigarette between his mittenlike fingers, giving the distinct impression that the only rolling paper worthy of such an indulgence is Modiano. It's a very rare and spectacular design—its curves feeding into yet more curves, its color scheme brash but not off-putting, and its brand name spelled out overhead very much in the manner of a neon sign. Additionally, Federico Seneca's art deco potentate calls to mind Turkish tobacco, a design choice that completely unifies the poster and justifies the use of fiery colors— colors that more than accurately echo the hue of smoldering tobacco. Saul Modiano began manufacturing high-quality rolling paper in 1889 in Trieste and Bologna, Italy.

Modiano, ca. 1929
Sándor Bortnyik (1893–1976)
49½ x 36¾ inches (125.7 x 93.3 cm)
Athenaeum, Budapest

According to an article in the January 1994 issue of *Plakat Journal,* Sándor Bortnyik "brought into Hungary the constructivist and functionalist principles of the Weimar school, of which his first posters for Modiano are a good example.... Before long the new Modiano posters which appeared every month were a daily sensation in Budapest, anticipated with great excitement by the public, passersby, and the press." In this design, every element, including the type, is composed of circles (or portions thereof), cylinders, and straight lines. Bortnyik's geometric purism even turns the pair of hands operating the tobacco-loading mechanism into a detached, purely functional, machinelike apparatus. The result is a stunning modernist design that sets our focus entirely on Modiano.

Modiano: Cartine e Tubetti per Sigarette, ca. 1936
Franz Lenhart (1898–1992)
55⅛ x 39⅜ inches (140 x 100 cm)
Grafiche Modiano, Trieste

After fleeing his native Greece to escape Ottoman persecution, Saul Modiano relocated to Trieste, Italy, where he founded the Modiano rolling paper and playing card company in the late 1800s. Hiring only the most talented local artists, Modiano commissioned promotional posters that are some of the finest creations in graphic design history. This image is no exception. The height of effortless elegance, the mysterious lady in black is made up of an intriguing combination of cutouts. Her hat and jacket are merely hinted at; they lack any real characteristics other than the absence of green. Meanwhile, the jade background serves as the negative space where the lady's blouse and hand should be. On the latter, three hash marks imply the presence of gloves. This leaves her face and the actual cigarette—where a smoldering cherry on the burning end echoes the glow of her cheeks and lips—as the only truly defined elements in the composition. And yet, despite the disembodied head floating amid Matisse-like cutouts, the cool sensuality of this woman elevates her to the level of an art deco siren. As a woman, we want to be her; as a man, we want to have her—and as consumers, we all want whatever product she is selling.

Modiano, ca. 1932
Róbert Berény (1887–1953)
49¼ x 37⅜ inches (125.1 x 94.9 cm)
Athenaeum, Budapest

In 1932, business was so good for the Modiano brand that a new factory was built in Budapest. At the time, the Hungarian market was already saturated with domestic brands of rolling paper; however, Saul Modiano believed that his methods of advertising, which had been so successful in Italy, would be just as successful in a foreign country. Needing a revolutionary design to launch the product in Hungary, he sought an equally revolutionary artist. Róbert Berény had been head of the painting department for the communist regime's Art Directorate in 1919 and was a seasoned master of effective propaganda. Prior to that, he had been a leading member of a Hungarian avant-garde movement known as The Eight. Being able to straddle both sides of seemingly incompatible styles of art, Berény was the ideal candidate for the job. The result is this incredible poster, as bold and eye-catching as any political banner and at the same time a composition so cutting-edge that it pushes the art deco aesthetic to new graphic heights. Containing no actual shading or definable detail, the poster is entirely executed through geometry. And among the shapes in the design, the circles are the most important elements. There is a monocle for sophistication; a mouth, which exhales a line of smoke, drawing the viewer's eye beyond the page; and a cherry of a smoldering cigarette, which acts both as a means of bringing one's attention to the product and as a dot on the *i* in the brand's name.

MODIANO

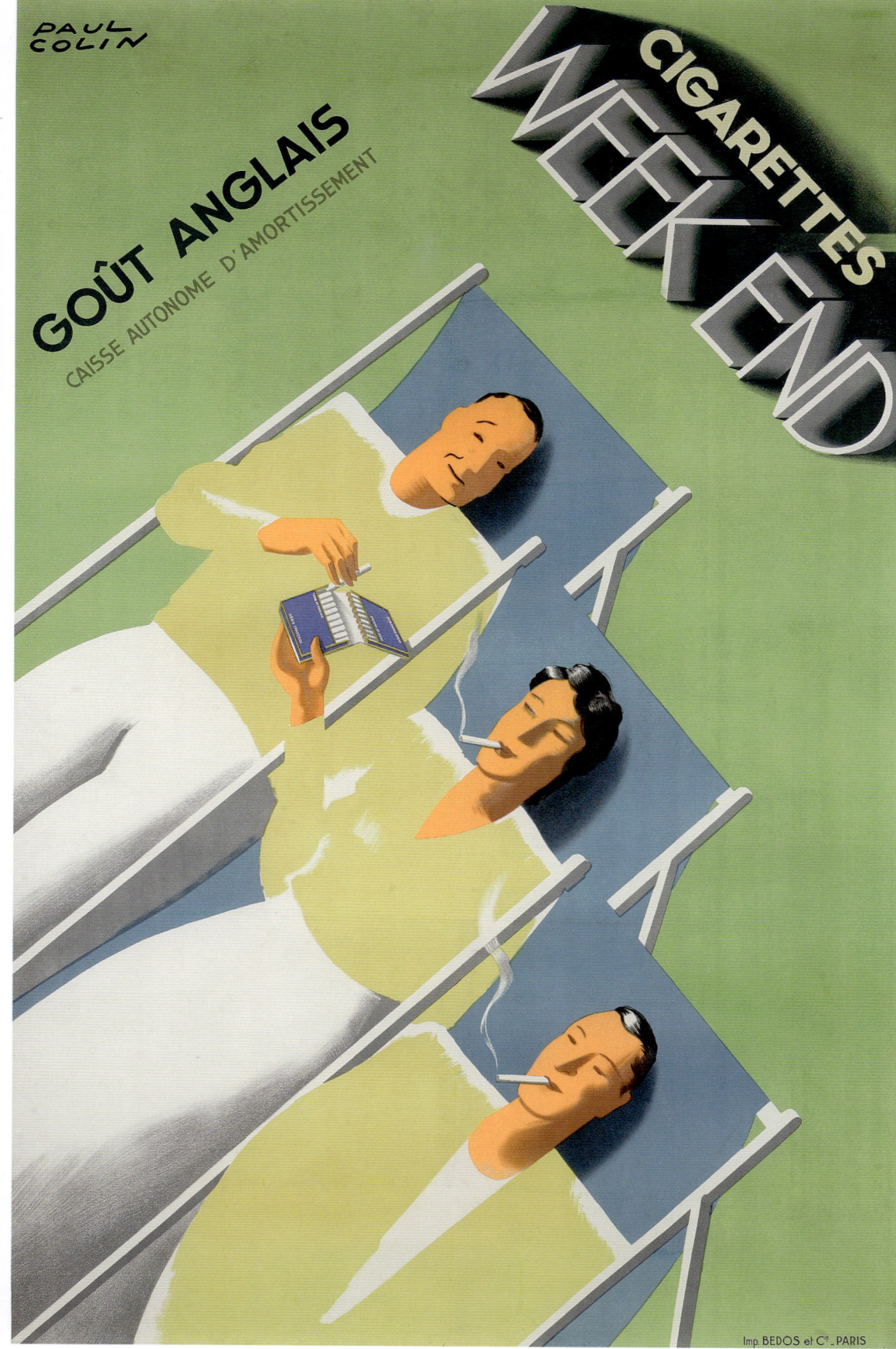

Week End Cigarettes, 1933
Paul Colin (1892–1985)
44¾ x 28½ inches (113.7 x 72.4 cm)
Imprimerie Bedos et Cie., Paris

A trio of relaxed smokers, blissfully taking a sunny nicotine break in the comfort of their reclining canvas deck chairs, have chosen Week End cigarettes, the brand in the snazzy, hinged, two-compartment pack, as their preferred puff. This is a great example of Paul Colin's art deco skills, executed with complementary diagonals, inviting, soft pastels, and a sense of pure smoking pleasure. During this era, according to *Affiche Réclame,* "light tobacco found in Europe was usually a blend referred to as English. Mainly Virginia tobacco, it had a pure, slightly sophisticated taste—not overly aromatic, not strong, with a very pronounced bright yellow color. The leading brands—Craven and Player's—came from Great Britain. In 1932, SEITA [the French government's tobacco monopoly] took the same tack with a brand they called Week End, which was on the market until 1971."

Offrez les Tabacs de la Régie Française, ca. 1930
Marc Real (n.d.)
62½ x 44½ inches (158.7 x 113 cm)
Imprimerie Bedos et Cie., Paris

In this poster, rather than singling out any particular brand, SEITA promotes French-made smokes en masse, advertising their output with three oversize cigars thrusting diagonally skyward and an open flip-top package of cigarettes alongside them. The art deco image by Marc Real is simple but powerful. Although the term "Régie Française" (which translates roughly as "French-owned company") never appeared in any official law or decree, it was prominently used in SEITA's numerous posters and was commonly used by the company's employees. In 1999, SEITA merged with its Spanish equivalent, Tabacalera, forming Altadis, which itself was acquired in 2008 by Imperial Tobacco, a global tobacco company based in Bristol, England.

OCEAN LINERS

THE FIRST HALF OF THE twentieth century constituted the golden age of the ocean liner. Burgeoning transoceanic commerce (particularly over the Atlantic), an expanding middle class, and advances in the technology of shipbuilding and engine design gave birth to this era. By the 1960s, transcontinental jet travel had consigned the ocean liner to a travel niche. Bookended by the two world wars, this golden age reached its zenith during the twenty years of the art deco period, despite the worldwide Great Depression during the 1930s.

The ocean liner is a nearly perfect icon of the art deco movement. The ships represent the triumph of modern design and technology over the hazards and hardships of ocean travel, and their massive scale, unprecedented speed, elegant lines, and unequaled comfort epitomize the principles of art deco design. The faraway destinations to which these ships traveled fulfilled the desires and dreams of the public and symbolized the mind-set from which art deco arose.

During the 1920s and 1930s, ocean-liner firms from France, Germany, the United Kingdom, and Italy vied for preeminence over their competitors, striving to prevail by operating the largest, fastest, and most elegant ships. Together these firms placed orders for and took deliveries of some of the most historically significant oceangoing vessels ever built, including the *Normandie*, *Statendam*, *Nieuw Amsterdam*, *Balderan*, *Queen Mary*, *Queen Elizabeth*, and *Empress of Britain*, all of which are pictured in this book. The competition among the lines is clearly evident in their poster advertising: liberal borrowing of themes and "poaching" of the most prominent poster artists were commonplace. The companies' efforts to top the successful campaigns of rival lines provide an insight into the competitive nature of the travel market between the wars.

Normandie: Voyage Inaugural, 1935
A. M. Cassandre (Adolphe Mouron, 1901–1968)
39¼ x 24½ inches (99.7 x 62.2 cm)
Alliance Graphique, Paris

Cassandre's iconic image of the *Normandie* is one of his finest and best known designs, and this poster, for the ship's "Voyage Inaugural," is the earliest and rarest of a series that subsequently appeared with a number of different texts. Cassandre's use of cubist angles and symmetry is striking, as is his placement of the massive ship confidently atop the innovative typeface. A flock of seagulls at the bottom of the ship's bow provides scale in this deceptively simple design, which perfectly captures the vessel's magnificence, comfort, and speed. *Normandie*, named after the province of her home port, Le Havre, was the largest and fastest ship afloat and was built to be a showcase of French creativity, elegance, and power. She departed from Le Havre on her maiden voyage on May 29, 1935, stopping in Southampton, England, before making the crossing to New York at record-breaking speed. Her launch undoubtedly added to the excitement and glamour of ocean liner travel in the majestic golden age of transoceanic cruising. The United States used the vessel during World War II and renamed her the USS *Lafayette*. As she was being converted into a troop transport ship in 1942, the *Normandie* caught fire—a spark from a welding torch ignited thousands of flammable life jackets stored onboard. The ship capsized and sank while docked at New York's Pier 88. Fortunately, most of her fabulous and precious art deco artifacts were removed during the retrofitting and now reside in museums and private collections. Though the vessel was salvaged, her restoration was deemed too costly, and she was scrapped in October of 1946.

Compagnie Générale Transatlantique: Normandie, 1937
Jean Auvigne (1859–1952)
39½ x 24½ inches (100.3 x 62.2 cm)
Éditions l'Atlantique

The *Normandie*, Compagnie Générale Transatlantique's famous ocean liner, is depicted here in the center of a compass rose, surrounded by the names of various destinations the ship served—North America, Spitzberg (Norway), the Baltic, Tunisia, Algeria, Morocco, the Antilles, and Central America. Jean Auvigne designed this poster for the 1937 Exposition Internationale des Arts et Techniques dans la Vie Moderne (International Exposition of Art and Technology in Modern Life) in Paris. The Compagnie Générale Transatlantique, or CGT—known outside of France as the French Line—was established in 1861 in an attempt to revitalize the French merchant marine. In addition to its ocean liners, CGT also operated a substantial freighter fleet. While the company survived both world wars, it was unable to withstand the ever-growing popularity of jet travel and in 1973 merged with the Compagnie des Messageries Maritimes to form Compagnie Générale Maritime.

Right: The stately first-class dining room in the *Normandie* was three decks high, three hundred feet long, and could accommodate seven hundred diners. Its lighting fixtures included twelve illuminated columns of Lalique glass.

Holland America Line: Statendam, 1928
Adriaan van't Hoff (1893–1939)
41⅞ x 30⅞ inches (106.4 x 78.4 cm)
S. Lankhout & Co., Den Haag

In total, five ships bore the *Statendam* name in the history of the Holland America line. This poster was used to advertise the first transatlantic crossing of the *Statendam III*, which became the flagship of the Holland America Line in April of 1929. Adriaan van't Hoff's design is filled with contrasting elements—massive chains in front of gently lapping waves; geometrically stacked color blocks that make up the ship; a row of seabirds flying in formation under a steeply angled, towering derrick (the birds' forward-focused motion recalls Edward McKnight Kauffer's *Daily Herald* flock; see page 102). Van't Hoff creates an art deco composition that radiates power and stateliness, one that heralds the *Statendam III* as an ideal combination of form and function. It's quite a contrast to the funnels-and-cowlings approach taken by Cassandre in his advertisement for the ship that same year (right). Construction on the *Statendam III* actually began in 1921, but changes in American immigration laws forced the Holland America Line to undertake a costly conversion of the ship's immigrant compartments. After her launch in 1924, the *Statendam III* once again encountered delays due to financial difficulties. Finally, eight years after construction began, she took to the seas on the Rotterdam–New York run. For the next ten years the vessel would service that route in summer and cruise out of New York to the Caribbean in winter. Laid up in Rotterdam in 1939, the *Statendam III* caught fire during the German invasion of the Netherlands in May of 1940, either set ablaze by the Dutch resistance in order to keep her from falling into German hands or the target of a German artillery barrage. Regardless, the ship was a total loss and was scrapped in August.

Statendam, 1928
A. M. Cassandre (Adolphe Mouron, 1901–1968)
41⅜ x 31¼ inches (105.1 x 79.4 cm)
Nijgh & Van Ditmar, Rotterdam

Seven years before Cassandre used a ship's sheer size to make an impact on passersby with his poster for the *Normandie* (page 224), he created a dramatic close-up of ventilation cowlings and funnels to call attention to the transatlantic voyage of the SS *Statendam III*. In contrast to the rigid geometry of the ship's lines, the wavy trail of smoke lends a wonderful sense of motion to the design. The poster refers to the *Statendam III* as "new" because it was ordered by the Holland America Line to replace its predecessor, the *Statendam II*, which had been taken over by the British during World War I.

Holland-America Line, 1937
Willem Frederick Ten Broek (1905–1993)
38 x 25⅛ inches (96.5 x 63.8 cm)
Joh. Enschedé en Zonen, Haarlem

In this poster for the Holland America Line, Willem Ten Broek decides to accentuate the size of the ship, not as Cassandre does—by placing a miniature flock of seagulls next to the hull for scale (see his *Normandie*, page 224)—but rather by placing a single diminutive sailboat in front of the massive ocean liner, which not only effectively creates an impression of grandeur but also keeps matters exclusively boat-related. Ten Broek does, however, follow Cassandre's lead by emphasizing the towering hull of the majestic vessel. He makes another stylistic decision in presenting the ship at a slight angle, a choice that not only shows the vessel's height but the entirety of its length as well. It is interesting to compare this Ten Broek design to the other Holland America advertisement he created two years later, for the line's service to the 1939 New York World's Fair (page 233). The two works are completely different in their execution: the simplified lines and extreme perspective seen here perfectly emphasize the ship, while the greater detail and broader scope of the world's fair design focus on the destination.

Rotterdam-Zuidamerika Lyn, ca. 1928
Adriaan van't Hoff (1893–1939)
41 x 27¾ inches (104.1 x 70.5 cm)
Boudier, Den Haag

Originally founded in 1905 as a timber transportation service between the Baltic and Holland, Van Nievelt, Goudriaan & Co.'s Stoomvaart Maatschappij line joined forces with the Holland America Line in 1920 to provide all manner of maritime transportation from Hamburg, Rotterdam, and Antwerp to Argentina. In 1928, the Holland America Line withdrew from the collaboration, leaving Van Nievelt, Goudriaan & Co. to form the Rotterdam Zuid Amerika Lyn on its own. Despite the size of the vessels, the company by no means had a large passenger clientele—the average ship only carried between twelve and twenty-four passengers at any given time—leaving its mail and freight services to dominate the transatlantic business. Van't Hoff's image for this inaugural year of the line's independent service is without a doubt a fanciful masterpiece—the towering hull of a ship bursts into the bright South American landscape with its anchor raised, seagulls seeming to roll over the undulating waves created by its immense forward thrust toward port. Van't Hoff was a well-known member of the Dutch arts and crafts movement; he often combined elements of art deco and Jugendstil, as he did in this composition. Birds were among his favorite subjects to put to paper, a preference evident in their prominence within this poster.

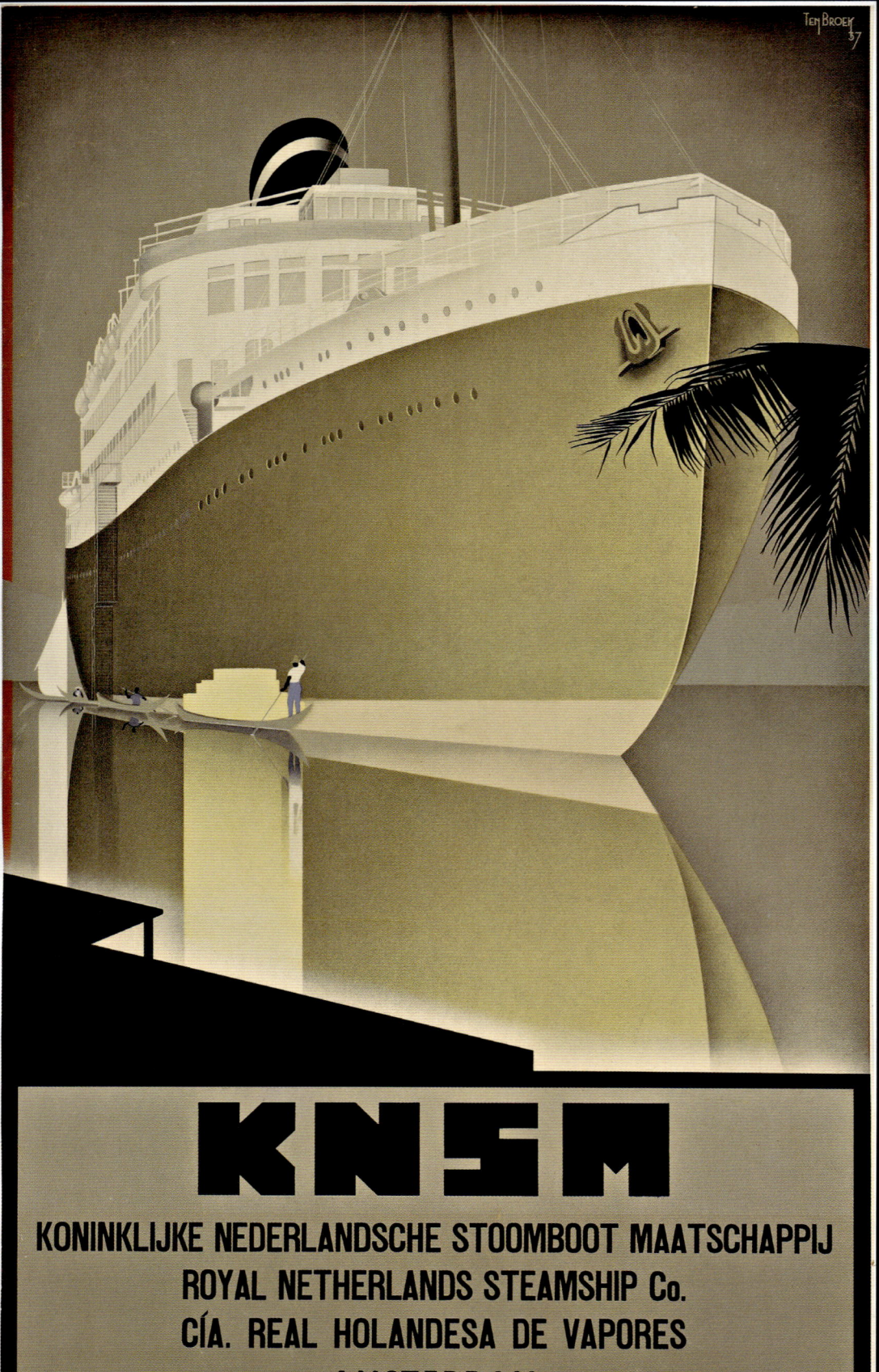

KNSM: Royal Netherlands Steamship Co., 1937
Willem Frederick Ten Broek (1905–1993)
41⅞ x 30⅞ inches (106.4 x 78.4 cm)
Printer unknown

This docked behemoth, its golden hull reflecting off the mirrored waters of some far-flung port, its bulk dwarfing the goods-laden delivery skiffs beside it, provides the Royal Netherlands Steamship Company with an ideal icon of oceanic superiority: romantic, powerful, and seemingly impervious to harm. Willem Ten Broek's trilingual lithographic calling card offers the company's name as its sole text. No other information must have been necessary for a firm whose pedigree stretches back to 1856, when Royal Netherlands began to provide regular steamship service from northwestern Europe to ports of call in North America, the West Indies, Central America, and the northern and western coasts of South America. In 1981, KNSM was amalgamated into the Dutch shipping company Nedlloyd. Both this and the artist's poster for the Holland America Line (page 228) emphasize the awe-inspiring size and towering majesty of the vessels that ruled the seas during the bygone golden era of transoceanic travel.

Rotterdamsche Lloyd, 1931
Johann von Stein (1886–1965)
28½ x 17½ inches (72.4 x 44.4 cm)
Nederlandse Rotogravure Maatschappij, Leiden

Johann von Stein's sleek, cinematic art deco design places a frame around the Rotterdam Lloyd steamship *Balderan*—a device that, with its series of towering vertical elements, cleverly and deftly pulls the viewer's gaze directly toward the ship. The eye glides from the airbrushed columns in the right-hand foreground directly to the silhouetted palm tree and onward to the *Balderan*'s foremast, each component precisely proportioned to suit the slick diminishing perspective. As Willem Ten Broek does in his poster for the Royal Netherlands Steamship Company (left), von Stein extends the hull of his vessel by reflecting it regally off the mirror-still water of the port in which it is moored. Launched in 1930, the *Balderan* was captured by the Germans in Rotterdam a decade later. Converted into a hospital ship and renamed *Strassburg,* she would be beached near IJmuiden, Holland, after being hit by a mine. The ship was later destroyed by British torpedo boats. Founded in 1839, Rotterdam Lloyd was a Dutch shipping company that sailed worldwide but placed its primary focus on the Dutch East Indies and the Far East. Starting in 1902, in cooperation with other shipping companies, the line began to service the Java–China–Japan route. After World War II, the company was afforded the honor of adding Koninklijke ("royal") to its name; however, in 1948, it merged with a number of other firms to form Nedlloyd, which maintained service from the Gulf of Mexico to the Persian Gulf, Pakistan, and India.

Liverpool Belfast: Night Passenger Service, ca. 1930
Harry Hudson Rodmell (1896–1984)
40 x 25 inches (101.6 x 63.5 cm)
Carew Wilson Massey, Ltd., London

Harry Hudson Rodmell's art deco design for the promotion of the Belfast Steamship Company's night passenger service between Liverpool and Belfast is a busy but punchy design. In 1917, the company had been one of many smaller services to be absorbed by Coast Lines, Ltd., which, as primarily a mail shipping service, appreciated the Belfast Steamship Company's original intention of providing swifter transportation across the Irish Sea. In an effort to grow the company even further, three ships were added to the fleet around 1930—the *Ulster Monarch*, the *Ulster Queen*, and the *Ulster Prince*. Using a visual economy of expression, Rodmell instantly conveys the information that these two ships passing in the night—the *Ulster Monarch* and the *Ulster Prince*—have just left the beacons of their respective cities, the frothy surf tracking silently behind them. The crescent moon in the upper right corner glistens over the water, creating gentle, geometric striations of waves, which serve as atmospheric accents as well as a means of directing one's eye toward the central text. The *Ulster Monarch* would be the only member of the original diesel trio to survive World War II.

New York: Holland-America Line, 1938
Willem Frederick Ten Broek (1905–1993)
37⅝ x 24¼ inches (95.6 x 61.6 cm)
Joh. Enschedé en Zonen, Haarlem

While they don't absolutely dwarf everything that surrounds them, as they do in Joseph Binder's *World of Tomorrow* poster (page 108), the Trylon and Perisphere from the 1939 New York World's Fair are centrally featured in this Willem Ten Broek design for the Holland America Line's expo-specific excursions. Sharing the lithographic limelight are the New York skyline, the flags of the United States and Holland, and the newest ship in Holland America's fleet—the aptly named *Nieuw Amsterdam*. It's a fascinating composition, possessing a peculiar yet altogether attractive sepia-toned luminosity. In fact, it rather resembles an alabaster sculpture, a scene that could easily have been part of the utopian diorama contained within the fair's Perisphere. Fondly known as the Darling of the Dutch, the *Nieuw Amsterdam* was the second ship of that name to be constructed by the Holland America Line. Built in 1936, she had cabin accommodations for more than twelve hundred passengers and could cruise at a top speed of twenty-one knots (approximately twenty-four miles per hour). Between October of 1939 and May of 1940, the *Nieuw Amsterdam* was used exclusively to carry passengers to and from the New York fair and Rotterdam. She was in Venezuela when the Germans overran Holland and subsequently traveled a total of 530,452 miles as an Allied troop transport ship during World War II. The ship returned to passenger service following the war and remained in service until she was scrapped in Kaohsiung, Taiwan, in September of 1974.

East Asiatic Co., ca. 1934
Initialed M.B.; artist unknown
33½ x 24½ inches (85.1 x 62.2 cm)
Dansk Papirvarefabrik, København

East Asiatic Co. Passenger Service, ca. 1935
M. Erlinger (n.d.)
39¾ x 24⅜ inches (101 x 61.9 cm)
Dansk Papirvarefabrik, København

Batavier Lijn, 1928
C. Claussen (n.d.)
40¾ x 25½ inches (103.5 x 64.8 cm)
N.v. Geuze & Co.'s Drukkerij, Dordrecht

Originally founded in 1897 as a passenger and freight service between Copenhagen and the Far East, the East Asiatic Company offered routes to myriad global destinations through a host of partner shipping lines by the 1920s. Even then, though, their ships always sailed under the Danish flag. Here we see one of its passenger ships cutting through the flat sea like an arrow through space. This elongated, heavily angled view of the ship was more the company's trademark than an individual expression of the artist (who identifies himself only as "M.B."); similar compositions were executed for the fleet by a variety of artists up through the 1950s. It does seem impossible, though, that "M.B." was unaware of Cassandre's design for the Nord Express (page 254), as both images share that same plunging angle toward infinity as well as the two-toned sans-serif typography and an identical palette. However, what makes Cassandre's work an art deco masterpiece is its kinetic force and energy, both of which are lacking in this otherwise static but piercing design. This poster manages to distill Cassandre's Nord Express into its essential eye-catching elements without drawing you in with its dynamism—an excellent example of the differences between a magnificent art deco design and a perfectly lovely one.

This poster for the East Asiatic Company gives us pure, monolithic power—a stark white vessel passing silently across an ice-flat sea. This is no-frills art deco, all planes and clean angles. It is a tidy, crisp imagining of a ship's steady journey from Europe to the lands across the northern Pacific Ocean, the only indication of nature being the small flock of gulls swooping across the hull (compare Cassandre's Normandie, page 224). The mirrored effect of the water makes the ship seem double its size (a technique used in Rotterdamsche Lloyd, page 231; KNSM, page 230; and Suède via Londres, page 237)—another testament to the vessel's dominance over the ocean and a clever means of creating an arrowlike composition that stretches the ship's length toward the horizon. In essence, the boat takes over every visual plane as far as the eye can see. At the time, the East Asiatic Company's passenger routes carried travelers out of New York through the then-Dutch territory of the West Indies, across the Atlantic to Europe, through the Mediterranean and the Suez Canal, and under India to the northern Pacific. Today, the East Asiatic Company still exists as a cargo shipping service: its passenger divisions were discontinued in 1969, after air travel had eclipsed ocean-liner travel in popularity.

Geometric shapes and simplified forms pleasingly converge in this rare design for the Batavier Line, a Dutch shipping company. Apart from a simple gull thrown in for good maritime measure, the poster consists of little more than bands of color, monochromatic circles, and a wavy gray sea. Claussen's midship focus makes it clear that there is more to the picture than meets the eye—both fore and aft—which ultimately presents the vessel in an either-or manner: either she's heading to London from Rotterdam or she's heading home to Rotterdam from London. The Batavier Line operated from 1830 until 1958. Established as the Nederlandsche Stoomboot Maatschappij with a single wooden paddle steamer named De Batavier, the enterprise was acquired by William H. Müller & Co. in 1896. Müller renamed the company, changed the funnel mark to an M to indicate ownership, and initiated the practice of naming all the ships in the Batavier Line Batavier (a total of fifteen ships would bear the name). Essentially a feeder service—a regional shipping line that conveyed people and cargo to larger international carriers—the Batavier Line emerged from World War II with a single ship, which carried passengers until the line was dissolved in 1958.

SAL: Svenska Amerika Linien, 1935
Ake Rittmark (1910–1987)
39 3/8 x 23 5/8 inches (100 x 60 cm)
Oscar Isacsons Tryckeri, Göteborg

Cassandre's high-seas influence stretches to Sweden in this Ake Rittmark poster for the Swedish American Line, or SAL. Instead of calling upon seabirds or sailboats to stress the towering grandeur of the vessel, Rittmark uses nothing but the company's name, which—even though it appears in large letters—is dwarfed by the utter mass of the ship. The artist also uses a bit of stylized cubism in his design: isolating the vessel against a flat-black background, he plays with perspective in order to add a bit of additional curvature to the prow, affording us a more complete view of the ship. However, due to the ship's immensity and our fairly low point of view, SAL's identifying funnel mark—three crowns contained within a blue ball—remains obscured. Rittmark rectifies the situation by flanking the minimal text with a pair of triple crowns. The Swedish American Line was created in 1914; it operated passenger and cargo service between Gothenburg, Sweden, and New York City. Because of Sweden's neutrality during World War I, SAL managed to thrive while other lines floundered. Its success would continue through the 1960s, at which time the increasing popularity of air travel began to cut into its viability. During the early 1970s, SAL concentrated its efforts exclusively on cruising, but in 1975 the company sold its last two ships, and SAL disappeared from the seas forever.

Suède via Londres: Swedish Lloyd, 1930
Harry Hudson Rodmell (1896–1984)
40 x 25 inches (101.6 x 63.5 cm)
Ronald Massey Ltd., London

Artist Harry Hudson Rodmell graphically plays the strict angles of the Swedish Lloyd vessel and Gothenburg's Masthugget Church—both the stylized structures themselves and their equally angular reflections—off the gentle curves of the ship's star-in-a-circle stack and the hill in the background, creating a superb art deco vision for Swedish Lloyd's service to London. While the majority of Rodmell's maritime images are realistic in nature, this poster creates a long-lasting impression with its distinctly art deco design (also see *Liverpool Belfast*, page 232). The color scheme is almost entirely that of the Swedish nation; the ship could be any of the three listed in the text (all were constructed by Swan Hunter & Wigham Richardson, Ltd., of Newcastle between 1926 and 1929), and the church is one of the primary symbols of Gothenburg and a popular tourist attraction. Swedish Lloyd's origins date back to 1869, but the company didn't enter the passenger market until 1916, when it purchased the Thule Line. In 1977, Swedish Lloyd finally went out of business, succumbing to pressure from much larger passenger lines in possession of much faster ships.

Cunard Line: États-Unis et Canada, 1929
Alexey Brodovitch (1898–1971)
36⅞ x 25¼ inches (93.7 x 64.1 cm)
Publications Willy Fischer, Paris

Alexey Brodovitch was one of the most talented graphic artists of his time. His image of the Cunard Line's *Mauretania* sailing the stylized seas is as rare as it is beautiful. Its classic art deco symmetry—the soft curve of the clouds, the triangular shadows on the ocean, and the geometry of the ship, which rises majestically in the middle ground between sea and sky—creates an atmosphere that is both soothing and irresistible. Completed in 1906, the *Mauretania* (also known as the *Maury*) was the largest and fastest ship in the world at that time and inaugurated Cunard's service out of Southampton, England. During the First World War, it served as both a troopship during the Gallipoli campaign and a hospital ship for the many soldiers injured in that battle. The most popular ship to ever sail the North Atlantic, she continued crossing and cruising until September 26, 1934. On that day, the *Queen Mary* was launched, and the "Grand Old Lady" set out from New York on her final voyage. She was scrapped in Rosyth, Scotland, in July of 1935, much to the dismay of her many loyal passengers, including President Franklin Roosevelt, who had written a letter urging Cunard to salvage rather than scrap the vessel—to no avail.

Cunard White Star, ca. 1939
A. Roquin (n.d.)
39¾ x 25¼ inches (101 x 64.1 cm)
Publimp-Nadal, Paris

To announce the launch of the Cunard White Star line's biweekly luxury liner service between New York and Cherbourg, Roquin created this handsome composition, visually equating two behemoths of the sea—the RMS *Queen Mary* and the RMS *Queen Elizabeth*—with one of the ultimate symbols of the art deco era, the Chrysler Building. As the British response to the superliners being built by French and German transport companies at the time, the two ships were constructed to break all existing records for size and speed. Indeed, the RMS *Queen Mary* captured the prestigious Blue Riband, an award given for the fastest Atlantic passenger crossing, from the *Normandie*, and the RMS *Queen Elizabeth* became the largest passenger liner ever built, a position it held for fifty-six years. Roquin treated the poster as a collage, layering the two ships over the cityscape to give the illusion of a photomontage. The ships themselves—their hulls presented at a highly raked angle, emphasizing their mass and power—give a heavy nod to Cassandre. The New York City skyline in the background creates the illusion of a giant anchor. Both vessels would be converted to troopships during World War II, only to be sold and transformed into tourist attractions in the early 1970s.

R.M.S.P.: South American Service, 1921
Frederick C. Herrick (1887–1970)
39 x 24 inches (99.1 x 61 cm)
The Baynard Press, London

Frederick C. Herrick's design for the Royal Mail Steam Packet Company (RMSP) is an interesting study of contrasting artistic styles: an abstract sea rolls almost in the manner of a plowed field toward the horizon, upon which a fairly realistically rendered vessel sails; ominous-looking serrated edges, perhaps belonging to partially hidden blades, make heavy vorticist waves, yet the boat slices through them with the greatest of ease. Ultimately, all styles unite to create an appealing art deco promotion for the British shipping concern. The RMSP began operating in 1841 after receiving the mail contract for the West Indies, serving not only as a carrier to the Caribbean region from Great Britain but also as an interisland service. South American service was added in 1850. At the time of this poster's production, the RMSP sailed to South American ports in Montevideo, Buenos Aires, and Santos, Brazil. In 1921, the Royal Mail began a joint service with the Holland America Line (see pages 228 and 233), which extended their routes to the western coast of North America. However, in 1932, the Kylsant shipping empire—Owen Philipps, Baron Kylsant, was the chairman of RMSP—collapsed amid a financial scandal, leading to the liquidation of the Royal Mail Steam Packet Company. As a result, Royal Mail Lines, Ltd., was formed from RMSP assets as well as those of several other smaller shipping concerns.

Empress of Britain: World Cruise, 1936
O. Schlienger (n.d.)
35¾ x 24 inches (90.8 x 61 cm)
Printer unknown

By some accounts, the *Empress of Britain*—the crown jewel of the Canadian Pacific Steamship Company fleet—was the most luxuriously appointed ship that ever sailed. Yet Schlienger chose to promote her and her 1937 around-the-world cruise rather modestly: a simple white silhouette of the vessel and her reflection set against a single vertical band of blue sea in front of a partially obscured orange globe. The combination resembles nothing so much as the pendulum of a clock, implying that the viewer had better book passage before time runs out. The period between the two world wars was the heyday of luxury cruising. During these years, Canadian Pacific operated more than 350 cruises to the West Indies, the Mediterranean, the Canary Islands, Scandinavia, and around the world. Each year between 1931 and 1939, the *Empress of Britain* would make nine round trips between Southampton and Quebec before signaling the end of her cruising season with a 128-day global cruise. The route took her out of New York City to the Mediterranean, North Africa, and the Middle East; then through the Suez Canal and into the Red Sea; then onward to India, Ceylon, Southeast Asia, and the Dutch Indies; then to China, Hong Kong, and Japan; then across the Pacific to Hawaii and California; then back through the Panama Canal and finally home to New York.

United States Lines, ca. 1935
Edmond Maurus (n.d.)
39½ x 24⅛ inches (100.3 x 61.3 cm)
Création Publix, Paris

This inspired art deco image for the United States Lines, which does away with the depiction of the mode of transportation altogether, employs an approach similar to the one Cassandre used in his posters for the Route Bleue bus service (page 305) and the Étoile du Nord railway system (page 255), both of which focus on suggestion over representation. Whereas the Cassandre Route Bleue design tempts the viewer with the lure of the open road, this poster draws us in with an expansive promise of high-seas intrigue. Instead of a ship, all we're given is a spreading wake and a plume of smoke that rises from beyond the horizon to form a puffy white cloud. The romance of travel is left entirely to the imagination. The United States Lines was a transatlantic shipping company formed in 1921 with three ships from the failed United States Mail Steamship Company. The line would go on to operate a total of sixty vessels—many of them named after American presidents—during the course of its history. Although the increased popularity of air travel would lead to the discontinuation of passenger service in 1969, the United States Lines survived as a container ship business until 1986. The company was formally liquidated in 1992.

Lloyd Sabaudo: Mediterranean America, 1930
Cap (n.d.)
43 x 28½ inches (109.2 x 72.4 cm)
Barabino & Graeve, Genova

Much as Willem Ten Broek did in his promotion for the Holland America Line (page 228), the designer of this rare poster, identified only as Cap, uses sailboats to emphasize the monumental grandeur of the vessel that dominates the image. Cap, however, ups the ante by setting two sailboats—as opposed to the single one used by Ten Broek—atop the glassine water in order to stress the oceanic majesty of the Lloyd Sabaudo ship. As Ten Broek did, Cap presents the ship at a slight angle in order to show off its full splendor. But he gives the viewer far more detail, not only presenting the public with exceedingly stylish art deco advertising but also giving them a more realistic image of the ship. Lloyd Sabaudo was formed in Turin, Italy, in 1906 and began sailing from Genoa to New York via Naples and Palermo the following year. By 1932, intense competition and the global economic depression led to the government-encouraged merger of Lloyd Sabaudo, the Cosulich Line (right), and Navigazione Generale Italiana into a new company named Italia di Navigazione.

Italia-Cosulich, 1936
A. M. Cassandre (Adolphe Mouron, 1901–1968)
37⅜ x 23¾ inches (94.9 x 60.3 cm)
Alliance Graphique/Imprimerie de Léonard Danel, Paris and Lille

The Trieste-based Cosulich Line boasts that it "covers the entire world," and Cassandre, with his image of a trio of liners steaming in unison around the globe, uses pure geometric form and symmetry to illustrate that point perfectly. The incongruity of the three oversize ships precariously placed on top of the world—a placement that speaks to perspective on several levels—adds eye-catching impact to the design. This was one of the posters that Cassandre created during a working summer holiday at Lake Maggiore, in northern Italy. The Mussolini regime had passed a law banning Italian companies from commissioning French artists. To get around this law, Cassandre's future publisher in Italy, Augusto Coen, invited him to work there. Though stylistically the artist's identity was something of a dead giveaway, Cassandre had to play along with the charade and use the monogram AMC to conceal his French name. The Cosulich Line was founded in 1903 by the shipping company Fratelli Cosulich in Trieste, which at that point was still part of the Austro-Hungarian Empire. Originally called Unione Austriaca di Navigazione, the company discontinued its service with the outbreak of World War I. Following the armistice, Trieste became an Italian city, and Unione Austriaca was reestablished as the Cosulich Line. It operated passenger service from Mediterranean ports to destinations in the United States and South America.

Nordamerika-Express, ca. 1937
Renato Cenni (1906–1977)
37½ × 25 inches (95.2 × 63.5 cm)
Printer unknown

In 1937, the Italian Line was formed by a government-directed merger of three smaller shipping companies. Although this gave the newly named operation a nine-ship fleet to work with, two additional ships had already been commissioned in preparation for the merger: the SS *Rex* and the SS *Conte di Savoia*, both jewels of the sea meant to compete against award-winning German vessels. Because they looked so much alike, it is impossible to say whether the *Conte di Savoia* or the *Rex* is depicted in this poster. The two were the only two passenger ships in the Italian Line fleet that made the round-trip voyage between Genoa and New York. While many other advertisements for the crossing between America and Europe focused on Lady Liberty in all her glory, Cenni turns this trope on its head. Instead, the Statue of Liberty appears to be glancing down at the magnificence that is this ship: here, the focus is no longer the excitement of one's destination but rather the perfection of the vessel getting you there.

Hamburg-Amerika Linie: Cuba und Mexico, 1933
Ottomar Anton (1895–1976)
33¼ × 23⅛ inches (84.4 × 58.7 cm)
Mühlmeister & Johler, Hamburg

The Hamburg America Line serviced extensive routes, from the Arctic Circle to the tropics. Here, by means of a specifically pinpointed route map overlaid on the ship's hull, Ottomar Anton firmly fixes our attention not on the ship itself but rather on the line's service to Cuba and Mexico. The skyward thrust of nationalistic stacks of black, red, and gold, and the text announcing German express service ("Deutscher schnelldienst"), complete the design. Established in Hamburg, Germany, in 1847, the Hamburg America Line (formally the Hamburg Amerikanische Packetfahrt Actien-Gesellschaft, or HAPAG) rapidly developed into the largest transatlantic shipping enterprise in Germany—and, at one point, the largest in the world. Although its routes were extensive, HAPAG flourished with the demand brought about by German emigration to the United States. After 123 years of independent operation, HAPAG merged in 1970 with North German Lloyd to create Hapag-Lloyd AG. Launched in 1928 and named after a river that flows through Venezuela and Colombia, the *Orinoco* serviced HAPAG's South American routes until 1941, at which time she was seized by Mexico and rechristened *Puebla*.

3ª Mostra del Mare, 1935
Urbana Corva (1901–1986)
39 × 26½ inches (99.1 × 67.3 cm)
Tipo-Litografia Leghissa di Mario Cozzi, Trieste

In his promotion for Trieste's third Maritime Festival, Urbana Corva calls upon a stylized futurist sailor to be more than a primary indicator of the high-seas theme—he uses him to direct the flow of visual information as well. Beginning with the city's upheld coat of arms at the top, the viewer's eye smoothly travels from the headline downward along the flowing wave of the navy blue figure's arms. The to-the-point text is wonderfully incorporated into the art deco design, and the unobtrusive background schooner adds the perfect touch of romance to the advertisement. Though the festival's theme is "Triestine June," it would appear as if the annual maritime celebration ran from the end of May until mid-August, judging from the dates on the bottom—the period during which attendees could obtain reduced rail fares to the festival. The XIII in the lower right-hand corner refers to Mussolini's thirteenth year in power, a reference that was required by the government. Trieste was a natural choice to host this sort of event: as part of the Hapsburg Monarchy from 1382 until 1918, it was one of the most prosperous seaports in the Mediterranean.

RAILWAYS

THE USE OF RAIL TRANSPORTATION dates to the early nineteenth century and the invention of the steam engine. Trains carried only freight until 1825, when the Stockton and Darlington Railway in England became the first rail system to transport both goods and passengers on a regular schedule. In 1867, George Pullman introduced a luxurious sleeping car called the *President*, making overnight passenger travel much more comfortable and popular.

By the 1930s, automobiles and airplanes began to replace trains for long-distance journeys, largely because of the speed of air travel and the flexibility provided by cars. Today, railways play an important role in hauling freight, but passenger service is primarily focused on carrying commuters to and from major metropolitan areas.

Urban rail systems throughout the world typically incorporate below-ground railways to complement surface transportation and ease roadway congestion. The world's oldest and most famous subway is the London Underground, which celebrates its 150th anniversary in 2013. The Underground consisted of several independent lines until 1933, when the London Public Transport Board (LPTB) consolidated them. The system now has 270 stations and 249 miles of track.

This collection contains one United States railroad poster—the streamlined *20th Century Limited* by Leslie Ragan—and one each from Japan and Australia. The balance is from Europe and includes posters by A. M. Cassandre, Alexandre Alexeieff, and Machiel Wilmink. The London Underground posters include outstanding and rare works by Man Ray, Edward McKnight Kauffer, Alan Rogers, and Frederick Manner. Each poster was ingeniously designed to entice the viewer to ski, play golf, or visit a specific destination—and always, of course, to travel there by rail.

Dine on the L.N.E.R., 1928
Alexandre Alexeieff (1901–1982)
40⅛ x 50¼ inches (101.9 x 127.6 cm)
Dobson Molle & Co., Ltd., Edinburgh

The advertising manager for the London and North Eastern Railway (LNER), William M. Teasdale, began a campaign that took travel posters to an entirely new height of sophistication and elegance. He encouraged graphic creativity, resulting in some of the most stunning travel images of the twentieth century. This design by Alexandre Alexeieff, promoting the luxurious dining opportunities available on the LNER's trains and in their hotels, is one of the finest of that campaign. (The LNER owned not only several railway lines but also several ships, canals, tramways, and hotels.) As if in a dream, the viewer comes across a single dining table patronized by an anonymous gentleman in white tie and tails. His head has been deliberately cut off so that the focus is entirely upon the anticipated meal rather than the guest. No particular food is shown, either, allowing the viewer to imagine his or her favorite dish, soon to be served on the finest china. The only real lure is the lone bottle of red wine and a full glass. Meanwhile, these tasteful comforts float effortlessly over a set of train tracks, as if somehow a table at the Ritz has managed to find its way onto an LNER dining car.

The Night Scotsman, 1932
Alexandre Alexeieff (1901–1982)
39⅞ x 50⅛ inches (101.3 x 127.3 cm)
Waterlow & Sons, Limited, London and Dunstable

Strikingly different from the artist's surreal design for the London and North Eastern Railway's dining car services (left), this highly simplified silhouette of an engine (outlined in the preliminary sketch at right) can be seen either as quietly rumbling across the British terrain, passing between a lake and a mountain, or as taking flight, effortlessly floating over the evening landscape far below its wheels. There is a watercolor quality to the palette and soft outlines of the background, creating the visual equivalent of a lullaby. The Night Scotsman was the London and North Eastern Railway's overnight passenger service between London and Edinburgh. It left King's Cross station every evening at 10:25 and arrived in Scotland around breakfast the next morning. Alexeieff's design is wildly ambitious, perfectly in line with the philosophy of LNER's advertising manager, William M. Teasdale. This image redefines the way one could advertise a railway—so frequently presented as a roaring monolith of the Machine Age rather than an elegant ambassador of technology.

Right: Alexeieff's original black-ink tracing of *The Night Scotsman* poster is oriented in reverse for direct transfer to a lithographic plate.

LNER: Take Me by the Flying Scotsman, 1932
Alfred Reginald Thomson (1894–1979)
40 x 24½ inches (101.6 x 62.2 cm)
S. C. Allen & Company, Ltd., London

In operation since 1862, the Flying Scotsman (the daytime counterpart to the Night Scotsman, page 249) was a daily express passenger service running between London and Edinburgh. Overseen by the London and North Eastern Railway (LNER), the line became known for its luxury and speed: in 1932, it could make the journey in a mere seven and a half hours. This poster's brilliance lies in its ability to poke fun at itself. On the one hand, the engine is beautifully rendered, its sleek black carriage and glistening wheels a geometric homage to art deco aesthetics. But the addition of two diminutive human figures—the little girl in awe of the train and the megaphone-wielding conductor—distracts the viewer from the impressive nature of the train and instead offers a playful knock at the posters of A. M. Cassandre, known for their exaggerated scale. The humor is perhaps best displayed, however, in the fine print on the lower right-hand corner of the page. There, the LNER apologizes to the Southern Railway for offering the Flying Scotsman as a travel option, as if by merely existing, such a remarkable service must be an embarrassment to every other line's obviously subpar fleet. This tongue-in-cheek ribbing actually stems from the famous railway "races" of the late 1800s, in which each of the many railway lines in service at the time tried to be faster than its competitors—a rivalry that obviously still existed, even in jest, in the 1930s.

LMS: The Best Way, 1928
A. M. Cassandre (Adolphe Mouron, 1901–1968)
43½ x 28½ inches (110.5 x 72.4 cm)
Imprimerie de Léonard Danel, Paris and Lille

As he did in his design for the Étoile du Nord express train (page 255), Cassandre chooses not to include an actual train or destination in this poster, an advertisement for the London, Midland & Scottish Railway (LMS). Instead we are given a dramatic close-up of an otherwise mundane object: the points lever, an ordinary manual railroad switch. In reality, this mechanism is neither sexy in its design nor particularly interesting; however, Cassandre's rendering of the object gives it the glamour of a Hollywood icon, all macho and powerful in its pure functionality. This cinematic quality is further emphasized in the grayscale tones of the design, which are enhanced by the burning brilliance of the tangerine-colored letters spelling out the company's initials. Behind the points lever, as far as the eye can see, are row upon row of train tracks, alluding in their seemingly infinite presence to the myriad places the LMS, the largest transportation company in the world at the time, could take you. Graphically, the tracks provide a visual rhythm against which the points lever appears even more emphatic and deliberate. Its artful simplicity anchors a powerful composition that seems to revel in the idea of traveling by night.

Southern Electric, 1935
Patrick Cokayne Keely (d. 1970)
39⅝ x 24¾ inches (100.6 x 62.9 cm)
Printer unknown

Starting in 1923, Britain's Southern Railway began the long task of gradually converting its many lines from steam to electric power. It would be the first mass electrification venture of the modern era. Any service using this newfangled third-rail system was subsequently referred to as Southern Electric, adding a glamorously modern sense of power and speed to those particular routes. Once the greater London area was electrified, the focus shifted to expanding the venture out to various coastal cities. In the early 1930s, the London-to-Brighton route was completed—the first electric intercity line in the world. This poster advertises that long journey between the capital and the coast. Pat Keely uses the haunting glow of the traffic signal, its muted green standing out against the night sky, as a focal point, inviting the viewer to continue traveling down the track toward the glowing city off in the distance. In addition to the many posters Keely created for Southern Electric, he produced works for the Great Western Railway and London Transport, each of them defined by a rich use of color and simple, bold graphics.

South for Sunshine, 1929
Edmond Vaughan (1906–1996)
40⅛ x 25¼ inches (101.9 x 64.1 cm)
The Baynard Press, London

This is the more whimsical of two gloriously prismatic images Edmond Vaughan created for the Southern Railway. Although it was the smallest of Britain's Big Four railway companies, Southern Railway was the one that ran to England's most attractive seaside resorts, the best known of which was Brighton. This distinction meant that Southern Railway was the only line whose income came primarily from passenger service rather than freight. As such, appealing travel posters were all the more important to its survival. Vaughan's design certainly does not leave the viewer dissatisfied: it manages to make the rather ethereal concept of sunshine a solid entity, physically altering all it touches. Like golden fingers stretching down from the sky, the beams of light wash warmth over the land-

Nord Express, 1927
A. M. Cassandre (Adolphe Mouron, 1901–1968)
41⅝ x 29½ inches (105.7 x 74.9 cm)
Hachard et Cie., Paris

It's hard to believe, but this is the only railway poster by Cassandre in which he depicts a complete engine. In fact, unlike his more abstract train designs, so dominated by suggestion and inference, this composition looks like his images for grand ships, in which the vessel is glorified as a larger-than-life symbol of the art deco era. Compare this poster with the artist's *Normandie* (page 224): in both designs, the viewer is positioned at an extremely low angle, nearly lying on the ground beside the conveyance. Here, one is overwhelmed by the sheer size of the steel beast as it rushes toward the seemingly limitless horizon. This emphasis on speed is visually echoed in the sharp parallel lines of track racing toward a single point. Breaking up this composition of right angles is the soft undulation of text describing the route at the bottom—the seven possible destinations converge and then separate like waves on the sea, connecting England, France, and Belgium with Germany, Latvia, and Poland. Although it is not indicated here, the original purpose of the Nord Express was to link Saint Petersburg with the rest of Europe, a goal that was deemed impractical and risky after World War I.

Étoile du Nord, 1927
A. M. Cassandre (Adolphe Mouron, 1901–1968)
44½ x 29⅝ inches (113 x 75.2 cm)
Hachard et Cie., Paris

Run by the Compagnie Internationale des Wagons-Lits, the North Star was an express train that went from Paris to Amsterdam via Brussels. Although the journey was not exceptionally long, the passenger accommodations were held to the highest luxury standards. Travelers could take advantage of Pullman sleeping cars and a variety of grand dining options. Cassandre's design, however, does not focus on any of that. In fact, one does not see a powerful locomotive, a map of an exotic destination, or even any real indication that this is a promotion for a train service. Once one reads the text, though, the composition manifests itself as an advertisement. It is not only one of Cassandre's most ambitious artistic executions but also, arguably, one of the most boundary-pushing travel posters of the twentieth century. Crowning the horizon is the North Star, an asymmetrical celestial body teetering like a ballerina upon a stage of darkness. Rushing toward it is a sweeping network of train tracks, looking more like trails behind a shooting star than steel beams traversing the ground. Their arrangement is entirely artistic, meant to imply swift movement and not to imitate reality. Yet suspended disbelief is a concession we're willing to make when viewing this poster, reality being far less interesting than Cassandre's brilliant reimagining of it.

Chemin de Fer du Nord, 1929
A. M. Cassandre (Adolphe Mouron, 1901–1968)
39¼ x 24½ inches (99.7 x 62.2 cm)
Imprimerie de Léonard Danel, Paris and Lille

Under the direction of the Baron James Mayer de Rothschild, the Compagnie des Chemins de Fer du Nord was responsible for exponentially expanding the French railway network from its founding in 1845 up through the late 1860s. Based out of the Gare du Nord, the company's lines ran up as far as the English Channel and eventually as far away as Belgium. The principal point of the company's advertising was that if one wished to travel north of Paris, the Chemin de Fer du Nord was the most practical and versatile option. Here, Cassandre distills that message into a handsome, eye-catching poster in which the exaggeratedly large needle of a compass points almost due north as it flies over the train tracks. The composition is almost entirely based on reemphasis. Although the dial cuts through the *N* in "Nord," the additional *N* on the face of the compass drives home the idea of traveling north. Meanwhile, the word "speed" (*vitesse*) in the tagline below is echoed in the motion lines slicing through the sky. The concept of luxury is implied in the metallic brass of the fulcrum, which brings to mind a modern train compartment outfitted with chic fixtures and sophisticated decor. Similarly, the idea of comfort is suggested by Cassandre's impossibly straight tracks, down which one imagines gliding smoothly toward one's destination.

Wagon-Bar, 1932
A. M. Cassandre (Adolphe Mouron, 1901–1968)
40⅜ x 24⅞ inches (102.5 x 63.2 cm)
Imprimerie de Léonard Danel, Paris and Lille

As standards for train service climbed higher, the restaurant car was considered to be on a par with the sleeping car: an expression of the utmost luxury and convenience for the passenger. Everything from the table linens to the silverware to the food itself was presumed to be of the best quality. Tables were often set with the likes of Christofle and Limoges, while white-gloved staff attended to one's every need. The allure of these moving restaurants was so great that pamphlets were produced encouraging patrons to spend Christmas and other holidays in the train's dining cars, which were wondrous destinations in and of themselves. This concept—that food service is a train's greatest attraction—is perfectly expressed in Cassandre's incomparable design. Neither a time of year nor a particular route is mentioned—the viewer is simply presented with the glorious temptations of dining on the train. In what must have been a startling composition for the time, one sees a photomontage rendering of a steel wheel halted on a small stretch of track. Hovering over it in impossible space are the makings of a delightful meal: a warm baguette, a glass of some sweet aperitif next to a soda siphon, and a full glass of wine with its accompanying bottle. These tantalizing fixtures of a fine dining experience were previously only available in the comforts of a high-end restaurant. Now, though, they are the standard amenities on any trip aboard a Compagnie Internationale des Wagons-Lits train.

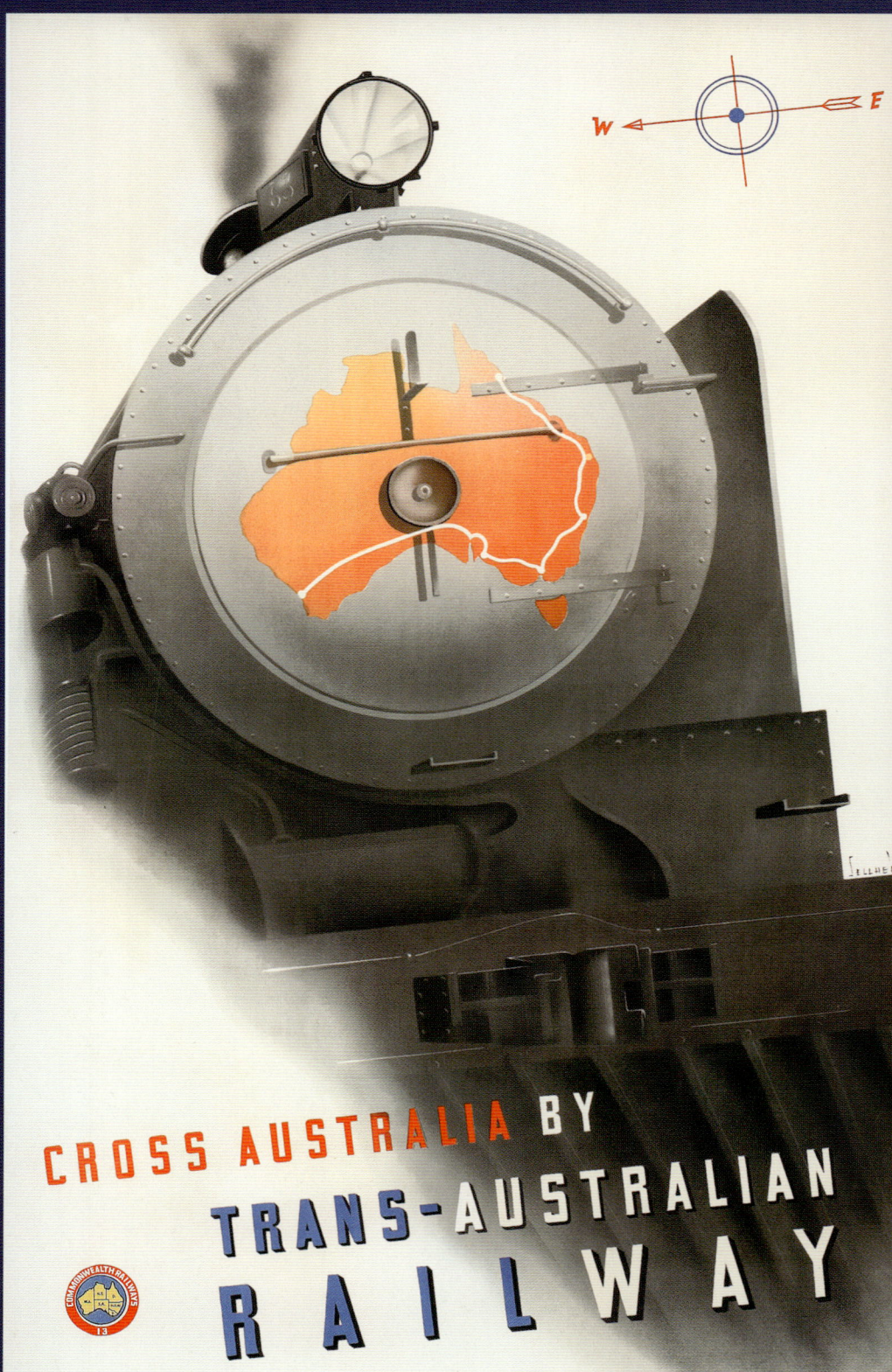

Trans-Australian Railway, 1936
Gert Sellheim (1901–1970)
39½ x 24½ inches (100.3 x 62.2 cm)
F. W. Niven Pty., Ltd., Melbourne

Possessing the world's longest single stretch of completely straight track (297 miles), the Trans-Australian Railway is considered one of the most historically significant train lines ever built. Running from Kalgoorlie to Port Augusta, a distance of 1,052 miles, it also links the Transcontinental Railway's routes from Sydney, on the continent's eastern coast, to Perth, on the western coast. This ability to swiftly connect one side of the commonwealth to the other is what fueled the construction of the line between 1912 and 1917: when Australia united its six colonies to form a single country in 1901, the biggest incentive for Western Australia to join was the promise of a federally funded railroad between remote Perth and the other major cities. This design directly advertises what twenty years before had been a complete fantasy. All rivets and steel, the photomontage of the engine sets the stage for the modern feel behind the poster. But the true focal point is the orange map of the country plastered across the train's nose like a light illuminating a dark path. Echoing the compass pointing due west in the upper right corner, the white line of the railway's route hugs the coastline, visually elucidating the tagline below.

Exactitude, 1932
Pierre Fix-Masseau (1905–1994)
39¼ x 24½ inches (99.7 x 62.2 cm)
Edita, Paris

For a two-year period between 1926 and 1928, Pierre Fix-Masseau worked in A. M. Cassandre's studio as his assistant. Of the many posters Fix-Masseau subsequently created, many show off the master's influence—but this is the single work in which Cassandre's hand is most obvious. There is a notably similar use of extreme foreshortening and heavily raked angles, an implied infinite horizon, and a powerful glorification of the mighty machine, shown in all its art deco glory. In fact, the composition as a whole is nearly a mirror image of Cassandre's *Nord Express* (page 254). However, there are aspects of the design that are distinctly unlike Cassandre, and these may be the best indicators of Fix-Masseau's true creative style. For example, the diamond-shaped pattern of the platform, which gradually fades off into the distance, contrasts with the usual flat planes of color used in similar posters. It gives the foreground a subtle texture that works to make the image more habitable, more real. This invitation to enter the design is further emphasized by the engineer peeking his head out of the side of the train as it leaves the station. By contrast, not a single one of Cassandre's railroad posters depicts an actual human being. The engineer's presence also brings a level of accountability to what is being advertised—the precision and timely nature (exactitude) of the state-run French railway service (Chemins de Fer de l'État, or État). That tiny figure, haloed by the governing hands of a clock, is the person who keeps everything running smoothly.

Dänemark: Die Dänischen Staatsbahnen, ca. 1935
Anonymous
39¼ x 25 inches (99.7 x 63.5 cm)
S. L. Møllers Bogtrykkeri, København

Similar in style to designs by Pierre Fix-Masseau and A. M. Cassandre, this poster for the Danish state-owned railway possesses a visual rhythm that elevates its anonymous artist to the level of those art deco masters. Although the boat and the train are individually defined, the image's color palette and regimentally placed lines unify them graphically, so that they appear almost as one giant mode of transport. The railway company itself is the largest railroad in Scandinavia, and, even in the 1930s, it had routes crossing into Sweden and Germany, as the map in the lower left indicates. Given that Denmark is a peninsula with a shoreline peppered by various small islands, one of the nation's most difficult travel challenges in the early twentieth century was the need to switch vessels when moving from land to sea and then back to land. Thus this poster attempts to indicate with its visual unity a seamless flow between train and ship as one traverses the country and beyond. The railroad is portrayed as not only a highly practical form of transport but also a superior one, in which not a single beat is skipped in the transfer from one vehicle to the other. They may be separate travel methods, but they work in tandem.

Lloyd Rapide, 1927
Machiel Wilmink (1894–1963)
44⅞ x 27¼ inches (114 x 69.2 cm)
Nederlandse Rotogravure Maatschappij, Leiden

Rotterdam Lloyd was one of many firms to emerge in response to the growing need for reliable mail delivery from the Netherlands to its East Asian colonies in the late 1800s. By the time this poster was printed, steamships were no longer the only method of mail transport, as trains had been used to supplement the various overseas routes since World War I. Dutch mail often was brought via ship as far as Marseilles or Genoa, where it would then be picked up by trains owned by the shipping company and brought to Rotterdam. These trains, like the ships, offered passenger service, a mode of transport that became all the more appealing with the launch of superfast express trains such as the Lloyd Rapide, advertised here. The Lloyd Rapide ran regular service from The Hague to Paris to Marseilles and back, promising, as noted in the tagline, the "fastest connection to Holland." With motion lines radiating from the nose of the engine, and with the engine coming at the viewer head-on, the design almost bursts off the page. The highly geometric structure of the train gives the poster a prismatic beauty while maintaining an aura of fierce modernity and strength. It is that balance between the decorative and the functional that makes this rare image an art deco masterpiece.

Ook's Winters per Spoor, ca. 1935
Kees van der Laan (1903–1983)
39⅝ x 24⅝ inches (100.6 x 62.5 cm)
Printer unknown

Best known for his dynamic aviation posters, Kees van der Laan developed his unique take on art deco style during a three-year stay in Paris (1924–1927), when he was living among those who were at the forefront of the aesthetic movement. After returning home to Holland, he discovered the work A. M. Cassandre had done for Dutch clients, further adding to his deco education. Van der Laan created this design for winter railway service after he published his more famous images for the Nationale Luchtvaartschool (see page 30), and this work shows a more mature and ambitious take on composition and line. Cutting through the night, the train wages war against the fury of a storm. The sky is pitch black, save for the occasional white blast of lightning that illuminates the landscape. Yet while trees bend in the winds and rain relentlessly streaks through the sky, the engine forges on, the lone figure of its steadfast conductor shown in silhouette against the glow of burning coals. Below, the four *V*s of the winter railway service are announced: safe, quick, cheap, and heated. As northern European winters can be quite harsh, this type of advertisement would not have discouraged potential clients: rather, it would have presented a realistic picture of an unwieldy season, finally tamable by the indestructible modern train.

The New 20th Century Limited, 1938
Leslie Ragan (1897–1972)
41 x 27 inches (104.1 x 68.6 cm)
Latham Litho and Printing Company, Long Island City

While Cassandre was the heralded master of train posters in Europe, Leslie Ragan was responsible for capturing the majesty of railroad travel in the United States. Each of his railway designs, bathed in a Norman Rockwellesque light, presents a perfect beacon of homegrown industry calmly traversing the serene American landscape. Although rail service between Chicago and New York was no groundbreaking concept in 1938, that summer saw the debut of a new, streamlined style of train designed by Henry Dreyfuss. No longer a clunky piece of machinery, the new 20th Century Limited, with its clean lines and simple shape, redefined how the world looked at locomotives, leading the New York Central Railroad to dub it the "most famous train in the world." The trip between the two cities took a mere sixteen hours, allowing businessmen—the service's primary market—to fall asleep in New York and wake up in Chicago. The finest attention to detail was present, right down to the matchbooks available onboard. Even before one got on the train, a red carpet was rolled out to make the service feel all the more exclusive and posh. Those incidental luxuries, however, are not alluded to in this poster: the image of the engine quietly rolling by the Hudson River toward New York's Grand Central Station is itself enough to fill the viewer with a sense of awe.

THE GOLDEN ARROW PULLMAN

LONDON
VICTORIA
DEP ·· 11·00
PARIS
NORD
ARR ·· 5·40

SHEP
SOUTHERN RAILWAY ADVERTISING

The "Golden Arrow" Pullman, 1931
Shep (Charles Shepherd, 1892–?)
39 3/8 x 24 3/4 inches (100 x 62.9 cm)
The Baynard Press, London

The Golden Arrow was the British equivalent of France's Flèche d'Or. Each operated as a luxury rail service between the coast and its nation's capital. In 1926, the French version, which ran between Calais and Paris, was unveiled. Three years later, England's Southern Railway released its answer to this posh service—a train consisting solely of ten first-class Pullman cars that ran from London to Dover in just over an hour and a half. Passengers could then transfer to the equally luxurious *Canterbury* ferry to cross the Channel and connect with the Flèche d'Or in Calais. By 1931, however, air travel was drastically undercutting the popularity of both lines among the upper classes, so much so that modifications rendering the accommodations less luxurious had to be made to the carriages and ship in order to keep the route operational. This poster, produced that same year, emphasizes the speed of the service rather than its former elitist cachet. The image—which, with its bold, stark lines and palette, was versatile enough to look good in both large and small formats—appeared with an alternative black background in a variety of magazines.

XX.Mustermesse, 1933
M. Egersdorfer (n.d.)
37 7/8 x 24 7/8 inches (96.2 x 63.2 cm)
Z. T. Narodnih Novina, Zagreb

This is an exceedingly rare poster by a little-known artist for train service to a livestock fair held in the Socialist Federal Republic of Yugoslavia. Despite the fact that 1933 was a particularly turbulent time for the country politically, events like this still took place, though public sentiment toward them was becoming less and less enthusiastic. This feeling of uncertainty is perhaps best expressed in the various economic incentives offered at the bottom of the poster for anyone who wished to attend the event— one could get a free round trip with the purchase of any animal at the fair or a 25–33 percent discount for travel to a neighboring country, such as Italy, Austria, Romania, Bulgaria, Hungary, Albania, or Greece. The design itself is relatively simple compared to its Western European counterparts. We see the silhouette of an engine at some transitional time of day—either dusk or just before dawn—and the ghostly aura of white steam tracing its outline. A rectangular block of red streaks along the top of the train, a sharp geometric nod to the burning embers smoldering inside the engine. The most eye-catching element in the composition is the pair of initials, ZZ, which stand for *železnice Zagreb*—the train to Zagreb.

Power: The Nerve Centre of London's Underground, 1931
Edward McKnight Kauffer (1890–1954)
39 x 25 inches (99.1 x 63.5 cm)
Vincent Brooks, Day & Son, Ltd., London

The graphic work of Edward McKnight Kauffer revolutionized the face of the London Underground. During the twenty-year period between 1915 and 1935 he not only created a total of 141 posters for the company but also revitalized portions of the subway stations throughout the city with murals and other examples of public art. This remains one of his most ambitious and rare compositions, fusing images of man and machine to best express the raw energy behind London's electrified train service. The focal point of the poster is a muscular arm thrusting violently out of a rapidly spinning turbine. As it grips an unseen lever, the kinetic energy of the gears is so great that blue streaks of electricity shoot from the source down through the arm's veins, emerging as three lightning bolts leaping from the closed fist. Additional little blue zaps of electricity skid along the outskirts of the image, most notably as vibrating streaks on the left-hand side of the word "power." In the upper right, blocks of electric-blue water flow into a simplified rendering of the Battersea Power Station—construction of which was the first stage of the London Power Company's effort to nationalize electric service. The power station was also an important component in the reliable electrification of the country's trains. At the heart of the turbine is the iconic symbol for the Underground, as if it is the spark from which all this dynamic activity is born.

Keeps London Going, 1939
Man Ray (Emmanuel Radnitzky, 1890–1976)
40 x 25 inches (101.6 x 63.5 cm)
Waterlow & Sons, Limited, London and Dunstable

In a genre so rife with variety, it seems impossible to claim that a single poster stands apart from other London Underground images; however, this startling and rare design by Man Ray does just that. Unlike the multitude of other posters made for the company that utilize eye-catching color palettes, this one subverts the viewer's expectations by relying on a soft gray scale to serve as the background. This image is an example of what the artist called a rayograph: he placed objects—in this case, sculptures of the London Transport logo and Saturn—on top of light-sensitive photographic paper. When exposed to light for long stretches of time, the paper would record the negative impressions of the objects on the page. This is how the design achieves its three-dimensional quality—it is technically a photograph, even if that photograph does not capture a slice of reality with the click of a shutter. Two panels of this poster were actually created—the first with the words "London Transport" at the bottom, so that the two posters displayed together would create a complete sentence. Not only was Man Ray enhancing the London Transport logo visually, by suggesting its similarity to Saturn, he was also making it necessary for advertisers to display two posters at once, reinforcing the metaphorical message.

Play between 6 and 12: The Bright Hours, 1930
Edward McKnight Kauffer (1890–1954)
39¾ x 24⅝ inches (101 x 62.5 cm)
Vincent Brooks, Day & Son, Ltd., London

Shop between 10 and 4: The Quiet Hours, 1930
Edward McKnight Kauffer (1890–1954)
39¾ x 24½ inches (101 x 62.2 cm)
Vincent Brooks, Day & Son, Ltd., London

Congestion has always been an issue on public transportation. The London Underground attempted to solve this problem by encouraging its customers to use the subways during off-peak hours for certain activities. Several posters promoting this idea were created from the late 1920s up through the mid-1930s, of which this set by Edward McKnight Kauffer may be the most handsome. Each design targets a specific demographic, informing them that their activity of choice is best served by rail at certain times of day. The first encourages those interested in leisurely recreation to use the trains between 6:00 p.m. and 12:00 midnight. The weighty, barrel-shaped pastel blue and pink trails behind the numbers convey the idea that these are the "bright hours," when the lights of the city are shining, ideal for playing and fun. Meanwhile, the color scheme characterizing the hours between 10:00 a.m. and 4:00 p.m. is muted, suggesting that these "quiet hours" are the perfect time for housewives to use the Tube for shopping. Note the juxtaposition of colors: what's blue in the "quiet" poster is pink in the "bright" poster, and what's blue in the "bright" poster is orange in the "quiet" poster. Each design is careful not to encourage train use during the morning and evening commute so that everyone's subway experience can be as pleasant and stress-free as possible. Companion pieces without being identical, these posters are also some of the earliest works in which Kauffer uses his newfound love of typographic airbrushing. This technique gives a very precise, machine-driven feel to the posters, especially given Kauffer's previous switch from diagonal to linear lines of text. These are images that reflect the orderly clock of the Machine Age, when even one's most mundane task merits a time stamp.

Safety, 1930
Alan Rogers (n.d.)
40 x 25 inches (101.6 x 63.5 cm)
The Broadway Press Ltd., London

Speed, 1930
Alan Rogers (n.d.)
40 x 25 inches (101.6 x 63.5 cm)
The Broadway Press Ltd., London

Dissatisfied with the bland imagery offered to him by various advertising agencies, London Underground publicity officer Frank Pick sought out individual artists directly and commissioned them to create posters advertising the company's services. What resulted was one of the greatest and longest-lasting contributions to public art ever made by a corporation. The only real restriction Pick placed on his artists was that the message within the poster had to be clear—other than that, the compositions could be as straightforward and literal or as wildly imaginative as the artist wanted. This pair fits within the former category. It presents with utmost graphic simplicity the two greatest selling points of the Underground: speed and safety. Both posters feature a bare-bones geometric symbol of a man drawn in the subway's signature colors. In the first, a medieval-style warrior straddles a subway platform, raising a shield stamped with the Underground's logo to ward off a lightning bolt that snakes toward him. Electrical accidents were not uncommon outside the city at the time, so emphasizing the safety of the railway was essential in winning over skeptical customers. In the second poster, an archer draws a lightning bolt (identical to the one in the first poster) from his London Underground–branded quiver, implying that the train could zip its passengers across the city faster than they ever thought imaginable. Together, these posters are a handsome example of the soft-sell approach used to persuade customers to embrace the subway and its myriad useful services.

Underground Gets You There, 1935
Zero (Hans Schleger, 1898–1976)
40 x 25 inches (101.6 x 63.5 cm)
The Baynard Press, London

One of the earliest proponents of the concept of corporate identity, Hans Schleger turned the circle-and-bar emblem of the London Underground into a streamlined, instantly recognizable symbol. Rather than consign it to the corner of the poster as an afterthought, as do so many other Underground images, Schleger incorporated it into the center of the design. This poster is one of a pair—the only difference between it and its mate is the sex of the figure. Here, a man is shown gazing intently down at his watch. The viewer is forced to follow that same line of sight and peer over the man's shoulder. The watch, depicted in bright red and blue amid a sea of muted tones, is essentially the Underground emblem itself—its bar has morphed into a wristband, and the circle has become the face of the watch. The text surrounding the image presents the answer to an implied question: Am I in time for the next train? It does not matter, as the trains run so frequently and efficiently that the London Underground will (always) get you there on time.

No Wet, No Cold, 1929
Frederick Manner (1889–1961)
39½ x 24½ inches (100.3 x 62.2 cm)
Printer unknown

Any visitor to London knows that barely a day in the city goes by when the sky does not at some point cloud over and a persistent drizzle begin to fall. At the very moment it does, hundreds of pedestrians open their black umbrellas in unison, populating the streets with a seemingly infinite sea of miniature charcoal tents. This poster captures the essence of that moment perfectly—an unending stretch of slick gray wherein the viewer can barely make out the difference between one object and the next. Although the image is graphically attractive, the underlying message is that no one wants to be outside in the English rain, all cold and miserable. Thus the bright red logo of the London Underground shines like a beacon of hope against the wretched storm, a warm symbol of respite from the elements. We don't even need to see the entire emblem in order to be drawn to it—its signature shape and color attract us, like moths to a flame, into its warm, dry shelter. When compared to the experience of walking in a cold rain, the Underground seems downright luxurious—the obvious, most pleasant choice for getting to and from one's destination.

UNDERGROUND

MANNER

NO WET · NO COLD

TRAVEL AND TOURISM

DURING THE 1920S AND 1930S, with the growth of the automobile and railroad industries and the advent of airplane travel, tourism experienced a rapid increase in popularity. Demand for travel-related goods and services was also fueled by signs of recovery from the Great Depression, the desire to forget the hardships and sacrifices of World War I, and the widespread impulse to enjoy life again.

Posters commissioned to support the travel industry were designed by many of the prominent art deco graphic artists of this period, including A. M. Cassandre, Roger Broders, Léo Marfurt, Gert Sellheim, Sascha Maurer, Dorothy Waugh, Munetsugu Satomi, and Aladár Richter. Their geometric designs, stylized figures, crisp typography, and bold colors resulted in arresting posters that enticed and seduced postwar pleasure seekers to travel to distant lands, discover exotic vacation spots, and enjoy rest, relaxation, and even adventure in their own countries and overseas. The collection shown here includes not only outstanding examples of European posters, advertising holiday retreats such as Dunkirk, Ostend and Dover, and Saint-Jean-de-Luz, but also remarkable designs made for destinations in Australia, Japan, and Argentina—places that, during the 1920s and 1930s, could only be reached from Europe and North America by means of a long seafaring journey. Regardless of the distance, though, travelers responded to advertisers' inducements with enthusiasm, and the notion of the "tourist" was born.

Orient Calls: Oriental Tourist Conference, 1936
Munetsugu Satomi (1900–1995)
39 x 25 inches (99.1 x 63.5 cm)
The Toppan Printing Co., Ltd.

In order to promote the broad scope of Tokyo's 1936 Oriental Tourist Conference, Munetsugu Satomi presents a wide array of Asian populations (including an unobtrusive elephant) in a universally understood, nonthreatening manner—as paper dolls and finger puppets. Each figure is reduced to its mostly featureless geometric basics, and each is representative of citizens both indigenous and colonial. Satomi (see his poster for KLM airlines, page 21) then proceeds to place them one beside another in the flattest perspective possible, fits them within the linear map of Asia beneath their feet, and then finishes off the composition by depicting the modes of transportation that can be used to travel to the conference. Satomi may not have included many facial features, but his choice of colors is exquisite and expressive, ranging from soft yellows to vibrant oranges to ruddy earth tones.

Osaka Railways, ca. 1935
Toyonosuke Kurozumi (1908–1955)
42 x 30½ inches (106.7 x 77.5 cm)
Printer unknown

Although frequently considered a Western movement, art deco had just as much a place in Japanese graphic design as it did in the famous images decorating the streets of Paris throughout the 1920s and 1930s. In fact, whereas art nouveau fetishized the Orient and often contained elements of Japonisme, the deco craze in the East could be seen as an inverted form of that visual dialogue. It borrowed signature aspects of European popular design and reinterpreted them in a particularly Asian way. For example, to advertise the fast (two hours and fifty-two minutes) rail service between Osaka and Yamada, Toyonosuke Kurozumi presents three highly stylized trains in profile, so simple in their execution that they appear toylike. The colors are striking without being off-putting, forcing the eye to bounce from shape to shape in rapid delight. This choice of palette is no accident, as fuchsia and bright blue appear repeatedly in Japanese posters from the era—a distinct difference from the highly varied color choices made in Europe at the time. And yet despite the giddy nature of this poster's colors, the composition is highly regimented—an eerie nod to the militarism that shortly thereafter would reshape the country's cultural landscape. The poster advertises increased railway access to the Ise Grand Shrine from the Kyoto-Osaka-Kobe metropolitan area (a.k.a. Keihanshin). The Ise Grand Shrine, located in Ise City, Mie Prefecture, is one of the most important Shinto shrines in Japan and is purportedly the home of the Sacred Mirror, one of three pieces of imperial regalia (along with a jewel and a sword) that represent the three primary virtues: wisdom, benevolence, and valor.

Preceding pages
Australia: Surf Club, 1936
Gert Sellheim (1901–1970)
40½ x 25½ inches (102.9 x 64.8 cm)
Sands & McDougall Pty., Ltd., Melbourne

Australia: Sunshine and Surf, ca. 1936
Gert Sellheim (1901–1970)
39½ x 25 inches (100.3 x 63.5 cm)
Troedel & Cooper Pty., Ltd., Melbourne

Australia: Great Barrier Reef, 1937
Gert Sellheim (1901–1970)
39½ x 25 inches (100.3 x 63.5 cm)
F. W. Niven Pty., Ltd., Melbourne

Gert Sellheim created a number of incredible art deco posters for the Australian National Travel Association, each a paragon of masterful concision and artistic economy. He uses repeated images, attractive geometric patterns, cheerful colors, and playful lettering to compose posters that entice without going overboard. They present idyllic locales in the simplest, most figurative terms, a tactic that gently persuades the viewer to step out of the everyday and into the world of the poster. Sellheim's rarest and most famous poster in this group is *Surf Club*. It depicts a team of five female lifeguards performing a reel-and-line rescue exercise, a subtle way to assure seaside visitors that they will be safe while they enjoy all the thrills the sea has to offer. The blue surf, accentuated by stylized waves, the sandy yellow beach, and the bronzed lifeguards all combine with Sellheim's expert use of diagonals and geometric patterns to result in a true art deco masterpiece. This advertisement was posted on kiosks, in shop windows, and on walls throughout London and San Francisco as well as in Australia. In *Sunshine and Surf,* no specific locale is singled out—though Sellheim might have been envisioning the state of Queensland, in the continent's northeast section, nicknamed the Sunshine State for its largely tropical climate. In this poster, the artist conveys a love of the beach with utmost clarity. The strong diagonals of softly lapping waves and the upside-down right triangle of sand not only clearly delineate surf from sunshine, they also create an illusion of motion for a trio of female swimmers who, by diving into the sea, demonstrate a compelling reason to vacation at the Australian seaside. Another spectacular Sellheim design is his advertisement for the glories of the Great Barrier Reef, located in the Coral Sea off the coast of Queensland, in northeastern Australia. The Great Barrier Reef is the world's largest reef system—composed of 900 islands and 2,900 individual reefs, and home to 1,500 species of fish, 500 species of seaweed, and 400 coral species. But Sellheim re-creates it for the passerby in manageable terms: a small school of three angelfish, carefully arranged on the diagonal; four strands of seaweed, which divide the poster into five neat segments as they rise to the surface; three pristine tropical islands, each with a sole palm tree; and one bright red underwater plant. The result is an easily understood, extremely attractive invitation to discover the wonders of nature. Sellheim, born in Estonia to parents of German descent, won the 1939 Sir John Sulman prize for designing the interior of the Victorian Government Tourist Bureau building in Melbourne. In 1942, however, he was briefly interned as a Nazi sympathizer, despite his insistence that he abhorred Hitler's actions.

Below: Lifeguards stand in formation on Bondi Beach (Sydney, New South Wales, Australia), with a brass band playing and flags flying, during the Bondi Carnival in 1933.

Page 280
The Seaside Calls: Go by Train, ca. 1938
Gert Sellheim (1901–1970)
39 x 25 inches (99.1 x 63.5 cm)
F. W. Niven Pty., Ltd., Melbourne

Page 281
By Train for Seaside Holidays, 1936
Gert Sellheim (1901–1970)
40 x 24½ inches (101.6 x 62.2 cm)
F. W. Niven Pty., Ltd., Melbourne

As is the norm in Gert Sellheim's travel posters, the essentials of the assigned message—here, that the Australian coast is a wonderful holiday destination—are magnificently expressed with succinct artistry in these two posters. In the image of a single female swimmer in mid-dive (page 280), Sellheim manages to convey the siren call of the sea in the most uncomplicated, captivating, and elegant manner. Additionally, the composition—the breaking blue wave paralleled by the tanned and toned diver—builds anticipation by withholding the moment of entry into the surf from the viewer. In the image on page 281, Sellheim employs a pair of cubist-influenced Oceanids—saltwater nymphs—frolicking in the sea to entice viewers into the water. One doesn't even need to be literate to understand that it might be a good time to go on vacation at the shore. To make these scenes a reality, all you have to do is go by train—specifically, aboard Victorian Railways—and it might not be a bad idea to bring a Kodak camera along to photograph the good times. Victorian Railways was a government-run company established in 1859 to take over the operations of failed private railroad firms within the state of Victoria. This series of Sellheim posters commissioned by the railroad, which ceased operations in 1983, proves that swimming, surfing, and sunshine are not mere pastimes in Australia but rather an integral part of life Down Under.

Antwerpen: Inhuldiging der Tunnels onder de Schelde, 1933
Léo Marfurt (1894–1977)
39 x 24 inches (99.1 x 61 cm)
Printer unknown

The Belgian city of Antwerp called upon Léo Marfurt to announce the inaugural festivities for its latest engineering marvel—the Waasland Tunnel, a roadway that travels beneath the Scheldt River—in 1933. Marfurt rose to the occasion with this stylish geometric composition in which the tunnel is actually portrayed twice: representationally, in an essentially traditional artistic depiction, and abstractly, in the white stripe that bisects the poster and visually references the road beneath the water. A trio of stylized ships on a field of blue nicely indicates the river and its traffic, while the striped banner echoes Antwerp's own red-and-white flag and adds a bit of civic pride and visual flair to the creation. The Waasland Tunnel was designed by Ole Singstad (1882–1969), the Norwegian-American civil engineer who also led the construction of the passage. Although he's not precisely a household name, Singstad is responsible for creating the ventilation system that made long underwater roadway tunnels—including New York City's Lincoln Tunnel, Holland Tunnel, Brooklyn Battery Tunnel, and Queens Midtown Tunnel—a reality. An interesting historical side note: retreating Belgian forces in 1940 and withdrawing German troops in 1944 attempted to blow up the Waasland Tunnel, but both attempts failed and the tunnel held. It remains in service today.

Antwerpen: Wereldhaven en Kunststad, 1934
Lucien De Roeck (1915–2002)
39½ x 24¼ inches (100.3 x 61.6 cm)
Fr. de Smet, Antwerpen

Lucien De Roeck created this classic art deco design for Antwerp, Belgium—a "center of tourism"—before he had graduated from the Institut Supérieur des Arts Décoratifs in Brussels. He stops our wandering eyes with a universally understood upraised hand, letting us know at a glance that we need look no further than Antwerp if we're seeking a "world port and city of the arts." The hand also references the legend that gave rise to the city's name: according to Jac Guerts, in his essay "Myth, History, and Image in the Low Countries," a giant named Antigon occupied a site along the Scheldt River from which he demanded a toll from all boatmen carrying goods. But a Roman hero, Silvius Brabo, chopped off the giant's hands and flung them into the river, marking the place where the city would eventually be built. In Dutch, the words *hand werpen* mean "to throw hands," and this eventually became the name of the city—Antwerpen. It's easy to appreciate the clever simplicity of this poster's design: a stylized ocean liner is incorporated into the "cuff" below the palm of the hand, and the silhouetted spire of the Cathedral of Our Lady rises like an emphatic architectural exclamation point through the poster's center. This was the winning entry in a 1934 poster competition organized by Camille Huysmans (1871–1968), the popular mayor of Antwerp. The initials HISK underneath De Roeck's signature likely stand for Antwerp's Hoger Instituut voor Schone Kunsten, or Institute for Higher Arts.

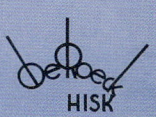

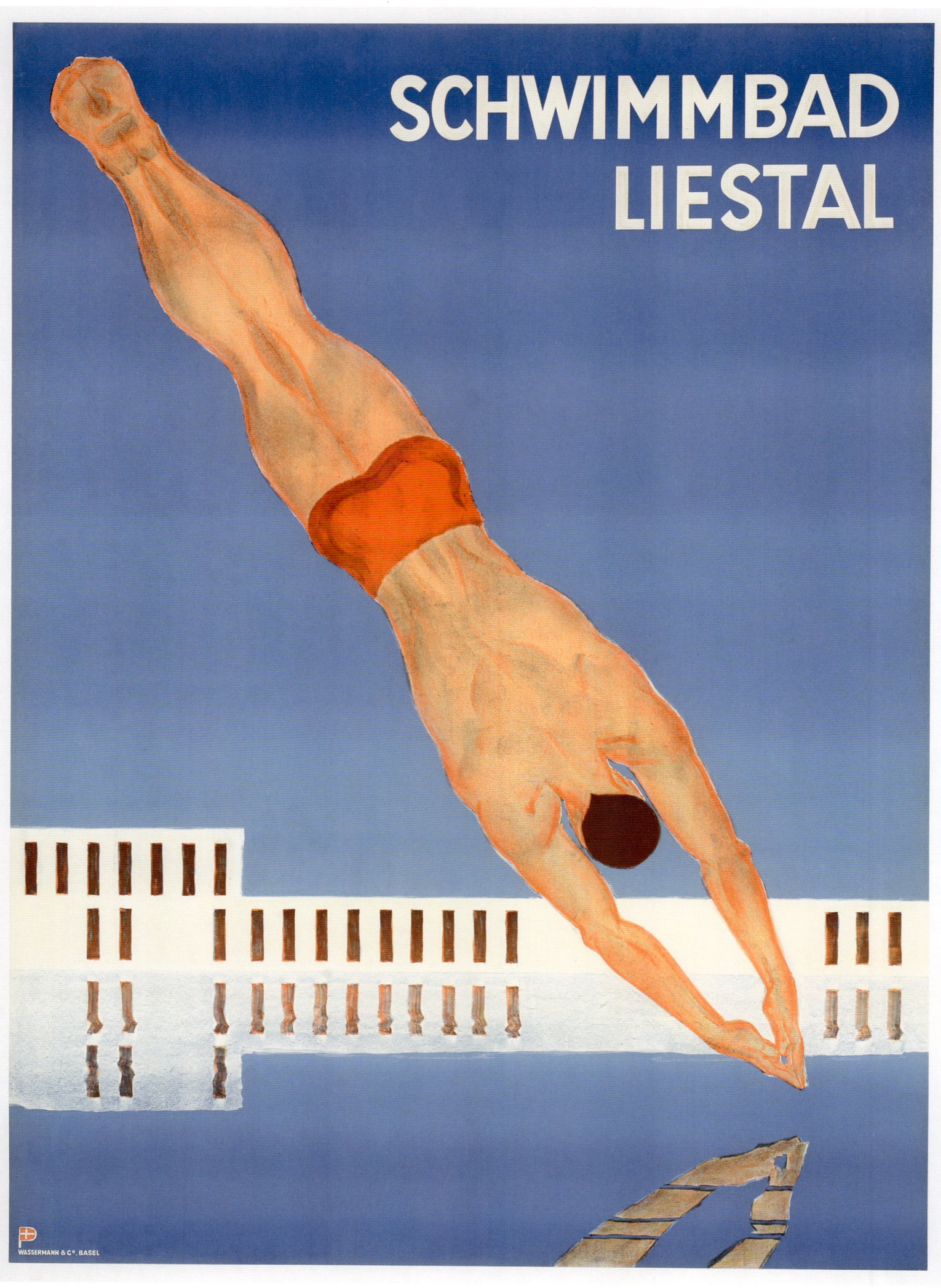

Schwimmbad Liestal, ca. 1930
Otto Jacob Plattner (1886–1951)
51¼ x 35½ inches (130.2 x 90.2 cm)
Graphische Anstalt W. Wassermann, Basel

In northwestern Switzerland, ten miles to the southeast of Basel and not far from the borders of France and Germany, one will find Liestal, the capital of the Basel-Landschaft canton, known for its mild summers and cold, snowy winters. This spectacular poster promoting Liestal's public swimming pool is a muscular display of art deco prowess, angularly defining the pre-impact moment of a diver about to slice into the pool's mirrored waters.

Strandbad Davos, 1933
Willy Trapp (1905–1984)
50⅜ x 35⅜ inches (127.9 x 89.8 cm)
J. E. Wolfenberger AG, Zürich

This stunningly simple but dynamic design by Willy Trapp advertises a public outdoor swimming pool and beach club in Davos, Switzerland. One is instantly drawn to the art deco image of the female diver jack-knifed in the air above the pool. Davos is located on the Landwasser River in the Swiss Alps, in the canton of Graubünden. At nearly one mile above sea level, it is the highest city in Europe. It hosts the well-known World Economic Forum, an annual gathering of global political and business leaders. Davos is also a famous and popular international ski resort.

Széchenyi Strandfürdő, 1935
Aladár Richter (b. 1898)
49¾ x 37¼ inches (126.4 x 94.6 cm)
Piatnik R.T., Budapest

The Széchenyi thermal baths in Budapest, supplied by two hot springs, are the largest medicinal baths in Europe. The neo-Baroque structure that houses the spa was designed by celebrated Hungarian architect Győző Czigler (1850–1905) and was built in the Városliget ("city park") in 1913, after his death. The building, however, is relegated to the background in this Aladár Richter poster. It lies behind the peaked art deco waves of one of the "three big pools" that create the "bathing beach" portion of the baths—which, the poster promises, provides patrons of the spa with "secluded sun-bathing" opportunities. Richter doesn't force the issue in his design, but rather holds to the leisurely spirit of the activity by depicting a pair of beach umbrellas and an expanse of unspoiled sand just awaiting the arrival of the viewer.

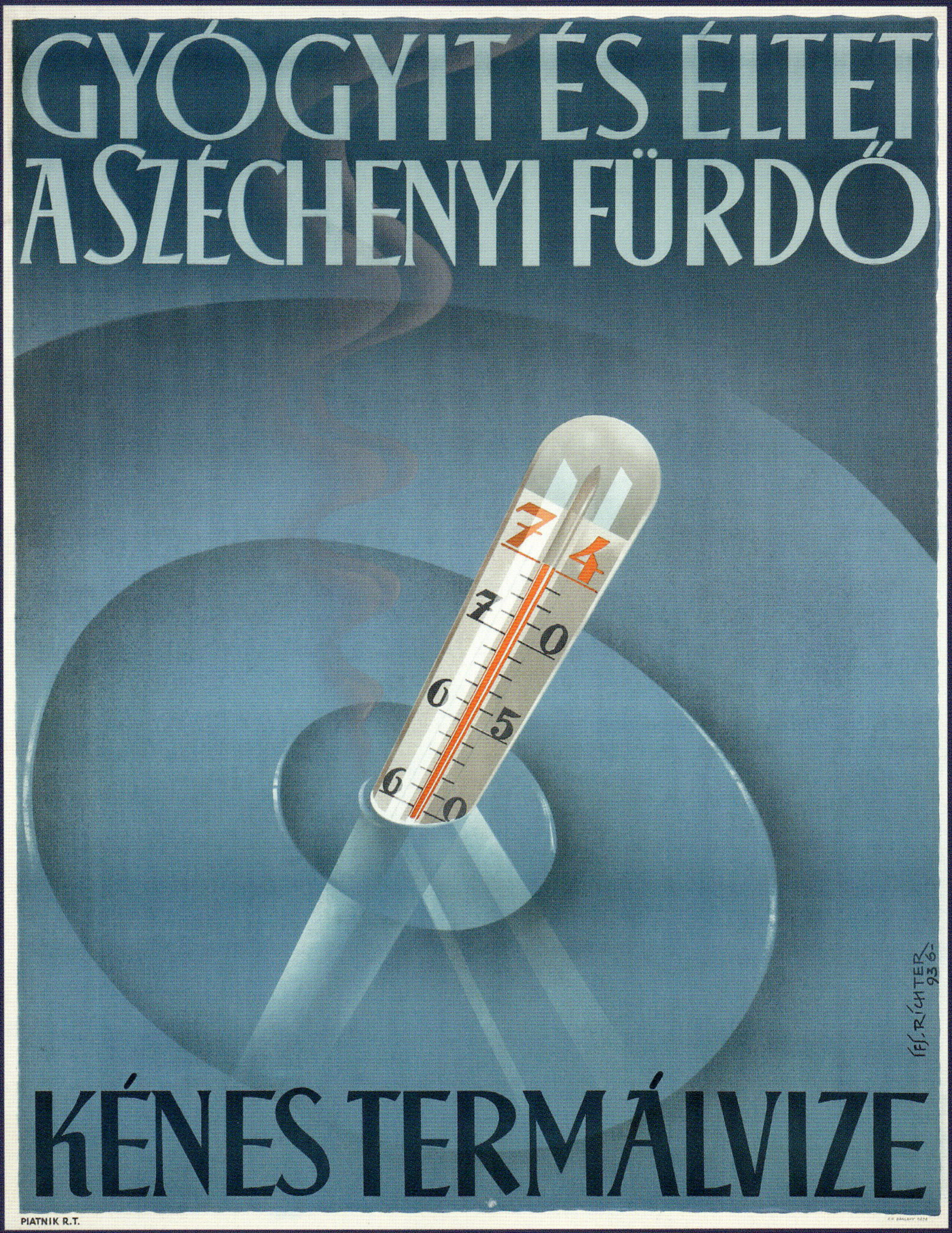

Széchenyi Fürdő, 1936
Aladár Richter (b. 1898)
49⅜ x 37¼ inches (126 x 94.6 cm)
Piatnik R.T., Budapest

According to the text in this superb Aladár Richter poster, the Széchenyi thermal sulfur spring baths are both curative and invigorating. But if you take Richter's artwork literally, they're nicely hot as well, registering a solid 74 degrees Celsius—that's 165 degrees Fahrenheit—on the thermometer. If that isn't hot enough for you, the spa's other spring registers even higher—76 degrees Celsius, or 171 degrees Fahrenheit—although Richter doesn't include that information on the poster. The gentle concentric ripples in the therapeutic waters, the hint of wispy steam, and the deep teal blue color seem to soothe the viewer at a glance. The Széchenyi baths are named after István Széchenyi (1791–1860), the Hungarian politician, theorist, and writer. Széchenyi was also one of the greatest statesmen in Hungarian history, a key figure in the establishment of the Hungarian Academy of Sciences and instrumental in turning Buda and Pest (and, later, the unified Budapest) into a major political, economic, and cultural center. The Széchenyi Chain Bridge—which spans the Danube River, connecting Buda with Pest—is also named after Count Széchenyi, and can be seen in the background of Károly Gerster's 1936 Budapest Grand Prix poster (page 171).

Right: Construction of the Széchenyi thermal baths in Budapest, Hungary, began in 1909. After an expansion in 1927, the complex grew to include three outdoor and fifteen indoor swimming pools.

Sables d'Or les Pins, 1926
Monogrammed LEC; artist unknown
39 x 25 inches (99.1 x 63.5 cm)
Publicité Générale, Rennes

Located in Brittany, in northwestern France, the seaside resort of Sables-d'Or-les-Pins was established in 1921 and was intended to compete with other French resorts, such as Deauville and La Baule. Its developer, Roland Brouard, hired the architect Yves Hémar to design the vacation spot in an "Anglo-Breton" style that would feel familiar and welcoming to visitors from England. The resort grew to include shops, restaurants, hotels, a casino, and, naturally, a golf course. The stained-glass-window approach of this advertisement—created by an artist identified only as LEC—strikes a chord with those who view the game as a pastime that falls somewhere between an obsession and a near-religious experience.

Cortina, 1938
Mario Puppo (1905–1977)
39½ x 27 inches (100.3 x 68.6 cm)
Arti Grafice Pizzi & Pizio, Milano and Roma

Cortina (or, more formally, Cortina d'Ampezzo) is a northern Italian winter resort town of global repute. Situated in the heart of the Dolomites—the rugged and grandiose limestone alpine massif whose yellow-and-pink tints can come across as either harsh or soft, depending on the way the daylight strikes them—Cortina is as popular for its scenery, accommodations, and après-ski scene as it is for the world-class skiing it provides. Mario Puppo's sole focus in this poster, however, is the skiing: the pink-hued Dolomites serve as a mere backdrop for the serious yet energetic art deco pair who appear to be chiseled from the same rock as the mountains behind them. There's nothing forced about the poster, yet its purposeful composition makes it clear at a glance that Cortina caters to both the competitive and the social skier. The incline of the mountains, the typeface, and the figures leave little doubt as to the region's alpine intensity.

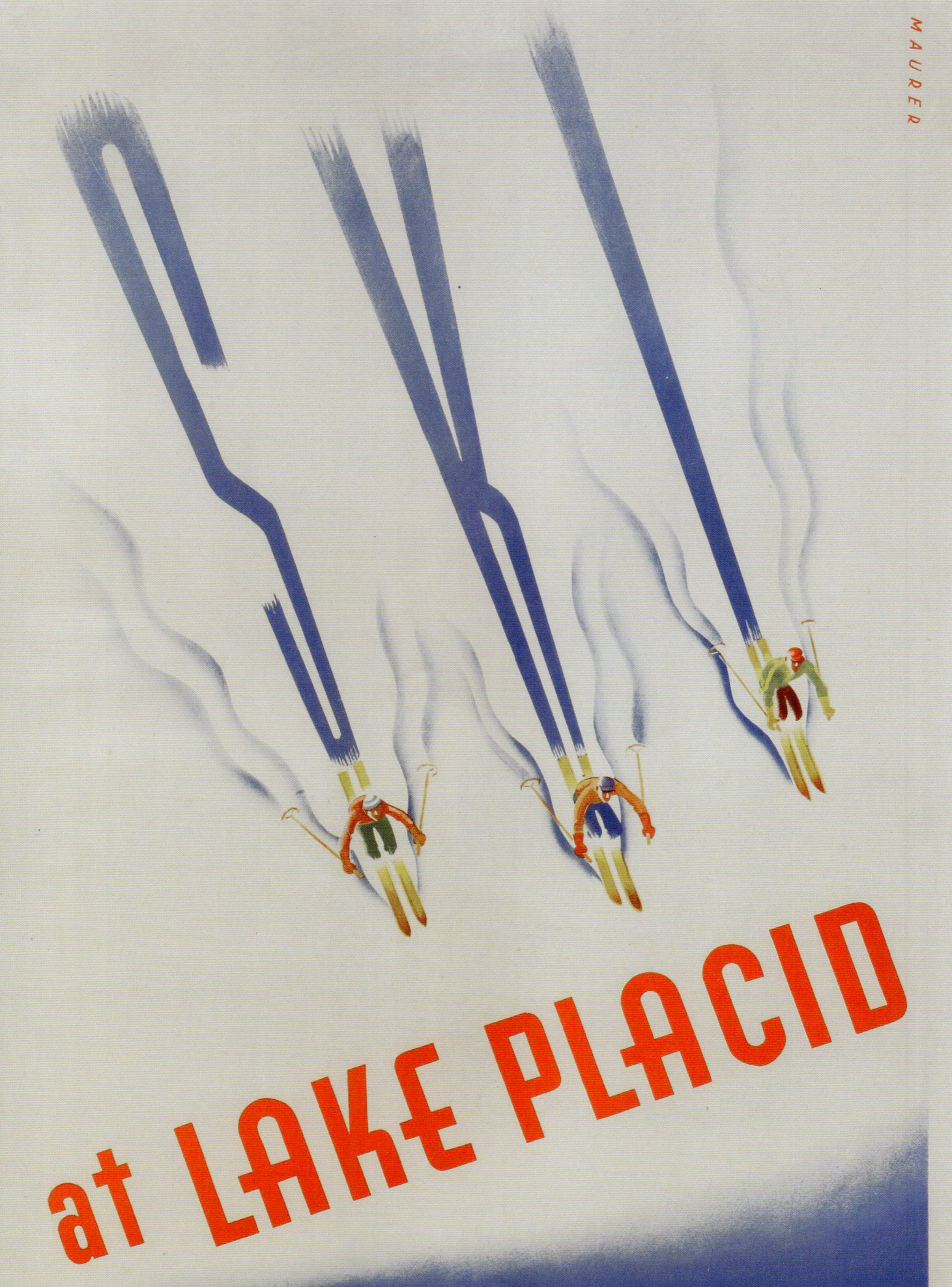

Ski at Lake Placid, 1938
Sascha Maurer (1897–1961)
25 x 18 inches (63.5 x 45.7 cm)
Printer unknown

Sascha Maurer's poster advertising Lake Placid, the New York State winter sports hot spot tucked into the Adirondack Mountains, is as easily understood as it is brilliant—a towering vantage point allows the viewer to peer down upon a trio of skiers carving the name of their favorite pastime into the snow as they roar down the mountain. The text at the bottom identifies the location, and with that the impressive simplicity of the design is complete. Although this poster takes a far less iconographic approach than is evident in the Witold Gordon poster for the third Winter Olympics in Lake Placid (page 118)—there, Gordon uses an in-flight ski jumper set against a globe to convey a sense of worldwide focus on the village—both designs make it abundantly and immediately clear that Lake Placid is *the* superior destination for winter sporting activity.

National and State Parks, ca. 1934
Dorothy Waugh (1896–1996)
40 x 27¼ inches (101.6 x 69.2 cm)
U.S. Government Printing Office, Washington, D.C.

The Works Projects Administration, called the Works Progress Administration until 1939, was a New Deal agency that attempted to jump-start the economy during the Great Depression by funding various activities with federal grants. Created by Franklin Delano Roosevelt's presidential order, the WPA employed millions of people and affected almost every locality in the United States until Congress and the wartime economic boom of 1943 shut down the initiative. Dorothy Waugh designed at least sixteen posters for the WPA, each of which promoted the year-round fun to be had in national and state parks around the country. This and the poster above right focus specifically on wintertime recreational activities. Here a dynamic central constructivist figure stoically publicizes the "four *S*'s" of winter fun. Although Waugh tended to use a subdued color scheme in the majority of her WPA works, this poster is awash in vibrant, warm hues. The clear implication is that even though skiing, skating, sliding, and sleighing are cold-weather activities, the action in the country's national and state parks is definitely hot.

National and State Parks: Winter Sports, ca. 1934
Dorothy Waugh (1896–1996)
40 x 27 inches (101.6 x 68.6 cm)
U.S. Government Printing Office, Washington, D.C.

Dorothy Waugh's design touting the wonders of winter sports activities in America's national and state parks focuses on a pair of enthusiasts whose love of cold weather and cross-country skiing appears to have literally turned them into snow people—an unadorned, strikingly simple approach that elevates the figures to the status of iconic art deco sculptures. The national parks system was born in 1872, when President Ulysses S. Grant established Yellowstone National Park, the nation's first. Today, the United States has fifty-nine national parks.

TRAVEL AND TOURISM

Historic National Parks and Monuments, ca. 1934
Dorothy Waugh (1896–1996)
40 x 27 inches (101.6 x 68.6 cm)
U.S. Government Printing Office, Washington, D.C.

This Dorothy Waugh design is literally striped with suggestions intended to persuade the American populace to visit the nation's historic national parks and monuments. The all-American color scheme of red, white, and blue makes it impossible to ignore the patriotic feel of the message. However, this poster's "stars" don't represent the states in the union; rather, in classic bust form, they represent the individuals who helped form the union, including Davy Crockett, Robert E. Lee, Abraham Lincoln, George Washington, and Captain John Smith. Each figure is associated with a park or monument—Davy Crockett with his birthplace near Limestone, Tennessee; Robert E. Lee with his memorial in Virginia's Arlington National Cemetery; Lincoln with his birthplace in Hodgenville, Kentucky; George Washington with his birthplace in Westmoreland County, Virginia; and Captain John Smith with the first permanent English settlement in North America at Jamestown, Virginia. It's a wonderful historic document, but more than anything it's a spectacular synthesis of styles—the conventional busts set against a gently undulating background that in turn contrasts with the bold art deco lettering. It's modernism in the service of tradition—and vice versa.

Internationale Verkehrs-und Turistik Ausstellung: Poznań, 1930
Janusz Alchimowicz (n.d.)
35 x 23¼ inches (88.9 x 59.1 cm)
F. K. Ziółkowski, Poznań

Planes, trains, and automobiles carry the workload in this German-language version of Janusz Alchimowicz's poster for an international transportation and tourism exhibition in Poznań, Poland. A silhouetted globe unobtrusively hugs the right-hand margin to indicate the international nature of the event. Once more it's difficult not to notice Cassandre's influence on this generation of graphic designers. With geometric precision and without clutter, a clearly defined field of color and curvilinear accents concisely convey the message and create strong visual appeal. Poznań is one of the oldest cities in Poland and an important center of trade, education, and industry. Since 1925, Poznań, which has the most extensive exhibition and conference facilities in Poland, has hosted multiple international trade fairs, a tradition that continues to this day.

Marseille: Point de Départ de la Côte d'Azur, ca. 1929
Roger Broders (1883–1953)
39⅜ x 24¾ inches (100 x 62.9 cm)
Imprimerie Lucien Serre et Cie., Paris

The message here is that the Marseilles rail terminal is the departure point for the PLM (Paris à Lyon et à la Méditerranée; see *La Route Bleue,* page 305) open-air motor coach service to other destinations along the Côte d'Azur. The sleek simplification of forms, and the way the angled text serves as the "road" up which the car and train travel out of the tunnel and toward the sea ahead of them, make for a powerful Machine Age design, one in which Cassandre's influence is apparent. It is interesting to compare this Broders poster to the one Arduino Colato created for an Italian travel company's round-trip motor excursions around Italy's Lake Garda (right). Both posters have a similar composition: vehicles emerge from a tunnel into a landscape featuring a body of water and mountains in the distance. But whereas the Colato design focuses as much on speed and automotive excitement as it does on the scenery, Broders's promotion overflows with a sense of ease and open spaces—an advertisement for the power of relaxation as much as for travel.

Garda Seerundfahrten: Bonomini-Verona, 1932
Arduino Colato (1880–1954)
55 x 39¼ inches (139.7 x 99.7 cm)
F.I.C.I.S., Milano

This is the German-language version of a poster produced for the Bonomini travel company of Verona to promote their round-trip motor excursions around Italy's largest lake—Lake Garda, a body of water located approximately midway between Venice to the east and Milan to the west. In this poster, the speeding Bonomini tour bus emerges from a tunnel like a bullet into a landscape of carefully graded colors and contrasting angles. It's a clever concept, one that holds the promise of both Italian alpine beauty and automotive excitement. The design was printed in several languages and was also used as the cover for

St Jean de-Luz, 1928
Robert Mallet-Stevens (1886–1945)
63 x 47½ inches (160 x 120.6 cm)
H. Chachoin, Paris

Robert Mallet-Stevens was France's most influential modernist architect between the wars. He designed the La Pergola casino complex in Saint-Jean-de-Luz, the central feature of this poster—the only poster Mallet-Stevens is believed to have created. In addition to the casino, La Pergola included elegant stores on the ground floor, a movie theater, and a hotel called the Atlantic. Its design, like that of many other examples of early modernist architecture, was influenced by the shapes and curves of the ocean liners of the period. Compared to the poster by Louis Floutier (right), this advertisement for the resort commune in the Basque Country of southwestern France takes passersby into the seaside environment from the opposite end of the esplanade. While the two posters depict almost exactly identical pieces of real estate, Mallet-Stevens simplifies matters even further than Floutier does, setting his scene with fields of flat, vivid colors—except for the sky, which slowly grades from white to blue. Also of note is the execution of the flower boxes, which pop like pixelated blocks of intense color in a manner not dissimilar to digital photography.

St Jean de Luz: Chemins de Fer du Midi, 1928
Louis Floutier (1882–1936)
41 x 30 inches (104.1 x 76.2 cm)
H. Chachoin, Paris

In order to promote the Chemins de Fer du Midi (French southern rail system) service to Saint-Jean-de-Luz, Louis Floutier created a lovely sun-baked seaside panorama that incorporates the town's sandy bay, the coral-tinted peak of Larrun—the mountain at the western end of the Pyrenees, on the border between France and Spain—and La Pergola, the resort and casino complex completed in 1924. While this rare poster's vibrant yet subdued color scheme and exacting geometric composition ensure that the viewer's gaze travels directly from the poster's largest flower box to its mountainous horizon, Floutier's esplanade, composed of interlocking geometric shapes, collage-style floral arrangements, and beachgoers, is especially worthy of mention. La Pergola is still in existence today, but as is the case with Saint-Tropez's Latitude 43 (see pages 298–299), it has been converted into an apartment building.

Latitude 43: St Tropez, 1932
Georges-Henri Pingusson (1894–1978)
31 x 46¾ inches (78.7 x 118.7 cm)
H. Chachoin, Paris

The text at the bottom of this poster advertises the opening of a new luxury hotel on the French Riviera—Saint-Tropez's Latitude 43, home to more than one hundred rooms, many with their own bathrooms, and a sports complex that included two pools and four tennis courts. The artwork, however, barely calls attention to the structure, which is represented here as a series of parallel lines and four stacked circles tidily placed into the background hills overlooking the Bay of Saint-Tropez. Instead, the artist chooses to focus on a schooner approaching the town—which, not coincidentally, is located at 43° latitude—an intriguing vantage point made somewhat turbulent by the interplay between the peaked geometry of swelling waves and the angles created by the linear rigging of the vessel upon which the viewer rides. This unusual on-deck perspective becomes a bit more comprehensible once it's revealed that French architect and urban planner Georges-Henri Pingusson also happens to be the individual who designed Latitude 43. Pingusson tended to work in what he called the Style Paquebot ("steamship style"), an approach he developed based on Le Corbusier's idea that a cruise ship is like a floating apartment building. In fact, the bright white Latitude 43, with its slightly off-kilter angles, neatly stacked floors, and rounded edges, gives off the appearance of a docked ocean liner rather than a hotel. Built completely of hollow, reinforced-concrete bricks, Latitude 43 opened its doors on July 14, 1932.

Ouverture: Latitude 43, 1936
Georges-Henri Pingusson (1894–1978)
28¼ x 20¾ inches (71.7 x 52.7 cm)
H. Chachoin, Paris

In this Pingusson design it appears as if he's discarded Latitude 43 altogether and simply presented the viewer with the mast, rigging, and sail of a schooner backed by a cloudless blue sky. However, as the eye grows accustomed to the ship, one notices that it's also a cleverly conceived cubist construct that provides a stylized map of the Saint-Tropez coastline with Latitude 43's location pinpointed on the left-hand side. The right-hand side of the design features the minimalist line drawing of Latitude 43 seen in Pingusson's poster for the hotel from four years earlier (above) as well as a depiction of the bay and the hotel's surroundings. Although Latitude 43 is considered one of the emblematic structures of the modern movement in architecture, it was operated as a hotel for only a few seasons: in 1937, the owners declared bankruptcy, and during the Second World War, the armies of France, Italy, the United States, and Germany successively occupied the building. Between 1945 and 1947, it served as a convalescent home for former concentration camp prisoners. In 1992, when it was declared a historic landmark, its facade was completely restored to resemble its appearance at the completion of its original construction in 1932.

Latitude 43, in Saint-Tropez, was converted from a hotel into an apartment building in 1948. Georges-Henri Pingusson designed not only the building itself but also the interiors and the staff uniforms.

CHEMINS DE FER BELGES

OSTENDE-DOUVRES
3 HEURES DE TRAVERSEE

LES CRÉATIONS PUBLICITAIRES 27 BOULEVARD DE DIXMUDE BRUXELLES

Ostende-Douvres, ca. 1938
Léo Marfurt (1894–1977)
49½ x 29½ inches (125.7 x 74.9 cm)
Les Créations Publicitaires, Bruxelles

Léo Marfurt was far and away the most innovative graphic artist in Belgium between the world wars. This beautiful and rare poster was commissioned by the Belgian national railroad—Société Nationale des Chemins de Fer Belges, which began operation in 1926—to promote the company's ferry service from the port city of Ostend, in the province of West Flanders, to the British port of Dover (Douvres). Ostend is the largest city on the Belgian North Sea coast and is noted for its seaside resorts. Dover, renowned for its chalk cliffs, is located in Kent, in southeastern England, and today claims to be the busiest passenger port in the world, handling sixteen million travelers annually. Marfurt glamorizes the three-hour crossing over the English Channel through his expertly portrayed figures of stylized, colorful, and elegantly dressed passengers and staff as they board the waiting ferry. Belgium was the first European country to adopt rail service, in 1834; ferry crossings between Ostend and Dover began in 1846, but were discontinued when the Eurotunnel opened in 1994. Ferries still operate between Calais and Dunkirk, in France, and Dover.

Mar del Plata, ca. 1930
Scotti (n.d.)
43¼ x 29 inches (109.8 x 73.7 cm)
Gráfico Argentino, Buenos Aires

Whereas the artist Pachelo used an art deco beach to set the scene for Mar del Plata's 1933 Copa Emilio Saint (see page 176), Scotti presents us here with a trio of art deco–inspired beachgoers to personify the three elements that have made the "great seaside resort" one of South America's most popular getaway destinations: plentiful deep-sea fishing opportunities, urban sophistication, and a thriving beach scene. Situated on the Atlantic coast some 249 miles to the south of Buenos Aires, Mar del Plata—which literally means "silver sea"—was founded on February 10, 1874, by Argentine businessman and landowner Patricio Peralta Ramos (1814–1887). In addition to its abundant tourist offerings, Mar del Plata is also home to the National University of Mar del Plata. This very rare and stunning poster was designed for the Argentine Association of Advertising and Promotion.

Bermuda in 5 Hours, 1937
Paul George Lawler (n.d.)
41¼ x 27 inches (104.8 x 68.6 cm)
Imprimerie Arts Graphiques, Nancy

Six hundred and forty miles southeast of Cape Hatteras, North Carolina, one finds the British island territory of Bermuda, which during the early part of the twentieth century became a popular destination for wealthy American, British, and Canadian tourists. Its subtropical climate and proximity to the eastern coastline of the United States made it an ideal getaway, thanks to the frequent steamboat crossings that serviced the island. However, once air service was established to Bermuda in the mid-1930s, tourism really began to escalate. In June of 1937, Pan American Airways and Imperial Airways inaugurated joint service to Bermuda departing from Norfolk, Virginia. Pan American flew Sikorsky S-40 Caribbean Clipper flying boats (amphibious aircraft), while Imperial used the C class Short Empire flying boat RMA *Cavalier* to deliver its passengers. It is this service that the artist extols, while also depicting the friendly response of the swimmers and sunbathers to the plane overhead, which is passing so close that it casts a giant shadow upon the surf below.

Soviet Armenia, ca. 1929
Anonymous
35¼ x 24¾ inches (89.5 x 62.9 cm)
Printer unknown

One does not naturally think of art deco glamour when imagining the satellite countries within the Soviet Union. But in this poster, Intourist, formerly the Soviet Union's official state-run travel agency, brings Gatsbyesque drama to the newly christened capital of the Armenian Soviet Socialist Republic. In a matter of just a few decades, Yerevan grew from a town of a few thousand residents to a bustling metropolis of more than a million, becoming the cultural and intellectual center of the country. While the town peppering the background may appear sleepy and small next to Mount Ararat, the towering overpass, speeding train, and sleek vehicle in the foreground bathe the city in a glow of modernity.

Dunkerque: Chemin de Fer du Nord, ca. 1930
Roger Broders (1883–1953)
39½ x 25 inches (100.3 x 63.5 cm)
Imprimerie Lucien Serre et Cie., Paris

During the period between the two world wars, Roger Broders was considered the finest designer of European art deco travel posters. His style could vary dramatically, ranging from realistic sun-splashed representations of mountain ranges to stylized depictions of fashion plates who appear to have stepped from the pages of *Vogue*. Broders's sole and very rare design for the Compagnie des Chemins de Fer du Nord railway service to Dunkirk, a small town on the shore of the North Sea at the northernmost tip of France, is something of a combination of these styles. The chic couple in the foreground, arriving at Dunkirk's port, are definitely *en vogue*, but they are also essentially two-dimensional. However, as we allow our gaze to venture deeper into the poster, the features of the landscape, such as the freestanding belfry and town hall, become more realistic and substantial, befitting a town so steeped in history. Dunkirk began life as a humble fishing village in the eighth century, but by the sixteenth century had become a haven for the pirates and privateers who pillaged ships in the North Sea. Although it would eventually evolve into a major international port and industrial center, it also became a popular seaside resort, primarily because of the town's impressive dunes.

La Route Bleue, 1929
A. M. Cassandre (Adolphe Mouron, 1901–1968)
39 x 24½ inches (99.1 x 62.2 cm)
Imprimerie de Léonard Danel, Paris and Lille

The Route Bleue was the luxury bus service operated by the PLM railway (Compagnie des Chemins de Fer de Paris à Lyon et à la Méditerranée), which connected London to the French Riviera via Paris (courtesy of a cross-Channel ferry) and Lyon. This extremely rare English-language version of Cassandre's design for the Route Bleue uses precision and geometry to convey the fascination of the journey to passersby. The focal point of the poster is the setting sun on the horizon at the end of a tree-lined allée. The viewer gets a real feeling of motion, as if he or she is seated on the bus and the trees are flying by. The spaces between the trees could even be the bus's windows. This is a spectacular example of travel advertising that

Passersby gather to read public notices below billboard-size posters on a busy street—a not uncommon sight in 1930s Paris.

ACKNOWLEDGMENTS

IT WOULD HAVE BEEN IMPOSSIBLE for me to amass the collection that lies at the heart of this book without the help of many people who facilitated the process along the way. Specifically, my gratitude goes out to the following auctioneers: Jack Rennert and Terry Shargel at Poster Auctions International, who also provided a few photographs for this book; Sophie Churcher and Nicolette Tomkinson at Christie's; Kristina Goodstadt and Nicholas Lowry at Swann Galleries; Guido Toen at Plakatauktion in Zurich; Udo Boersma at Van Sabben Poster Auctions in Hoorn; Joern Weigelt at Poster Connection in Clayton, California; Maurizio Piumatti at Bolaffi in Turin; Xavier Llach Moreno at Soler y Llach Subastas Internacionales in Barcelona; Frederic Lozada at Frederic Lozada in Paris; Florence Camard at Camard et Associés in Paris; and Patrick Bogue at Onslows Auctioneers in London.

In addition, I am grateful to several dealers who provided their assistance: Jim Lapides at the International Poster Gallery in Boston; Mickey Ross at the Ross Art Group in New York City; Mark Weinbaum at Mark J. Weinbaum Fine Posters and Prints in New York City; George Sells at Omnibus Galleries in Aspen; Eric Kellenberger in Geneva; Jean-Daniel Clerc at Galerie 123 in Geneva; Josef Lebovic at the Josef Lebovic Gallery in Sydney; Gail Chisholm at the Gail Chisholm Gallery in New York City; Nancy and Morris Steinbock at Nancy Steinbock Posters in Chestnut Hill, Massachusetts; Tony Singer at Vintage Auto Posters in Carmel Valley, California; and Burkhard Sülzen in Berlin.

As with my poster collection, this book wouldn't have been possible without the helpful efforts of several skilled professionals. Many thanks to Hiroaki Shigeta; Susanne Giezendanner at the Museum für Gestaltung, Zurich; Jerry Johnson; and my dear friend Colleen Hess, who found one of the rarest posters in my collection. My thanks also to Alain Weill, one of the world's leading poster experts, for his help and guidance, and to Rene Wanner of PosterPage.ch, who keeps the world abreast of important poster news through his website. I'm also grateful to Angelina Lippert, an art historian and specialist at Poster Auctions International, and Tim Gadzinski, a poster expert and former Poster Auctions International associate, both of whom provided essential assistance with the writing. Thank you to Michael Brown, who helped with research, managing the inventory of images, and myriad other tasks; Barbara Clark, who edited the text; Russell Hassell, who initially connected me with the right people at Vendome, created the book design, and shepherded the project through to completion; Robert Walch, who photographed the posters; Philip Reeser, who handled photo research; and Alastair Duncan, whose insightful introduction puts the collection in valuable historical perspective. Finally, I'd like to express my appreciation to the staff at Vendome, especially its chairman, Alexis Gregory, and its president, Mark Magowan.

—W.W.C.

BIBLIOGRAPHY

Belvès, Pierre. *100 ans d'affiches des chemins de fer.* Paris: Éditions NM-La Vie du Rail, 1980.

Brown, Robert K., and Susan Reinhold. *The Poster Art of A. M. Cassandre.* New York: E. P. Dutton, 1979.

Cadringher, Gabriel, and Anne Weallans. *Affiches des compagnies maritimes.* Paris: Citadelles & Mazenod, 2008.

Camard, Florence, and Christophe Zagrodzki. *Le train à l'affiche: les plus belles affiches ferroviaires française.* Paris: La Vie du Rail, 1989.

Cassandre, A. M. *A. M. Cassandre.* Paris: ADAGP (Société des Auteurs dans les Arts Graphiques et Plastiques); Tokyo: BCF (Bureau des copyrights français), 1991. Catalog of the exhibition held at the Tokyo Metropolitan Teien Art Museum, Tokyo, Japan, June 2–July 14, 1991.

Celant, Germano. *Marcello Nizzoli.* Milano: Edizioni di Comunità, 1968.

Cole, Beverly, and Richard Durack. *Railway Posters: 1923–1947.* New York: Rizzoli International Publications, 1992.

Crouse, William W. *Grand Prix Automobile de Monaco Posters—The Complete Collection: The Art, the Artists, and the Competition, 1929-2009.* New York: William W. Crouse, 2009.

Dailey, Victoria, and Steve Turner. *Danish Posters 1910–1940.* Los Angeles: William Dailey Antiquarian Books, 1988.

Duncan, Alastair. *Art Deco Complete: The Definitive Guide to the Decorative Arts of the 1920s and 1930s.* New York: Abrams, 2009.

Edelstein, Teri J., ed. *Art for All: British Posters for Transport.* New Haven: Yale University Press, 2010. Catalog of the exhibition held at the Yale Center for British Art, New Haven, Connecticut, May 27–August 15, 2010; at the Musée de l'Imprimerie, Lyon, France, October 15, 2010–February 13, 2011; and at the Wolfsonian-Florida International University, Miami Beach, Florida, April 15–August 14, 2011.

Eurelectric. *European Electricity: Flashback on a Momentous Era, Spotlight on an Exciting Future.* Brussels: Eurelectric, 2007.

Green, Oliver. *Art for the London Underground.* New York: Rizzoli, 1990.

Gregory, Alexis. *The Golden Age of Travel: 1880–1939.* London: Cassell, 1998.

Hartmann, Gérard, and Françoise Leloup-Perier. *Affiches de l'histoire d'aviation* (with English-language insert: *The History of Aviation in Posters*). Paris: Citadelles & Mazenod, 2009.

Haworth-Booth, Mark. *E. McKnight Kauffer: A Designer and His Public.* London: Gordon Fraser, 1979.

Hutchison, Harold F. *London Transport Posters.* London: London Transport Board, 1963.

Kauffer, E. McKnight, ed. *The Art of the Poster: Its Origin, Evolution & Purpose.* London: Cecil Palmer, 1924.

Kauffer, E. McKnight, *Memorial Exhibition of the Work of E. McKnight Kauffer, Born Montana 1890, Died New York 1954: October to November 1955.* London: Percy Lund, Humphries & Co., 1955. Catalog of the exhibition at the Victoria and Albert Museum.

———. *Posters by E. McKnight Kauffer.* Foreword by Aldous Huxley. New York: Museum of Modern Art, 1937. Catalog of the exhibition at the Museum of Modern Art, New York, 1937.

Kery, Patricia Frantz. *Art Deco Graphics.* New York: Harry N. Abrams, 1986.

Levey, Michael F., ed. *London Transport Posters.* Oxford: Phaidon Press, 1976.

Lopez, Emmanuel. *Affiches de l'automobile.* Paris: Citadelles & Mazenod, 2011.

Masutani, Yoko. *Every Face of the Great Master Cassandre.* Tokyo: Suntory Museum, 1995. Catalog of the exhibition held at the Suntory Museum, Osaka, Japan, June–August, 1995.

Mouron, Henri. *A. M. Cassandre.* New York: Rizzoli, 1985.

Pétry-Parisot, Claude. *Paul Colin et les spectacles.* Nancy: Musée des Beaux-Arts, 1994. Catalog of the exhibition at the Musée des Beaux-Arts, Nancy, May 2–July 31, 1994.

Remington, R. Roger, and Barbara Hodik. *Nine Pioneers in American Graphic Design.* Cambridge, Mass.: The MIT Press, 1989.

Remington, R. Roger, and Mark Resnick. *The American Image: U.S. Posters from the 19th to the 21st Century.* Rochester, NY: RIT Cary Graphic Arts Press, 2007. Catalog of the posters from the Mark and Maura Resnick Collection at the Rochester Institute of Technology, Rochester, New York.

Rennert, Jack. *100 Posters of Paul Colin.* New York: Images Graphiques, 1977.

———. *Cappiello: The Posters of Leonetto Cappiello.* New York: Poster Art Library, Posters Please, Inc., 2004.

Rennie, Paul. *Modern British Posters: Art, Design & Communication.* London: Black Dog Publishing, 2010.

Réunion des Musée Nationaux. *Quand l'affiche faisait de la rèclame! L'affiche française de 1920 à 1940. Musée national des arts et traditions populaires, 12 novembre 1991–3 février 1992.* Paris: Réunion des Musée Nationaux, 1991. Catalog of an exhibition organized by the Réunion des Musées Nationaux and the Musée National des Arts et Traditions Populaires of posters selected from the collection of the Musée de la Publicité.

Rothschild, Deborah, Ellen Lupton, and Darra Goldstein. *Graphic Design in the Mechanical Age: Selections from the Merrill C. Berman Collection.* New Haven: Yale University Press, 1998.

Sauvage, Anne-Marie. *A. M. Cassandre: oeuvres graphiques modernes, 1923–1939.* Paris: Bibliothèque Nationale de France, 2005. Catalog of the exhibition at Chaumont, May 21–July 23, 2005, and the Bibliothèque Nationale de France, Paris, September 20–December 4, 2005.

State Historical Society of Iowa. "Ellen Church: The Flying Nurse." *The Goldfinch* 2, no. 1 (September 1980).

Timmers, Margaret. *The Power of the Poster.* London: Victoria and Albert Museum, 1998. Catalog of the exhibition at the Victoria and Albert Museum, London, April 2–July 26, 1998.

Vergani, Guido. *Thirty Years and a Century of the Campari Company.* 3 vols. Milan: Davide Campari, 1900.

Weill, Alain. *Affiches art deco.* Paris: Inter-Livres, 1990.

———. *Cassandre.* Paris: Bibliothèque de l'Image, 2005.

———. *Retrospective Jean Carlu.* Paris: Musée de l'Affiche, 1980. Catalog of the exhibition at the Musée de l'Affiche, Paris, November 26, 1980–March 29, 1981.

Weill, Alain, and Israel Perry. *Roger Broders: Travel Posters.* New York: Queen Art Publishers, 2002.

Weill, Alain, and Jack Rennert. *Paul Colin: affichiste.* Paris: Éditions Denoël, 1989.

Weill, Alain, and Hiroshi Unno. *Graphiques d'Art Deco: affiches de 1920s.* Tokyo: Art Life, 1983. Catalog of the exhibition held in Tokyo, 1983.

Wlassikoff, Michel. *Histoire du graphisme en France.* Paris: Museé des Arts Décoratifs, 2005.

Zega, Michael E., and John E. Gruber. *Travel by Train: The American Railroad Poster, 1870-1950.* Bloomington: Indiana University Press, 2002.

INDEX

Italic page numbers refer to illustrations.

Acebo, Javier Gómez, 172
Aeroput Jugoslavija, *25*
Air Union, *26, 27*
Ala Littoria, *16*
Albi, Grand Prix, *169*
Alchimowicz, Janusz, 292
Alexeieff, Alexandre, 12, *247, 248, 249*
Alfa Romeo, 163
Allentown Air Meet, *37*
Allgemeiner Deutscher Automobil-Club (ADAC), *182*
Alliance Graphique, 11
Amsterdam RAI (De Rijwiel-Automobile Industrie), *67*
Anderson, John Stewart, 91
Andrieu, F., *169*
Andry-Farcy, Pierre, 104
Anton, Ottomar, 27, 244
Antwerp
    Waasland Tunnel, *282*
    World Port and Art City, *283*
Armenia, Soviet, *303*
Armsheimer, 120
Au Bûcheron, *139*
Austin Motor Company, *56*
Austin Reed, 133, *152*
Australia
    Great Barrier Reef, *278*
    Sunshine and Surf, *277*
    Surf Club, *276*
    Train to the seaside, *280–281*
Australian National Travel Association, 279
Automobile Club d'Auvergne, *170*
Automobile Club de France, Grand Prix, *168*
Automoto motorcycle, *63*
Automovil Club Argentino (ACA), *176*
Auto Union, 163
Auvigne, Jean, 225

Baker, Josephine, 11
Bakst, Léon, 8, *8*
Bal Fleuri, Le, *156*
Balla, Giacomo, 11, *11*
Ballets Russes, 8, *8*
Barberis, Franco, 153
Barbier, George, 8
Barcelona, Autodromo, *172*
Barcelona World's Fair (1929), 101
Batavier Line, *235*
Baumberger, Otto, 15, 34, 69
Beall, Lester T., 71, 84
Beckman, Anders, 15, 18, 21
Belfast Steamship Company, *232*
Benito, Edouard García, 8
Benton, M. F., 10
Berény, Róbert, 218
Beristain, 133, *140, 141, 142*
Berlin Jewelry Week, Trage Schmuck du Gewinnst show, *154*
Bernard, Francis, 15, 112

Bernhard, Lucian, 110
Besson, J., 29
Bicicletas Orbea, *129*
Binder, Joseph, 109
Blackbird Revue, The, 157
Boeing Air Transport, 15
Bofarull, Jacint, 141, 142
Bolales, J., 66
Bonfils, Robert, 8
Bonomini, *295*
Bortnyik, Sándor, 217
Bosio & Caratsch, *204*
Bouillon Kub, *212–213*
BP (British Petroleum), *92*
Brée, 36
Broders, Roger, 273, 294, 304
Brodovitch, Alexey, 48, 239
Brown, George Massiot, 195
Brunelleschi, Umberto, 8
Budapest, Grand Prix, *171*
Budapest, Thermal Baths, *286, 287*
Bugatti, 11, *55*, 163
Bühler, Fritz, 32

Calvados, *195*
Campari, 189, *190*, 191
Campeonato Abierto de Basket-Ball, *115*
Campeonato Mundial de Football, *114*
Campionati del Mondo di Ciclismo, *130*
Candee & Company, *153*
Cap (artist), 242
Cappiello, Leonetto, 9, 104, 189, 211
Cardinaux, Alfred, 46
Carlu, Jean, 9, 11, 15, 25, 71, 74, 160
Caroselli, 114
Cassandre, A. M. (Adolphe Mouron), 9, 10, 11, 12, *12*, 15, 29, 43, 66, 71, 78, 89, 96, 103, 116, 129, 139, 151, 189, 197, 203, 206, 207, 225, 242, 247, 251, 255, 256, 273, 304
Cavallero, Steph, 22
Cenni, Renato, 244
Chavepeyer, Albert, 65
Chelini, Franco, 127
Chemins de Fer Belges, 12, *300*
Chemins de Fer de l'État (France), 12, *259*
Chéret, Jules, 9
Chevrolet, *47*
Chicago World's Fair (1933), 101
Chrysler, *44, 45*
Church, Ellen, 15
Claussen, C., 234
Codognato, Plinio, 52
Colato, Arduino, 294
Colin, Paul, 9, 11, 133, 135, 156, 158, 189, 220
Compagnie Aérienne Française (CAF), 11, *24*
Compagnie des Chemins de fer de Paris à Lyon et à la Méditerranée, *305*
Compagnie des Chemins de Fer du Nord, *256, 257, 304*
Compagnie Générale Aéropostale, *28*
    Flèche d'Argent service, *29*
Compagnie Générale Transatlantique (CGT), *225*
Concentrum, *93*
Cooper, Austin, 12, 112
Coppa di Ferro del Duce: Regata Universitaria, *127*
Cora, *205*
Cortina d'Ampezzo, *288*
Corva, Urbana, 244

Cosulich Line, *243*
Coupe Davis, *117*
Coupe du Monde, FIFA, *116*
Créations Publicitaires, Les, 12
Crociera Aerea del Decennale, *38*
Cunard Line, *238*
Cunard White Star line, *239*
Cuneo (Italy), 3 Corsa Automobilistica, *177*
Cycles Brillant, *128*
Cycles Dilecta, *129*

Daily Herald, *102*
Dänischen Staatsbahnen (Danish railways), *260*
Dartmouth Winter Carnival, *120*
Davos (Switzerland), swimming pool, *285*
Delahaye, *58*, 163
Delval, Henri, 167
De Roeck, Lucien, 282
Desmé, D. H., 116
De Soto, 131
Deutsche Zeppelin-Reederei (DZR), *27*
de Valerio, Roger, 43, 44
Diaghilev, Sergei, 8
Diggelmann, Alex, 123
di Lazzaro, Umberto, 15, 17, 38
Diulgheroff, Nicolay, 106, 204
Dolbeau, 40
Dolder Kunsteisbahn, *122*
Donnet automobiles, *49*
Dubonnet, 189, 197, *198–202*
Duncan, Lisa (Elisabeth Milker), 133, *159*

Earhart, Amelia, 15
East Asiatic Company, *234*
Eastern Ski Championships, 120, *121*
Eckersley, Tom, 91
École des Beaux-Arts, Paris, 11
Egersdorfer, M., *265*
Eiropas Meistarsacīkstēs: Ātrslidošanā, *123*
Eisenwerk Clus, *98*
Empress of Britain, 241
Engelhard, Julius Ussy, 183
Erlinger, M., 234
Erma, 170
Ernst, Otto, 44
Étoile du Nord, 12, *255*
Exposition de l'Habitation, *112*

Fabrique Nationale (FN), *64, 65, 174*
Falcucci, Robert, 163, *164*
Favre, Georges, 94, 129
Femina magazine, 11
Fête Aviation
    Essey, *36*
    Nancy, *36*
Fiat, *52, 53*
Fix-Masseau, Pierre, 258
Floutier, Louis, 297
Fokina, Vera, 8
Fokine, Michel, *8*
Fontanet, Noël, 163, 185, 189, 195
Ford, V-8 engine, *46*
French Air Force, *36*
French Tobacco, *221*

Gaba, *78*
Galeries Barbès, *136*
Garmisch-Partenkirchen, *183*
Garretto, Paolo Federico, 92
Gellé Frères, *75*
General Motors, *47*
General Post Office (Britain), *106*
Geneva Grand Prix, *184*
Gerster, Károly, 170
Giornata del Prodotto Italiano, *99*
Gold Starry, 12, *72, 73*
Gorde, Gaston, 92
Gordon, Witold, 119
Gordon Bennett Cup, *32, 33*
Görey, Íhap Hulusi, 25
Grand Palais, 9
Grand-Sport, *150, 151*
Greif (artist), 51
Gris, Juan, *11*
Gronowski, Tadeusz, 32

Hamburg America Line, *244*
Havinden, Ashley, 51
Hengelosche Electrische en Mechanische Apparaten Fabriek (Heemaf), *96*
Herrick, Frederick C., 241
Hindenburg, 27
Historic National Parks and Monuments (USA), *292*
Hitler, Adolf, 9, 69
Holland America Line, *226, 228, 233*
Hydrogazo, *93*

Icart, Louis, 11
Illustration, L', 11
Imperial Airways, *22, 23, 302*
International Advertising Association, Reklame Schau, *110*
International Automobile and Motorcycle Exhibition, Berlin, *69*
International Auto Show, Milan, *66*
International Aviation Meeting
    Plzeň (Czech Republic), *39*
    Zürich, *35*
Internationale Hygiene Ausstellung, *77*
Internationale Tentoonstelling Klank en Beeld, *110*
International Transportation and Tourism Exhibition, Poland, *293*
Italian Aerial Lines, *17*
Italian Line, *244*

JH (monogram), 38
Joanethis, T. H., 120

Kalff, Louis C., 106
Kauffer, Edward McKnight, 12, 15, 22, 31, 71, 103, 106, 247, 266, 268
Keely, Patrick Cokayne, 253
Keimel, Hermann, 110
Keizer, L., 21
Kienast, Eugen, 69
Klausen Pass
    Course Internationale, *180*
    Internationales Klausenrennen, *181*
KLM (Royal Dutch Airlines), 15, *21*
Klotz, Anton, 69
Koelliker, Hermann Alfred, 204
Kraüss, 204
Kurozumi, Toyonosuke, 274

INDEX

Laborde, Guillermo, 114
Laffly, *57*
Lake Placid, New York
  ski resort, *290*
  Winter Olympics, *118*
Latitude 43 (building), Saint-Tropez (France), *298, 299*
Lawler, Paul George, 302
Leibow, Joe, 120
Lenhart, Franz, 218
Lenoble, M., 175
Lepape, Georges, 8
Leroy (optician), 133, *134, 135*
Liestal (Switzerland), swimming pool, *284*
Lindbergh, Charles Augustus, 15
Lloyd Rapide, *261*
Lloyd Sabaudo, *242*
Löbl, Otto, 208
Lombers, Eric, 91
London, Midland & Scottish Railway (LMS), *251*
London and North Eastern Railway, *248, 249, 250*
London Underground, 247, *266–271*
Louis, Robert, 48
Loupot, Charles, 9, 11, 43, 54, 56, 59, 71, 76, 137, 189, 192, 208
Lyra Extra, *215*

Maccabiah Games, 131
Mallet-Stevens, Robert, 297
Mambour, Auguste, 175
Mancioli, Corrado, 131
Manner, Frederick, 247, 270
Mar del Plata (Argentina), *301*
Marfurt, Léo, 12, 273, 282, 301
Marseilles, *294*
Martin, F. J., 63
Marton, Lajos, 135
Massachusetts, Auto Races, *187*
Matter, Herbert, 12, 146
Maurer, Sascha, 273, 291
Maurus, Edmond, 241
Mercedes-Benz, 163
Mezinárodní Letecký (International Aviation Meeting), *39*
Milan International Auto Show, *66*
Mira, *76*
Misr Airlines, *25*
Mistrzosostwo Świata: Krynica, *124*
Mistrzostwa Szermiercze Europy: Championnats D'Europe D'Escrime, *125*
Modiano, *216, 217, 218, 219*
Monaco, Grand Prix, *165*
Mondaini, Giacinto, 66
Monet-Goyon, *60*
Monsavon, 11, *74*
Monte Carlo, Rallye Automobile, *164*
Monvel, Bernard Boutet de, 8
Morach, Otto, 12, 146
Motor Comptoir (Zürich), *68*
Motosacoche, *61*
Mucha, Alphonse, 8
Muenchner Plakat Kunst, *111*
Munich, Bayer Automobil Club, *183*
Musée Galliera, 9
Mussolini, Benito, 9, 163

National and State Parks (USA), *291*
National Championship, Brattleboro, Vermont, *119*
Nationale Luchtvaartschool, *30*
Nazi Party, 163
New York Central Railroad, *263*
New York World's Fair (1939), 101
  Railroads on Parade, *109*
  The World of Tomorrow, *108*
Nice, Grand Prix Automobile de, *166*
Nicolas, *206*
Nilson, Gustav, 119
Nizzoli, Marcello, 12, 43, 60, 65, 189, 191
Nord Express, 12, *254*
Normandie, 12, *224*
Noveltex, *155*

Odéon Records, *161*
Olivier, Jean, 27
Olympiads, 101
Olympic Winter Games, *118*
Ook's Winters per Spoor, *262*
Oriental Tourist Conference, *274*
Orsi, 11–12, 71, 72
Osaka Railways, *275*
Osiecki, Stefan, 12, 125, 127
Owens, Jesse, 101
Oxford Blag's, *160*

Palais de la Nouveauté, *137*
Panchelo, 176
Paris Air Show, *40, 41*
Paris Opéra, 11
Pau Grand Prix Automobile, *167*
Pérot, Roger, 59, 60
Perugina (brand), *211*
Perugina Cup, *179, 180*
Petit Dauphinois, Le, *105*
Petzold, Willy, 76
Peugeot, *59*
Philips (brand), *106*
Pierce-Arrow, *48*
Pingusson, Georges-Henri, 298
Pivolo, *203*
PKZ, 12, 133, *144–146, 147, 148–149*
Planchaërt, M., 36
Plattner, Otto Jacob, 285
Plymouth, *51*
Poiret, Paul, 8, *9, 10, 10*
Pombo, A., 66
Pontiac Six, *50*
Ponty, Max, 63
Portier, Francis, 185
Pozzati, Severo (Sepo), 137, 155
Prentis, Terence, 51
Progrès, Le, *103*
Pullman "Golden Arrow," *264*
Puppo, Mario, 289
Purvis, Tom, 153

Radebaugh, Arthur C., 18
Ragan, Leslie, 109, 247, 262
Ray, Man (Emmanuel Radnitzky), 247, 266
Real, Marc, 220
Regina Palast Hotel, *160*
Reklame Schau (International Advertising Association), 110
Renaud, André, *158*
Revue Black Birds, La, 11, *157*
Riccobaldi del Baza, Giuseppe, 43, 52, 98
Richter, Aladár, 104, 273, 287
Rittmark, Ake, 237

Rodmell, Harry Hudson, 232, 237
Rogers, Alan, 247, 269
Roggero (artist), 56
Römer, Botho von, 183
Römer, Hans von, 183
Roquin, A., 239
Rosen, Fritz, 110
Rotterdam Lloyd, *231*
Rotterdam Zuid Amerika Lyn, *229*
Royal Aero Club, Air Race, *186*
Royal Auto Moto Club du Hainaut (RAMCH), 175
Royal Mail Steam Packet Company (RMSP), *240*
Royal Netherlands Steamship Company, *230*
Ruprecht, Ernst, 34, 163, 181
Rural Electrification Administration, *82–87*, 85

Sabena: Société Anonyme Belge d'Exploitation de la Navigation Aérienne, *20*
Sables-d'Or-les-Pins, *289*
Saint-Jean-de-Luz (France), *296*
  Railway Promotion, *297*
Saint-Tropez (France), Latitude 43 (building), *298, 299*
Salón del Automóvil, *66*
Salon de l'Aviation, *40, 41*
Sandeman, *194*
San Sebastián (Spain), *173*
Santamarta, Máximo Viejo, 172
Sato, *214*
Satomi, Munetsugu, 15, 21, 273, 274
Saturday Evening Post, The, 11
Savignac, Raymond, 163, 169
Savo, *151*
Savoia-Marchetti, *38*
Scandinavian Air Express, *21*
Schlienger, O., 241
Schnackenberg, Walter, 160
Schönholzer, E., 181
Scintilla, *34*
Scot (artist), 167
Scotti (artist), 301
Segrelles, Josep, 172
Sellheim, Gert, *276–278, 279, 280–281*
Seneca, Federico, 178, 189, 211, 217
Severin, Marc Fernand, 160
Severini, Gino, 11
Shea, Jack, 119
Shell, *31, 89, 90*
Shep (Charles Shepherd), 265
Shepard, Otis, 189, 210
Sissa, *204*
Skolimowski, Jerzy, 12, 125, 127
Southern Electric, *252*
Southern Railway (UK), *253*
Soviet Armenia, *303*
Spidoléine, *89*
Spirit of St. Louis, 15
Statendam, 12, *227*
Steinlen, Théophile-Alexandre, 8
Stoecklin, Niklaus, 71, 78, 85, 98, 146
Stout Air Lines, 15
St Raphaël (brand), *192, 193*
Styl'son motorcycle, *62*
Stypiński, Andrzej, 125
Svanlund, Olle, 94
Swedish Air Lines, *18*
Swedish American Line (SAL), *236*
Swedish Lloyd, *237*
Swiss Grand Prix, *185*

Tato (Guglielmo Sansoni), 15, 17
Tejada, Anibal, 129
Ten Broek, Willem Frederick, 12, 229, 232
Theodoro (Theodore Pfeifer), 40, 71, 72
Thomson, Alfred Reginald, 251
Thomson Electric, *97*
Thorpe, Jim, 101
Toulouse-Lautrec, Henri de, 8
Trage Schmuck du Gewinnst (Berlin Jewelry Week), *154*
Trans-Australian Railway, *258*
Trapp, Willy, 285
Trelleborg, *95*
Trieste, Maritime Festival, *245*
Triplex, *79*
Trompf, Percy, 163, 187
Tungsram, *85*
Twinings, *209*

United Air Lines, *19*
United States, posters in, 43
United States Lines, *241*

Vállalatának, *104*
Valvo, *85*
van der Laan, Kees, 12, 31, 262
Van Nelle (brand), *207*
van't Hoff, Adriaan, 226, 229
Vaughan, Edmond, 253
Venna, Lucio, 176
Vera Mint de Ricqlès, *196*, 197
Victoria and Albert Museum, Poster Show, *113*
Victoria Tee, *208*
Vie Parisienne, La, 11
Vincent, René, 11, 43, 54
Voisin automobile, *54*
von Stein, Johann, 230
Vov, 191

Wagula, Hans, 25
Waugh, Dorothy, *107*, 273, 291, 292
Weber, N., 155
Week End, *220*
Weissmuller, Johnny, 101
Wilmink, Machiel, 247, 260
Wioślarkie Mistrzostwa Europy, *126*
World War I, 15
World War II, 163
Wright, Orville, 15
Wrigley's Spearmint, *210*

Yugoslavia, Mustermesse, *265*
Yunge, 91

Zaharias, Babe Didrikson, 101
Zero (Hans Schleger), 270

On the cover
Front: Normandie: Voyage Inaugural, 1935, by A.M. Cassandre.
Back, clockwise from top left: Australia: Surf Club, 1936, by Gert Sellheim; Fête des 21ème et 33ème d'Aviation: Essey, 1935, by Brée; Grande Prix de Suisse, 1938, by Noël Fontanet; Lloyd Rapide, 1927, by Machiel Wilmink.

Pages 4–5: Detail of *Motorists Prefer Shell* by John Stewart Anderson (1936), page 90
Right: Actor Cary Grant on the set of the movie *Holiday* (1938)

Every effort has been made to locate copyright holders of photographs and other imagery included in this book. Credit, if and as available, is provided below. Errors or omissions in credit citations, or failure to obtain permission if required by copyright law, have been either unavoidable or unintentional. The authors, editor, and publisher welcome any information that would allow them to correct future reprints.

Picture credits
All poster photography © William W. Crouse, 2013; Opposite p. 1, © Estate of André Kertész / Higher Pictures; p. 1, © Christie's Images / Corbis; pp. 2–3, London Express / Getty Images; pp. 8l, 8c, Erich Lessing / Art Resource, NY; p. 8r, © E.O. Hoppe / Corbis; p. 9, Keystone-France / Getty Images; p. 10r, © Underwood & Underwood / Corbis; p. 11l, © CNAC / MNAM / Dist. RMN-Grand Palais / Art Resource, NY; p. 11r, Mondadori Portfolio / Electa / Art Resource, NY; p. 27b, Time Life Pictures / Getty Images; p. 32b, ullstein bild / The Granger Collection, New York; p. 40b, National Digital Archives, Poland; p. 52b, Licensed under the Creative Commons Attribution-Share Alike 3.0 Unported license; pp. 69b, 85b, 109b, 119l, 197, © Bettmann / Corbis; p. 81b, © BBC / Corbis; p. 92b, Mary Evans / IMAGNO / Austrian Archives (S); p. 147, © Keystone / Corbis; p. 156b, Licensed under the Creative Commons Attribution-Share Alike 3.0 Unported license; p. 207b, Licensed under the Creative Commons Attribution-Share Alike 3.0 Netherlands license; p. 225, Byron Company / Museum of the City of New York; p. 279, The Sydney Morning Herald / Getty Images; p. 287b, Education Images / Getty Images; p. 298b, © ENSBA / Cité de l'Architecture et du Patrimoine / Archives d'architecture du XXème siècle; pp. 306–7, © Lucien Aigner / Corbis; Opposite p. 312, John Kobal Foundation / Getty Images

Image copyrights
p. 11r, © 2013 Artists Rights Society (ARS), New York / pp. 12, 15, 22, 31, 71, 103, 106, 247, 266, 268 copyright © Simon Rendall / SIAE, Rome; pp. 24, 74–75, 93, 134, 156–59, 161, 164–65, 168, 220, 259, 261, 302, © 2013 Artists Rights Society (ARS), New York / ADAGP, Paris; pp. 29, 67, 79, 88, 96–97, 103, 117, 128, 138–39, 150–51, 196–203, 206–7, 224, 227, 243, 251, 254–57, 305 © MOURON. CASSANDRE. Lic 2013-28-05-04 www.cassandre.fr; pp. 35, 69, © 2013 Artists Rights Society (ARS), New York / ProLitteris, Zurich; pp. 54, 56, 59, 76, 136, 192–93, 208–9, © 2013 Artists Rights Society (ARS), New York / ADAGP; pp. 65, 174, © 2013 Artists Rights Society (ARS), New York / SABAM, Brussels; pp. 82–87, Art © Dumbarton Arts, LLC/ Licensed by VAGA, New York, NY; p. 94b, © 2013 Artists Rights Society (ARS), New York / OOA-S, Prague; pp. 105t, 212–13, © 2013 Artists Rights Society (ARS), New York; p. 110b, © 2013 Artists Rights Society (ARS), New York / VG Bild-Kunst, Bonn; p. 160r, © 2013 Artists Rights Society (ARS), New York / VG Bild Kunst, Bonn; p. 267, © 2013 Man Ray Trust / Artists Rights Society (ARS), NY / ADAGP, Paris; p. 296, © 2013 Estate of Robert Mallet-Stevens / Artists Rights Society (ARS), New York / ADAGP, Paris

First published in the United Kingdom in 2013 by
Thames & Hudson Ltd, 181A High Holborn,
London WC1V 7QX

This paperback edition first published in 2017

Copyright © 2013 The Vendome Press
Translation, Text, and Commentaries copyright © 2013 William W. Crouse
Introduction copyright © 2013 Alastair Duncan

All rights reserved. No part of the contents of this book may be reproduced or transmitted in any form or by any means, electronic or mechanical, including photocopy, recording or any other information storage and retrieval system, without prior permission in writing from the publisher.

British Library Cataloguing-in-Publication Data
A catalogue record for this book is available from the British Library

ISBN 978-0-500-29306-5

Printed and bound in China by OGI

To find out about all our publications, please visit **www.thamesandhudson.com**.
There you can subscribe to our e-newsletter, browse or download our current catalogue, and buy any titles that are in print.